THE

SPANISH

PHRASEBOOK

Compiled by

LEXUS

ROUGH
GUIDES

Credits

Compiled by Lexus with Fernando Léon Solís
Lexus Series Editor: Sally Davies
Rough Guides Reference Director: Andrew Lockett
Rough Guides Series Editor: Mark Ellingham

First edition published in 1995.
Reprinted in 1995, 1996, 1998 and 2004.
This updated edition published in 2006 by
Rough Guides Ltd,
80 Strand, London WC2R 0RL
345 Hudson St, 4th Floor, New York 10014, USA
Email: mail@roughguides.co.uk.

Distributed by the Penguin Group.

Penguin Books Ltd, 80 Strand, London WC2R 0RL
Penguin Putnam, Inc., 375 Hudson Street, NY 10014, USA
Penguin Group (Australia), 250 Camberwell Road, Camberwell,
Victoria 3124, Australia
Penguin Books Canada Ltd, 10 Alcorn Avenue, Toronto,
Ontario, Canada M4V 1E4
Penguin Group (New Zealand), Cnr Rosedale and Airborne Roads,
Albany, Auckland, New Zealand

Typeset in Bembo and Helvetica to an original design by Henry Iles.
Printed in Italy by LegoPrint S.p.A

British Library Cataloguing in Publication Data
A catalogue for this book is available from the British Library.

ISBN 13: 978-1-84353-628-4
10: 1-84353-628-5

The publishers and authors have done their best to ensure the
accuracy and currency of all information in The Rough Guide
Spanish Phrasebook however, they can accept no responsibility for
any loss or inconvenience sustained by any reader using the book.

Online information about Rough Guides can be found at our
website www.roughguides.com

CONTENTS

CONTENTS

Introduction

The Rough Guide Spanish phrasebook is a highly practical introduction to the contemporary language. Laid out in clear A-Z style, it uses key-word referencing to lead you straight to the words and phrases you want – so if you need to book a room, just look up 'room'. The Rough Guide gets straight to the point in every situation, in bars and shops, on trains and buses, and in hotels and banks.

The main part of the Rough Guide is a double dictionary: English-Spanish then Spanish-English. Before that, there's a section called **Basic Phrases** and to get you involved in two-way communication, the Rough Guide includes, in this new edition, a set of **Scenario** dialogues illustrating questions and responses in key situations such as renting a car and asking directions. You can hear these and then download them free from **www.roughguides.com/phrasebooks** for use on your computer or MP3 player.

Forming the heart of the guide, the **English-Spanish** section gives easy-to-use transliterations of the Spanish words wherever pronunciation might be a problem. Throughout this section, cross-references enable you to pinpoint key facts and phrases, while asterisked words indicate where further information can be found in a section at the end of the book called **How the Language Works**. This section sets out the fundamental rules of the language, with plenty of practical examples. You'll also find here other essentials like numbers, dates, telling the time and basic phrases. In the **Spanish-English** dictionary, we've given you not just the phrases you'll be likely to hear (starting with a selection of slang and colloquialisms) but also many of the signs, labels, instructions and other basic words you may come across in print or in public places.

Near the back of the book too the Rough Guide offers an extensive **Menu Reader**. Consisting of food and drink sections (each starting with a list of essential terms), it's indispensable whether you're eating out, stopping for a quick drink, or browsing through a local food market.

¡buen viaje!
have a good trip!

Basic
Phrases

Basic Phrases

yes
sí

no
no

OK
vale
[**ba**lay]

hello
¡hola!
[**o**la]

good morning
buenos días
[bw**ay**noss]

good evening
buenas tardes
[bw**e**nass t**ar**dess]

good night
bu**e**nas noches
[**no**chess]

goodbye
adiós
[ad-y**o**ss]

hi!
(hello) ¡hola!
[**o**la]

see you!
¡hasta luego!
[**a**sta lw**ay**go]

please
por favor
[fab**o**r]

thanks, thank you
gracias
[**gra**th-yass]

that's OK, don't mention it
no hay de qué
[ī day kay]

yes please
sí, por favor

no thanks
no gracias

how are you?
¿c**ó**mo est**á**s?

I'm fine, thanks
bien, gracias
[b-yen **gra**th-yass]

pleased to meet you
encant**a**do de conocerle
[day konoth**aí**rlay]

excuse me
(to get past)
con perm**i**so
(to get attention)
¡por favor!
[fab**o**r]
(to say sorry)
perdone
[pair**do**nay]

sorry
perdone
[pairdonay]

pardon (me)?
(didn't understand/hear) ¿cómo?

what?
¿qué?
[kay]

what did he say?
¿que ha dicho?
[kay a]

I see
(I understand) ya comprendo

I don't understand
no entiendo
[ent-yendo]

do you speak English?
¿habla inglés?
[abla]

I don't speak Spanish
¿no hablo español?
[ablo espan-yol]

could you say it slowly?
¿podría decirlo despacio?
[podree-a detheerlo despath-yo]

could you repeat that?
¿puede repetir eso?
[pwayday repeteer ayso]

could you write it down?
¿puede escribírmelo?
[pwayday eskreebeermaylo]

I'd like a ...
quisiera un/una...
[kees-yaira...]

could I have ...?
quisiera ...
[kees-yaira...]

how much is it?
¿cuánto es?
[kwanto]

cheers!
(toast) ¡salud!
[saloo]

when?
¿cuando?
[kwando]

where?
¿dónde?
[donday]

Scenarios

1. Accommodation

is there an inexpensive hotel you can recommend?
▶ ¿puede recomendarme un hotel que no sea caro?
[pwayday rekomendarmay oon otel kay no say-a karo]

lo siento, parece que todos están completos ◀
[lo s-yento parethay kay todoss estan komplaytoss]
I'm sorry, they all seem to be fully booked

can you give me the name of a good middle-range hotel?
▶ ¿puede decirme un hotel de precio normal?
[pwayday detheermay un otel day preth-yo normal]

déjeme un momento que mire ¿prefiere estar en el centro? ◀
[dayHaymay oon momento kay meeray pref-yeray estar en el thentro]
let me have a look, do you want to be in the centre?

if possible
▶ si es posible
[see ess posseeblay]

¿le importa estar un poco lejos del centro? ◀
[lay eemporta estar oon poko layHoss del thentro]
do you mind being a little way out of town?

not too far out
▶ no demasiado lejos
[no demass-yado layHoss]

where is it on the map?
▶ ¿dónde está en el mapa?
[donday esta en el mapa]

can you write the name and address down?
▶ ¿puede escribir el nombre y la dirección?
[pwayday eskreebeer el nombray ee la deerekth-yon]

I'm looking for a room in a private house
▶ estoy buscando una habitación en una casa privada
[estoy booskando oona abeetath-yon en oona kassa preebada]

2. Banks

bank account	la cuenta bancaria	[kwenta bankar-ya]
to change money	cambiar dinero	[kamb-yar deenairo]
cheque	el cheque	[chaykay]
to deposit	ingresar	[eengressar]
euro	el euro	[ay-ooro]
pin number	el pin	[peen]
pound	la libra	[leebra]
to withdraw	retirar	[reteerar]

can you change this into euros?
▶ ¿puede cambiarme esto a euros?
[pwayday kamb-yarmay esto a ay-ooross]

¿cómo prefiere el dinero? ◀
[komo pref-yairay el deenairo]
how would you like the money?

small notes
▶ billetes pequeños
[bee-yaytayss pekayn-yoss]

big notes
▶ billetes grandes
[bee-yaytayss grandayss]

do you have information in English about opening an account?
▶ ¿tiene información en inglés sobre cómo abrir una cuenta?
[t-yaynay eenformath-yon en eenglayss sobray komo abreer oona kwenta]

sí ¿qué tipo de cuenta quiere? ◀
[see kay teepo day kwenta k-yairay]
yes, what sort of account do you want?

I'd like a current account
quisiera una cuenta corriente
[keess-yaira oona kwenta korr-yentay]

permítame su pasaporte, por favor ◀
[pairmeetamay soo passaportay por fabor]
your passport, please

can I use this card to draw some cash?
▶ ¿puedo sacar dinero con esta tarjeta?
[pwaydo sakar deenairo kon esta tarHayta]

tiene que ir al mostrador de caja ◀
[t-yaynay kay eer al mostrador day kaHa]
you have to go to the cashier's desk

I want to transfer this to my account at the Banco Santander
▶ quisiera enviar esto a mi cuenta en el Banco Santander
[keess-yaira emb-yar esto a mee kwenta en el banko santandair]

de acuerdo, pero tendremos que cobrarle la llamada ◀
[day akwairdo pairo tendraymoss kay kobrarlay la yamada]
OK, but we'll have to charge you for the phonecall

14

3. Booking a room

shower	la ducha	[**doo**cha]
telephone in the room	teléfono en el cuarto	[tel**ay**fono en el **kwar**to]
payphone in the lobby	teléfono público en el vestíbulo	[tel**ay**fono **poo**bleeko en el bayss**tee**boolo]

do you have any rooms?
▶ ¿tiene habitaciones libres?
[t-**yay**nay abeetath-y**o**nayss **lee**brayss]

¿para cuántas personas? ◀
[**para** kw**antass** pair**so**nass]
for how many people?

for one / for two
▶ para una/para doss
[**para oo**na/**para** doss]

▶ sí, tenemos habitaciones libres
[see ten**ay**moss abeetath-y**o**nayss **lee**brayss]
yes, we have rooms

▶ ¿para cuántas noches?
[**para** kw**antass no**chayss]
for how many nights?

just for one night
sólo para una noche ◀
[**s**olo **para oo**na **no**chay]

how much is it?
▶ ¿cuánto es?
[**kwa**nto ess]

90 euros con baño y 70 sin baño ◀
[nob**enta** ay-**oo**ross kon **ban**-yo ee set**enta** seen **ban**-yo]
90 euros with bathroom and 70 euros without bathroom

does that include breakfast?
▶ ¿está incluido el desayuno?
[est**a** eenkl-w**ee**do el dessa-y**oo**no]

can I see a room with bathroom?
▶ ¿puedo ver una habitación con baño?
[pw**ay**do bair **oo**na abeetath-y**on** kon **ban**-yo]

ok, I'll take it
▶ vale, me la quedo
[**ba**lay may la **kay**do]

when do I have to check out?
▶ ¿cuándo tengo que salir?
[**kwa**ndo **te**ngo kay sal**eer**]

is there anywhere I can leave luggage?
▶ ¿puedo dejar el equipaje en algún sitio?
[pw**ay**do day**Ha**r el eekeepa**Hay** en alg**oon** **see**t-yo]

4. Car hire

automatic	automático	[owtomateeko]
full tank	depósito lleno	[deposseeto yayno]
manual	manual	[manwal]
rented car	el coche alquilado	[kochay alkeelado]

I'd like to rent a car
▶ quisiera alquilar un coche
[keess-yaira alkeelar oon kochay]

¿para cuánto tiempo? ◀
[para kwanto t-yempo]
for how long?

two days
▶ dos días
[doss dee-ass]

I'll take the ...
▶ me llevo el ...
[may yaybo el...]

is that with unlimited mileage?
▶ ¿es sin límite de kilómetros?
[ess seen leemeetay day keelometross]

sí ◀
[see]
yes

¿me permite su carnet de conducir? ◀
[may pairmeetay soo karnay day kondootheer]
can I see your driving licence please?

y su pasaporte ◀
[ee soo passaportay]
and your passport

is insurance included?
▶ ¿está incluido el seguro?
[esta eenkl-weedo el segooro]

sí, pero usted tendría que pagar los primeros cien euros ◀
[see pairo oostay tendreea kay pagar loss preemaiross th-yen ay-ooross]
yes, but you have to pay the first 100 euros

¿puede dejar una fianza de cien euros? ◀
[pwayday dayHar oona fee-antha day th-yen ay-ooross]
can you leave a deposit of 100 euros?

and if this office is closed, where do I leave the keys?
▶ y si esta oficina está cerrada ¿dónde dejo las llaves?
[ee see esta ofeetheena esta thairrada donday dayHo lass yabayss]

las pone en esa caja ◀
[lass ponay en ayssa kaHa]
you drop them in that box

5. Communications

ADSL modem	el modem ADSL	[modem a-day-**ay**say-**ay**lay]
at	arroba	[arroba]
dial-up modem	el modem de marcador manual	[modem day markador manwal]
dot	punto	[**poo**nto]
Internet	internet	[**ee**ntairnet]
mobile (phone)	el móvil	[mobeel]
password	la contraseña	[kontrassen-ya]
telephone socket adaptor	el adaptador para el teléfono	[adaptador para el telefono]
wireless hotspot	el punto de acceso inalámbrico	[**poo**nto day akth**ay**sso eena**lam**breeko]

is there an Internet café around here?
▶ ¿hay por aquí un cibercafé?
[i por ak**ee** oon theebairkaf**ay**]

can I send email from here?
▶ ¿puedo enviar emails desde aquí?
[pw**ay**do emb-y**ar** emailss desday ak**ee**]

where's the at sign on the keyboard?
▶ ¿dónde está la arroba en el teclado?
[donday esta la arr**o**ba en el tekl**a**do]

can you switch this to a UK keyboard?
▶ ¿se puede cambiar a teclado británico?
[say pw**ay**day kamb-y**ar** a teklado breet**a**neeko]

can you help me log on?
▶ ¿puede ayudarme a conectarme?
[pw**ay**day ayood**a**rmay a konekt**a**rmay]

can you put me through to ...?
▶ ¿puede ponerme con...?
[pw**ay**day pon**ai**rmay kon...]

I'm not getting a connection, can you help?
▶ no puedo conectarme ¿puede ayudarme?
[no pw**ay**do konekt**a**rmay pw**ay**day ayood**a**rmay]

where can I get a top-up card for my mobile?
▶ ¿dónde puedo comprar una tarjeta para el móvil?
[donday pw**ay**do kompr**ar** **oo**na tarH**ay**ta para el mobeel]

zero	five
cero	cinco
[th**ai**ro]	[th**ee**nko]
one	six
uno	seis
[**oo**no]	[say-eess]
two	seven
dos	siete
[doss]	[s-y**ay**tay]
three	eight
tres	ocho
[tress]	[**o**cho]
four	nine
cuatro	nueve
[kw**a**tro]	[nw**ay**bay]

6. Directions

hi, I'm looking for Calle Real
▶ hola, estoy buscando la Calle Real
[**o**la est**oy** boosk**a**ndo la k**a**-yay ray-**a**l]

lo siento, nunca he oído hablar de ella ◀
[lo s-y**e**nto n**oo**nka ay o**ee**do abl**a**r day **ay**-ya]
sorry, never heard of it

hi, can you tell me where Calle Real is?
▶ hola, ¿puede decirme dónde está la Calle Real?
[**o**la pw**ay**day deth**eer**may d**o**nday est**a** la k**a**-yay ray-**a**l]

yo tampoco soy de aquí ◀
[yo tamp**o**ko soy day ak**ee**]
I'm a stranger here too

hi, Calle
Real, do
you know
where it is?
hola, la
Calle Real,
¿sabe
dónde
está?
[**o**la la k**a**-yay
ray-**a**l s**a**bay
d**o**nday esta]

where?
¿dónde?
[d**o**nday]

which direction?
¿por dónde?
[por d**o**nday]

▶ a la izquierda en el segundo semáforo
[a la eethk-y**ai**rda en el seg**oo**ndo sem**a**foro]
left at the second traffic lights

▶a la vuelta de la esquina   ▶ luego es la primera calle a la derecha
[a la bw**e**lta day la esk**ee**na]   [lw**ay**go ess la preem**ai**ra k**a**-yay a la dair**ay**cha]
around the corner   then it's the first street on the right

a la derecha	cerca	justo después	siguiente
[a la dair**ay**cha]	[th**ai**rka]	[H**oo**sto	[seeg-y**e**ntay]
on the right	near	despw**e**ss]	next
		just after	
allí	delante de		
[a-y**ee**]	[dayl**a**ntay day]		todo recto
over there	in front of	más allá	[**to**do r**e**kto]
		[mass a-y**a**]	straight
atrás	en frente de	further	ahead
[atr**a**ss]	[en fr**e**ntay day]		
back	opposite		
		pasado el...	a la izquierda
calle	gire	[pass**a**do el...]	[a la eethk-
[k**a**-yay]	[H**ee**-ray]	past the ...	y**ai**rda]
street	turn off		on the left

7. Emergencies

accident	el accidente	[aktheedentay]
ambulance	la ambulancia	[amboolanth-ya]
consul	el cónsul	[konsool]
embassy	la embajada	[embaHada]
fire brigade	los bomberos	[bombaiross]
police	la policía	[poleethee-a]

help!
▶ ¡socorro!
[sokorro]

can you help me?
▶ ¿puede ayudarme?
[pwayday ayoodarmay]

please come with me! it's really very urgent
▶ ¡por favor, venga conmigo! es de verdad muy urgente
[por fabor baynga konmeego ess day bairda mwee oorHayntay]

I've lost (my keys)
▶ he perdido (las llaves)
[ay pairdeedo (lass yabayss)]

(my car) is not working
▶ (mi coche) no funciona
[(mee kochay) no foonth-yona]

(my purse) has been stolen
▶ me han robado (el monedero)
[may an robado (el monedairo)]

I've been mugged
▶ me han robado
[may an robado]

¿cómo se llama? ◀
[komo say yama]
what's your name?

¿me permite su pasaporte? ◀
[may pairmeetay soo passaportay]
I need to see your passport

I'm sorry, all my papers have been stolen
▶ lo siento, me han robado todos los documentos
[lo s-yento may an robado todoss loss dokoomayntoss]

8. Friends

hi, how're you doing?
▶ hola ¿qué tal?
[ola kay tal]

muy bien ¿y tú? ◀
[mwee b-yen ee too]
ok, and you?

yeah, fine
▶ pues bien
[pwess b-yen]

not bad
▶ no estoy mal
[no estoy mal]

d'you know Antonio?
▶ ¿conoces a Antonio?
[konothayss a antonio]

and this is Marta
▶ y ésta es Marta
[ee esta ess marta]

si, ya nos conocemos ◀
[see ya noss konothaymoss]
yeah, we know each other

where do you know each other from?
▶ ¿de qué os conocéis?
[day kay oss konothay-eess]

we met at Gonzalos's place
▶ nos conocimos en casa de Gonzalo
[noss konotheemoss en kassa day gonthalo]

that was some party, eh?
▶ menuda fiesta ¿eh?
[maynooda fee-aysta ay]

genial ◀
[Hayn-yal]
the best

are you guys coming for a beer?
▶ ¿venís a tomar una cerveza?
[bayneess a tomar oona thairbaytha]

estupendo, vamos ◀
[estoopendo, bamoss]
cool, let's go

no, he quedado con Lola ◀
[no, ay kaydado kon lola]
no, I'm meeting Lola

see you at Gonzalo's place tonight
▶ nos vemos esta noche en casa de Gonzalo
[noss baymoss esta nochay en kassa day gonthalo]

hasta luego ◀
[asta lwaygo]
see you

9. Health

I'm not feeling very well
▶ no me siento bien
[no may s-yento b-yen]

can you get a doctor?
▶ ¿puede llamar a un médico?
[pwayday yamar a oon maydeeko]

▶ ¿dónde le duele?
[donday lay dwaylay]
where does it hurt?

it hurts here
me duele aquí ◀
[may dwaylay akee]

▶ ¿es un dolor constante?
[ess oon dolor konstantay]
is the pain constant?

it's not a constant pain
no es un dolor constante ◀
[no ess oon dolor konstantay]

can I make an appointment?
▶ ¿puedo pedir cita?
[pwaydo pedeer theeta]

can you give me something for ...?
▶ ¿puede darme algo para...?
[pwayday darmay algo para]

yes, I have insurance
▶ sí, tengo seguro
[see tengo segooro]

antibiotics	el antibiótico	[anteeb-yoteeko]
antiseptic ointment	la pomada antiséptica	[pomada anteessaypteeka]
cystitis	la cystitis	[theesteeteess]
dentist	el dentista	[denteesta]
diarrhoea	la diarrea	[d-yarray-a]
doctor	el médico	[maydeeko]
hospital	el hospital	[ospeetal]
ill	enfermo	[enfairmo]
medicine	la medicina	[medeetheena]
painkillers	analgésicos	[analHayseekoss]
pharmacy	la farmacia	[farmath-ya]
to prescribe	recetar	[rethaytar]
thrush	las aftas	[aftass]

10. Language difficulties

a few words	unas palabras	[**oo**nass pala**bra**ss]
interpreter	el intérprete	[eent**air**praytay]
to translate	traducir	[tradoo**theer**]

le han rechazado la tarjeta de crédito ◀
[lay an rechat**ha**do la tar**Hay**ta day kr**ay**deeto]
your credit card has been refused

what, I don't understand; do you speak English?
▶ ¿cómo? no comprendo; ¿habla usted inglés?
[**ko**mo no kom**pre**ndo **a**bla oos**tay** eeng**lay**ss]

esto no es válido ◀
[**esto** no ess b**a**leedo]
this isn't valid

could you say that again?   slowly
▶ ¿puede repetir?   despacio ◀
[**pw**ayday repet**eer**]   [desp**a**th-yo]

I understand very little Spanish
▶ comprendo muy poco español
[kom**re**ndo mwee p**o**ko espan-y**ol**]

I speak Spanish very badly
▶ hablo español muy mal
[**a**blo espan-y**ol** mwee mal]

no puede pagar con esta tarjeta ◀
[no pw**ay**day pagar kon **e**sta tar**Hay**ta]
you can't use this card to pay

▶ ¿comprende?   sorry, no
[kom**pre**nday]   no, lo siento ◀
do you understand?   [no lo s-y**ento**i]

is there someone who speaks English?
▶ ¿hay alguien que hable inglés?
[i **a**lg-yen kay **a**blay eeng**lay**ss]

oh, now I understand   is that ok now?
▶ ah, ahora comprendo   ▶ ¿está todo bien ya?
[ah a-**o**ra kom**pre**ndo]   [est**a** t**o**do b-yen ya]

download these scenarios as MP3s from:

11. Meeting people

hello
▶ hola
[**o**la]

hola, me llamo Blanca ◀
[**o**la may **ya**mo bl**a**nka]
hello, my name's Blanca

Graham, from England, Thirsk
▶ soy Graham, de Thirsk, Inglaterra
[soy graham day thirsk eenglat**ai**rra]

no lo conozco ¿dónde está? ◀
[no lo kon**o**thko d**o**nday est**a**]
don't know that, where is it?

not far from York, in the North; and you?
▶ no lejos de York, en el norte, ¿y usted?
[no **lay**Hoss day york en el **no**rtay ee oost**ay**]

soy de Salamanca: ¿está aquí solo? ◀
[soy day salam**a**nka est**a** ak**ee** s**o**lo]
I'm from Salamanca; here by yourself?

no, I'm with my wife and two kids
▶ no, estoy con mi mujer y mis dos hijos
[no, est**oy** kon mee moo**H**air ee meess doss **ee**Hoss]

what do you do?
▶ ¿a qué se dedica?
[a kay say dayd**ee**ka]

a la informática ◀
[a la eenform**a**teeka]
I'm in computers

me too
yo también
[yo tamb-y**en**]

here's my wife now
▶ aquí está mi mujer
[ak**ee** est**a** mee moo**H**air]

encantada de conocerla ◀
[enkant**a**da day konoth**ai**rla]
nice to meet you

12. Post offices

airmail	correo aéreo	[korray-o a-airay-o]
post card	la postal	[postal]
post office	correos	[korray-oss]
stamp	el sello	[say-yo]

what time does the post office close?
▶ ¿a qué hora cierra Correos?
[a kay ora th-yaira korray-oss]

a las cinco entre semana ◀
[alass theenko entray semana]
five o'clock weekdays

is the post office open on Saturdays?
▶ ¿Correos abre los sábados?
[korray-oss abray loss sabadoss]

hasta mediodía ◀
[asta med-yodee-a]
until midday

I'd like to send this registered to England
▶ quisiera enviar esto certificado a Inglaterra
[keess-yaira emb-yar esto thairteefeekado a eenglatairra]

sí, claro, van a ser 10 euros ◀
[see klaro ban a sair d-yeth ay-ooross]
certainly, that will cost 10 euros

and also two stamps for England, please
▶ y también dos sellos para Inglaterra, por favor
[ee tamb-yen doss say-yoss para eenglatairra por fabor]

do you have some airmail stickers?
▶ ¿tiene pegatinas de correo aéreo?
[t-yaynay pegateenass day korray-o a-airay-o]

do you have any mail for me?
▶ ¿tiene correo para mí?
[t-yaynay korray-o para mee]

| cartas | paquetes | lista de correos |
| letters | parcels | poste restante |

13. Restaurants

bill	la cuenta	[kw**e**nta]	menu	el menú [men**oo**]
table	la mesa	[m**ay**ssa]		

can we have a non-smoking table?
▶ ¿nos da una mesa de no fumadores?
[noss da **oo**na m**ay**ssa day no foomad**o**rayss]

there are two of us　**there are four of us**
▶ somos dos　　　　▶ somos cuatro
[s**o**moss doss]　　　[s**o**moss kw**a**tro]

what's this?　　　　　　　　　　　es pescado ◀
▶ ¿qué es esto?　　　　　　　　　　[ess pesk**a**do]
[kay ess **e**sto]　　　　　　　　　　**it's a type of fish**

　　　　　　　　es una especialidad de la zona ◀
　　　　　　　　[ess **oo**na espeth-yaleed**a** day la th**o**na]
　　　　　　　　it's a local speciality

　　　　　　　　　　　　entre y se lo enseño ◀
　　　　　　　　　　　　[**e**ntray ee say lo ens**ay**n-yo]
　　　　　　　　　　come inside and I'll show you

we would like two of these, one of these, and one of those
▶ queremos dos de éstos, uno de éstos y uno de aquéllos
[kair**ay**moss doss day **e**stoss **oo**no day **e**stoss ee **oo**no day ak**ay**-yoss]

▶ ¿y para beber?　**red wine**　　　**white wine**
[ee p**a**ra beb**air**]　▶ vino tinto　　▶ vino blanco
and to drink?　　[b**ee**no t**ee**nto]　[b**ee**no bl**a**nko]

a beer and two orange juices
▶ una cerveza y dos zumos de naranja
[**oo**na thairb**ay**tha ee doss th**oo**moss day naranHa]

some more bread please
▶ un poco más de pan, por favor
[oon p**o**ko mass day pan por fab**o**r]

▶ ¿les ha gustado la comida?　　　　excellent, very nice!
[layss a goost**a**do la kom**ee**da]　¡estaba estupenda! ¡muy buena! ◀
how was your meal?　　　　　[est**a**ba estoop**ay**nda mwee bw**ay**na]

▶ ¿algo más?　　　　　　　　　　　**just the bill thanks**
[**a**lgo mass]　　　　　　　　　　sólo la cuenta, gracias ◀
anything else?　　　　　　　　[s**o**lo la kw**e**nta gr**a**th-yass]

14. Shopping

¿en qué puedo servirle? ◄
[en kay pwaydo sairbeerlay]
can I help you?

can I just have a look around?
▶ ¿puedo echar sólo un vistazo?
[pwaydo echar solo oon beestatho]

yes, I'm looking for ...
▶ sí, estoy buscando ...
[see estoy booskando]

how much is this?
▶ ¿cuánto es esto?
[kwanto ess esto]

treinta y dos euros ◄
[tray-eenta ee doss ay-ooross]
thirty-two euros

OK, I think I'll have to leave it; it's a little too expensive for me
▶ vale, creo que tendré que dejarlo; es demasiado caro para mí
[balay kray-o kay tendray kay deHarlo ess demass-yado karo para mee]

¿y esto? ◄
[ee esto]
how about this?

can I pay by credit card?
▶ ¿puedo pagar con tarjeta de crédito?
[pwaydo pagar kon tarHayta day kraydeeto]

it's too big
▶ es demasiado grande
[ess demass-yado granday]

it's too small
▶ es demasiado pequeño
[ess demass-yado pekayn-yo]

it's for my son – he's about this high
▶ es para mi hijo – es más o menos así de alto
[ess para mee eeHo ess mass o maynoss assee day alto]

▶ ¿va a querer algo más?
[ba a kerair algo mass]
will there be anything else?

that's all thanks
▶ eso es todo, gracias
[ayso ess todo grath-yass]

make it twenty euros and I'll take it
▶ si me lo pone a veinte euros me lo quedo
[see may lo ponay a bay-eentay ay-ooros may lo kaydo]

fine, I'll take it
▶ vale, me lo quedo
[balay may lo kaydo]

abierto	caja	cambiar	cerrado	rebajas
open	cashdesk	to exchange	closed	sale

26

15. Sightseeing

art gallery	la galería de arte	[galairree-a day artay]
bus tour	visita en autobús	[beesseeta en owtobooss]
city centre	el centro	[thentro]
closed	cerrado	[thairrado]
guide	la guía	[gee-a]
museum	el museo	[moossay-o]
open	abierto	[ab-yairto]

I'm interested in seeing the old town
▶ quisiera ver el casco antiguo
[keess-yaira bair el kasko anteegwo]

are there guided tours?
▶ ¿hay visitas guiadas?
[ī beeseetass gee-adass]

lo siento, está completo ◀
[lo s-yento esta komplayto]
I'm sorry, it's fully booked

how much would you charge to drive us around for four hours?
▶ ¿cuánto nos cobraría por darnos un paseo de cuatro horas?
[kwanto noss kobraree-a por darnoss oon passay-o day kwatro orass]

can we book tickets for the concert here?
▶ ¿podemos reservar aquí las entradas para el concierto?
[podaymoss resairbar akee lass entradass para el konth-yairto]

▶ sí ¿a qué nombre?
[see a kay nombray]
yes, in what name?

¿qué tarjeta de crédito? ◀
[kay tarHayta day kraydeeto]
which credit card?

where do we get the tickets?
▶ ¿dónde nos dan las entradas?
[donday noss dan lass entradass]

recójanlas a la entrada ◀
[rekoHanlass a la entrada]
pick them up at the entrance

is it open on Sundays?
▶ ¿abren los domingos?
[abrayn loss domeengoss]

how much is it to get in?
▶ ¿cuánto cuesta entrar?
[kwanto kwesta entrar]

are there reductions for groups of 6?
▶ ¿hay descuentos para grupos de seis?
[ī deskwentos para grooposs day say-eess]

that was really impressive!
▶ ¡ha estado genial!
[a estado Hen-yal]

16. Trains

to change trains	hacer transbordo	[athair transbordo]
platform	el andén	[andayn]
return	el billete de ida y vuelta	[bee-yaytay day eeda ee bwelta]
single	el billete de ida	[bee-yaytay day eeda]
station	la estación	[estath-yon]
stop	la parada	[parada]
ticket	el billete	[bee-yaytay]

how much is ...?
▶ ¿cuánto es ...?
[kwanto ess]

a single, second class to ...
▶ un billete de ida, en clase turista a ...
[oon bee-yaytay day eeda en klassay tooreesta a]

two returns, second class to ...
▶ dos billetes de ida y vuelta, en clase turista a ...
[doss bee-yaytayss day eeda ee bwelta en klassay tooreesta a]

for today	for tomorrow	for next Tuesday
▶ para hoy	▶ para mañana	▶ para el próximo martes
[para oy]	[para man-yana]	[para el prokseemo martayss]

El Talgo tiene suplemento ◀
[el talgo t-yaynay sooplemento]
there's a supplement for the Talgo

¿quiere reservar el asiento? ◀
[k-yairay ressairbar el ass-yento]
do you want to make a seat reservation?

tiene que hacer transbordo en Córdoba ◀
[t-yaynay kay athair transbordo en kordoba]
you have to change at Córdoba

is this seat free?
▶ ¿está libre este asiento?
[esta leebray estay ass-yento]

excuse me, which station are we at?
▶ perdone ¿en qué estación estamos?
[pairdonay en kay estath-yon estamoss]

is this where I change for Málaga?
▶ ¿es aquí donde tengo que hacer transbordo para Málaga?
[es akee donday tengo kay athair transbordo para malaga]

English

→

Spanish

A

a, an* un, una [oon, **oo**na]
about: about 20 unos veinte
it's about 5 o'clock son
aproximadamente las cinco
[aproxeem**a**damentay]
a film about Spain una
película sobre España
[**sobr**ay]
above ... encima de ...
[ent**hee**ma day]
abroad en el extranjero
[estran**hair**o]
absolutely (I agree) ¡desde
luego! [**des**day lw**ay**go]
accelerator el acelerador
[athelaira**dor**]
accept aceptar [athep**tar**]
accident el accidente
[aktheed**en**tay]
there's been an accident
ha habido un accidente [a
a**bee**do]
accommodation alojamiento
[aloHam-**yen**to]
accurate exacto
ache el dolor
my back aches me duele la
espalda [may dw**ay**lay]
across: across the road al otro
lado de la calle [ka-**yay**]
adapter el adaptador
address la dirección [deerekth-
yon]
what's your address? ¿cuál es
su dirección? [kwal]
address book la libreta de

direcciones [leebr**ay**ta day
deerekth-**yon**ess]
admission charge la entrada
adult el adulto
advance: in advance por
adelantado
aeroplane el avión [ab-**yon**]
after después (de) [desp**wess**
day]
after you usted primero
[oos**tay** pree**mair**o]
after lunch después del
almuerzo
afternoon la tarde [**tar**day]
in the afternoon por la tarde
this afternoon esta tarde
aftershave el 'aftershave'
aftersun cream la crema para
después del sol [**kray**ma para
desp**wess**]
afterwards después [desp**wess**]
again otra vez [beth]
against contra
age la edad [ay**dath**]
ago: a week ago hace una
semana [**ath**ay]
an hour ago hace una hora
agree: I agree estoy de
acuerdo [day akw**air**do]
AIDS el SIDA [**seed**a]
air el aire [a-**eer**ay]
by air en avión [ab-**yon**]
air-conditioning el aire
acondicionado [a-**eer**ay
akondeeth-yon**ado**]
airmail: by airmail por avión
[ab-**yon**]
airmail envelope el sobre
aéreo [**sobr**ay a-**air**ay-o]

airport el aeropuerto
[a-airopw**air**to]
to the airport, please al
aeropuerto, por favor
airport bus el autobús del
aeropuerto [owtob**oo**ss]
aisle seat asiento de pasillo
[as-y**en**to day pas**ee**-yo]
alarm clock el despertador
alcohol el alcohol [alk**ol**]
alcoholic alcohólico
Algeria Argelia [arH**ay**lee-a]
all: all the boys todos los
chicos
all the girls todas las chicas
all of it todo
all of them todos ellos
[**ay**-yoss]
that's all, thanks eso es todo,
gracias [**ay**so]
allergic: I'm allergic to ...
soy alérgico/alérgica a ...
[al**air**Heeko]
allowed: is it allowed? ¿está
permitido?
all right ¡bien! [b-yen]
I'm all right estoy bien
are you all right? (fam) ¿estás
bien?
(pol) ¿se encuentra bien? [say
enkw**ay**ntra]
almond la almendra
almost casi
alone solo
alphabet el alfabeto

a a	j Hota	s **ay**say
b bay	k ka	t tay
c thay	l **ay**lay	u oo

ch chay	m **ay**may	v **oo**bay
d day	n **ay**nay	w **oo**bay d**oo**blay
e ay	ñ **ayn**-yay	x **ay**kees
f **ay**fay	o o	y ee gr-y**ay**ga
g Hay	p pay	z th**ay**ta
h a**chay**	q koo	
i ee	r a**ir**ray	

already ya
also también [tamb-yen]
although aunque [a-**oon**kay]
altogether del todo
always siempre [s-y**em**pray]
am*: I am soy, estoy
a.m.: at seven a.m. a las siete
de la mañana [day la man-y**a**na]
amazing (surprising) increíble
[eenkray-**ee**blay]
(very good) estupendo
ambulance la ambulancia
[amboolanth-ya]
call an ambulance! ¡llame a
una ambulancia! [y**a**may]
America América
American (adj) americano
I'm American (man/woman) soy
americano/americana
among entre [**en**tray]
amount la cantidad [kant**ee**da]
(money) la suma
amp: a 13-amp fuse el fusible
de trece amperios [foos**ee**blay
day – amp**air**ee-oss]
amphitheatre el anfiteatro
[anfeetay-**a**tro]
and y [ee]
angry enfadado
animal el animal
ankle el tobillo [tob**ee**-yo]

anniversary (wedding) el aniversario de boda [aneebairsar-yo day]

annoy: this man's annoying me este hombre me está molestando [estay ombray may]

annoying molesto

another otro

can we have another room? ¿puede darnos otra habitación? [pwayday – abeetath-yon]

another beer, please otra cerveza, por favor [thairbaytha]

antibiotics los antibióticos [anteeb-yoteekoss]

antifreeze el anticongelante [anteekonнelantay]

antihistamine el antihistamínico [antee-eestameeneeko]

antique: is it an antique? ¿es antiguo? [anteegwo]

antique shop la tienda de antigüedades [t-yenda day anteegway-dadess]

antiseptic el antiséptico

any: have you got any bread/tomatoes? ¿tiene pan/tomates? [t-yaynay]

do you have any change? ¿tiene cambio? [kamb-yo]

sorry, I don't have any no siento, no tengo [s-yento]

anybody cualquiera [kwalk-yaira]

does anybody speak English? ¿habla alguien inglés? [abla alg-yen eenglayss]

there wasn't anybody there allí no había nadie [a-yee no abee-a nad-yay]

anything algo

dialogues

anything else? ¿algo más?
nothing else, thanks nada más, gracias

would you like anything to drink? ¿le apetece beber algo? [lay apetethay bebair]
I don't want anything, thanks no quiero nada, gracias [no k-yairo nada]

apart from aparte de [apartay day]

apartment el apartamento, el piso

appendicitis la apendicitis [apendeetheeteess]

appetizer la entrada

aperitif el aperitivo [apereeteebo]

apology la disculpa

apple la manzana [manthana]

appointment la cita [theeta]

dialogue

good afternoon, sir, how can I help you? buenas tardes, señor, ¿en qué puedo servirle? [bwenass tardess, sen-yor en kay pwaydo

sairb**ee**rlay]
I'd like to make an
appointment quisiera pedir
hora [kees-y**ai**ra ped**ee**r **o**ra]
what time would you like?
¿a qué hora le viene bien?
[a kay **o**ra lay b-y**ay**nay b-yen]
three o'clock a las tres
I'm afraid that's not
possible, is four o'clock
all right? me temo que no
será posible, está bien a las
cuatro? [may t**ay**mo kay no
s**ai**ra pos**ee**blay]
yes, that will be fine sí,
está bien
the name was ...? ¿su
nombre era ...? [n**o**mbr**ay**
aira]

apricot el albaricoque
[albarik**o**kay]
April abril
are*: we are somos; estamos
you are (fam) eres [**ai**ress];
estás
(pol) es; está
they are son; están
area la zona [th**o**na]
area code el prefijo [pref**ee**Ho]
arm el brazo [br**a**tho]
arrange: will you arrange it for
us? ¿nos lo organiza usted?
[organ**ee**tha oost**ay**]
arrival la llegada [yeg**a**da]
arrive llegar [yeg**a**r]
when do we arrive? ¿cuándo
llegamos? [kw**a**ndo yeg**a**moss]
has my fax arrived yet? ¿ha

llegado ya mi fax? [a yeg**a**do]
we arrived today llegamos
hoy [yeg**a**moss oy]
art el arte [**a**rtay]
art gallery el museo de bellas
artes [moos**ay**-o day b**ay**-yass
artess]
(smaller) la galería de arte
[galair**ee**-a]
artist (man/woman) el pintor/la
pintora
as: as big as tan grande como
[gr**a**nday]
as soon as possible lo antes
posible [**a**ntess pos**ee**blay]
ashtray el cenicero
[thayneeth**ai**ro]
ask preguntar [pregoont**a**r]
I didn't ask for this no había
pedido eso [ab**ee**-a – **ay**so]
could you ask him to ...?
¿puede decirle que ...?
[pw**ay**day deth**ee**rlay kay]
asleep: she's asleep está
dormida
aspirin la aspirina
asthma el asma
astonishing increíble [eenkray-
eeblay]
at: at the hotel en el hotel
at the station en la estación
at six o'clock a las seis
at Pedro's en la casa de
Pedro
athletics el atletismo
Atlantic Ocean el Océano
Atlántico [oth**ay**-ano]
attractive guapo, atractivo
[atrakt**ee**bo]

aubergine la berenjena
[beren**Hay**na]

August agosto

aunt la tía [**tee**-a]

Australia Australia [**owstral**-ya]

Australian (adj) australiano
I'm Australian (man/woman) soy
australiano/australiana

automatic (car) automático
[owtomat**eeko**]

automatic teller el cajero
automático [ka**Hai**ro]

autumn el otoño [o**ton**-yo]
in the autumn en otoño

avenue la avenida [abe**nee**da]

average (not good) regular
[regoo**lar**]
on average por término
medio [**tair**meeno **mayd**-yo]

awake: is he awake? ¿está
despierto? [desp-**yair**to]

away: go away! ¡lárguese!
[**lar**gaysay]
is it far away? ¿está lejos?
[lay**Hoss**]

awful terrible [te**rree**blay]

axle el eje [**ay**Hay]

B

baby el bebé [bay**bay**]

baby food la comida de bebé
[day]

baby's bottle el biberón
[beebai**ron**]

baby-sitter la niñera [neen-
yaira]

back (of body) la espalda

(back part) la parte de atrás
[**par**tay day]
at the back en la parte de
atrás
can I have my money back?
¿puede devolverme el
dinero? [**pway**day daybol**bair**may
el dee**nai**ro]
to come/go back volver
[bol**bair**]

backache el dolor de espalda
[day]

bacon el bacon [**bay**kon], la
panceta [pan**the**ta]

bad malo
a bad headache un fuerte
dolor de cabeza [**fwair**tay – day
ka**bay**tha]

badly mal
(injured) gravemente
[grabe**mayn**tay]

bag la bolsa
(handbag) el bolso
(suitcase) la maleta [ma**lay**ta]

baggage el equipaje
[ekeepa**Hay**]

baggage check la consigna
[kon**see**gna]

baggage claim la recogida
de equipajes [reko**Hee**da day
ekeepa**Hess**]

bakery la panadería
[panadai**ree**-a]

balcony el balcón
a room with a balcony una
habitación con balcón
[abeetath-**yon**]

bald calvo [**kal**bo]

Balearic Islands las Baleares

[balay-**a**ress]

ball (large) la pel**o**ta
 (small) la b**o**la
ballet el ballet
banana el pl**á**tano
band (musical) la orquesta
 [ork**e**sta]
 (pop) el grupo
bandage la venda
 [b**e**nda]
Bandaid® la tir**i**ta
bank (money) el b**a**nco
bank account la cuenta
 banc**a**ria [kw**e**nta]
bar el bar
 a bar of chocolate una b**a**rra
 de chocolate [day chokol**a**tay]
barber's el barbero [barb**ai**ro]
Barcelona Barcelona
 [barthayl**o**na]
basket el cesto [th**e**sto]
 (in shop) la c**e**sta
bath el b**a**ño [b**a**n-yo]
 can I have a bath? ¿puedo
 bañarme? [pw**ay**do ban-y**a**rmay]
bathroom el cuarto de baño
 [kw**a**rto]
 with a private bathroom con
 baño privado [pr**ee**bado]
bath towel la toalla de baño
 [to-**a**-ya day]
battery la p**i**la
 (car) la bater**í**a [batair**ee**-a]
bay la bah**í**a [ba-**ee**-a]
Bay of Biscay el G**o**lfo de
 Vizcaya [day beethk**a**ya]
be* ser [sair]; estar [ayst**a**r]
beach la playa [pl**a**-ya]
beach mat la esterilla de playa

[estair**ee**-ya]
beach umbrella la sombrilla
 [sombr**ee**-ya]
beans las judías [Hood**ee**-ass]
 runner beans las judías
 verdes [b**ai**rdess]
 broad beans las habas
 [**a**bass]
beard la b**a**rba
beautiful bon**i**to
because porque [p**o**rkay]
 because of ... debido a ...
 [deb**ee**do]
bed la c**a**ma
 I'm going to bed now me voy
 a acostar ya [may boy]
bed and breakfast habitación
 y desayuno [abeetath-yon ee
 desa-y**oo**no]
bedroom el dormitorio
 [dorme**eto**r-yo]
beef la carne de vaca [k**a**rnay
 day b**a**ka]
beer la cerveza [thairb**a**ytha]
 two beers, please dos
 cervezas, por favor
before antes [**a**ntess]
begin empezar [empeth**a**r]
 when does it begin? ¿cuándo
 empieza? [kw**a**ndo emp-y**e**tha]
beginner el/la principiante
 [preentheep-y**a**ntay]
beginning: at the beginning al
 principio [preenth**ee**p-yo]
behind detr**á**s
 behind me detrás de mí
beige beige [b**a**y-eess]
Belgium Bélgica [b**a**ylHeeka]
believe creer [kray-**a**ir]

below abajo [abaно]

belt el cinturón [theentooron]

bend (in road) la curva [koorba]

berth (on ship) el camarote [kamarotay]

beside: beside the ... al lado de la ...

best el mejor [meнor]

better mejor

  are you feeling better? ¿se siente mejor? [say s-yentay]

between entre [entray]

beyond más allá [a-ya]

bicycle la bicicleta [beetheeklayta]

big grande [granday]

  too big demasiado grande [demass-yado]

  it's not big enough no es suficientemente grande [soofeeth-yentemayntay]

bike la bicicleta [beetheeklayta]
  (motorbike) la motocicleta [mototheeklayta]

bikini el bikini [beekeenee]

bill la cuenta [kwenta]
  (US: banknote) el billete [bee-yaytay]

  could I have the bill, please? la cuenta, por favor

bin el cubo de la basura [koobo day]

bin liners las bolsas de basura

binding (ski) la atadura

bird el pájaro [paнaro]

biro® el bolígrafo

birthday el cumpleaños [koomplayan-yoss]

  happy birthday! ¡feliz cumpleaños! [feleeth]

biscuit la galleta [ga-yeta]

bit: a little bit un poquito [pokeeto]

  a big bit un pedazo grande [pedatho granday]

  a bit of ... un pedazo de ...

  a bit expensive un poco caro

bite (by insect) la picadura
  (by dog) la mordedura

bitter (taste etc) amargo

black negro [naygro]

blanket la manta

bleach (for toilet) la lejía [leнee-a]

bless you! ¡Jesús! [Haysooss]

blind ciego [th-yaygo]

blinds las persianas [pers-yanass]

blister la ampolla [ampo-ya]

blocked (road, pipe) obstruido [obstrweedo]
  (sink) atascado

block of flats el bloque de apartamentos [blokay day]

blond rubio [roob-yo]

blood la sangre [sangray]

  high blood pressure la tensión alta [tenss-yon]

blouse la blusa [bloosa]

blow-dry (verb) secar a mano

  I'd like a cut and blow-dry quisiera un corte y un marcado [kees-yaira oon kortay ee]

blue azul [athool]

blusher el colorete [koloraytay]

boarding house la casa de huéspedes [wespaydess]

boarding pass la tarjeta de embarque [tarHayta day embarkay]

boat el barco

body el cuerpo [kwairpo]

boil (water) hervir [airbeer]

boiled egg el huevo pasado por agua [waybo – agwa]

boiler la caldera [kaldaira]

bone el hueso [wayso]

bonnet (of car) el capó

book el libro [leebro]

(verb) reservar [resairbar]

can I book a seat? ¿puedo reservar un asiento? [pwaydo – as-yento]

dialogue

I'd like to book a table for two quisiera reservar una mesa para dos personas [kees-yaira resairbar oona maysa]

what time would you like it booked for? ¿para qué hora le gustaría reservarla? [kay ora lay goostaree-a resairbarla]

half past seven las siete y media

that's fine de acuerdo [day akwairdo]

and your name? ¿y su nombre es ...? [ee soo nombray]

bookshop, bookstore la librería [leebrairee-a]

boot (footwear) la bota

(of car) el maletero [maletairo]

border (of country) la frontera [frontaira]

bored: I'm bored estoy aburrido

boring aburrido

born: I was born in Manchester nací en Manchester [nathee]

I was born in 1960 nací en mil novecientos sesenta

borrow pedir prestado

may I borrow ...? ¿puede prestarme ...? [pwayday prestarmay]

both los dos

bother: sorry to bother you lamento molestarle [molestarlay]

bottle la botella [botay-ya]

a bottle of house red una botella de tinto de la casa [day]

bottle-opener el abrebotellas [abraybotay-yass]

bottom (of person) el trasero [trassairo]

at the bottom of the ... (hill/road) al pie del/de la ... [p-yay del/day]

box la caja [kaHa]

box office la taquilla [takee-ya]

boy el chico

boyfriend el amigo

bra el sujetador [sooHetador]

bracelet la pulsera [poolsaira]

brake el freno [frayno]

brandy el coñac [kon-yak]

bread el pan

  white bread el pan blanco

  brown bread el pan moreno [morayno]

  wholemeal bread el pan integral

break (verb) romper [rompair]

  I've broken the ... he roto el ... [ay]

  I think I've broken my ... creo que me he roto el ... [kray-o kay may]

break down averiarse [abairee-arsay]

  I've broken down he tenido una avería [ay – abairee-a]

breakdown la avería

breakdown service el servicio de grúa [serbeeth-yo day groo-a]

breakfast el desayuno [desayoono]

break-in: I've had a break-in han entrado los ladrones en mi casa [an – ladroness]

breast el pecho [paycho]

breathe respirar

breeze la brisa [breesa]

bridge (over river) el puente [pwentay]

brief breve [braybay]

briefcase el portafolios [portafol-yoss]

bright (light etc) brillante [bree-yantay]

  bright red rojo vivo [roHo beebo]

brilliant (idea, person) brillante [bree-yantay]

bring traer [tra-air]

  I'll bring it back later lo devolveré después [lo daybolbairay despwess]

Britain Gran Bretaña [bretan-ya]

British británico

  I'm British (man/woman) soy británico/británica

brochure el folleto [fo-yeto]

broken roto

bronchitis la bronquitis [bronkeeteess]

brooch el broche [brochay]

broom la escoba

brother el hermano [airmano]

brother-in-law el cuñado [koon-yado]

brown marrón

  brown hair el pelo castaño [castan-yo]

  brown eyes los ojos castaños [oHoss]

bruise el cardenal

brush (for hair, cleaning) el cepillo [thepee-yo]

  (artist's) el pincel [peenthel]

bucket el cubo [koobo]

buffet car el vagón restaurante [bagon restowrantay]

buggy (for child) el cochecito de niño [kochaytheeto day neen-yo]

building el edificio [edeefeeth-yo]

bulb (light bulb) la bombilla [bombee-ya]

bull el toro

bullfight la corrida de toros
[day]
bullfighter el torero [torairo]
bullring la plaza de toros
[platha day]
bumper el parachoques
[parachokess]
bunk la litera [leetaira]
bureau de change (oficina
de) cambio [ofeetheena day
kamb-yo]
burglary el robo con
allanamiento de morada
[a-yanam-yento]
burn la quemadura [kemadoora]
(verb) quemar [kemar]
burnt: this is burnt está
quemado [kemado]
burst: a burst pipe una cañería
rota [kan-yairee-a]
bus el autobús [owtobooss]
   what number bus is it to ...?
   ¿qué número es para ...? [kay
   noomairo]
   when is the next bus to ...?
   ¿cuándo sale el próximo
   autobús para ...? [kwando
   salay]
   what time is the last bus?
   ¿a qué hora es el último
   autobús? [kay ora – oolteemo]
   could you let me know
   when we get there? ¿puede
   avisarme cuando lleguemos
   allí? [pwayday abeesarmay
   kwando yegaymoss a-yee]

dialogue

does this bus go to ...?
¿este autobús va a ...?
[estay owtobooss ba]
no, you need a number ...
no, tiene que coger el ...
[t-yaynay kay koHair]

business el negocio [negoth-yo]
bus station la estación de
autobuses [estath-yon day
owtoboosess]
bus stop la parada de autobús
bust el pecho [paycho]
busy (restaurant etc) concurrido
I'm busy tomorrow estoy
ocupado mañana [man-yana]
but pero [pairo]
butcher's la carnicería
[karneethairee-a]
butter la mantequilla
[mantekee-ya]
button el botón
buy (verb) comprar
   where can I buy ...? ¿dónde
   puedo comprar ...? [donday
   pwaydo]
by: by bus/car en autobús/
coche
   written by ... escrito por ...
   by the window junto a la
   ventana [Hoonto]
   by the sea a orillas del mar
   [oree-yass]
   by Thursday para el jueves
bye ¡adiós! [ad-yoss]

cabbage el repollo [repo-yo]

cabin (on ship) el camarote [kamarotay]

cable car el teleférico [telefaireeko]

Cadiz Cádiz [kadeeth]

café la cafetería [kafetairee-a]

cagoule el chubasquero [choobaskairo]

cake el pastel [pastayl]

cake shop la pastelería [pastelairee-a]

call (verb) llamar [yamar]
(to phone) llamar (por teléfono)
what's it called? cómo se llama esto? [say yama]
he/she is called ... se llama ...
please call the doctor llame al médico, por favor [yamay]
please give me a call at 7.30 am tomorrow por favor, llámeme mañana a las siete y media de la mañana [yamamay man-yana]
please ask him to call me por favor, dígale que me llame [deegalay kay may yamay]

call back: I'll call back later volveré más tarde [bolbairay mass tarday]
(phone back) volveré a llamar [yamar]

call round: I'll call round tomorrow me paso mañana

[may]

camcorder la videocámara [beeday-o kamaira]

camera la máquina de fotos [makeena]

camera shop la tienda de cámaras fotográficas [t-yenda day]

camp (verb) acampar
can we camp here? ¿se puede acampar aquí? [say pwayday – akee]

camping gas canister la bombona de butano [bootano]

campsite el camping

can la lata
a can of beer una lata de cerveza [thairbaytha]

can*: can you ...? ¿puede ...? [pwayday]
can I have ...? ¿me da ...? [may]
I can't ... no puedo ...

Canada el Canadá

Canadian canadiense [kanad-yensay]
I'm Canadian soy canadiense

canal el canal

Canaries las Islas Canarias [eeslass kanar-yass]

cancel anular [anoolar]

candies los caramelos [karamayloss]

candle la vela [bayla]

canoe la piragua [peeragwa]

canoeing el piragüismo [peeragweesmo]

can-opener el abrelatas

cap (hat) la gorra

(of bottle) el tapón

car el coche [kochay]

by car en coche

carafe la garrafa

a carafe of house white, please una garrafa de vino blanco de la casa, por favor [day beeno]

caravan la caravana [karabana]

caravan site el camping

carburettor el carburador

card (birthday etc) la tarjeta [tarHayta]

here's my (business) card aquí tiene mi tarjeta (de visita) [akee t-yaynay – day beeseeta]

cardigan la rebeca [rebayka]

cardphone el teléfono de tarjeta [telayfono day tarHeta]

careful prudente [proodentay]

be careful! ¡tenga cuidado! [kweedado]

caretaker el encargado

car ferry el ferry, el transbordador de coches [kochess]

car hire el alquiler de coches [alkeelair day]

car park el aparcamiento [aparkam-yento]

carpet la moqueta [mokayta]

carriage (of train) el vagón [bagon]

carrier bag la bolsa de plástico [day plasteeko]

carrot la zanahoria [thana-or-ya]

carry llevar [yebar]

carry-cot el capazo [kapatho]

carton el cartón

carwash el lavacoches [labakochess]

case (suitcase) la maleta [malayta]

cash el dinero [deenairo] (verb) cobrar

will you cash this for me? ¿podría hacerme efectivo un cheque? [podree-a athairmay efekteebo oon chaykay]

cash desk la caja [kaHa]

cash dispenser el cajero automático [kaHairo owtomateeko]

cashier (man/woman) el cajero/ la cajera

cassette la cassette [kaset]

cassette recorder el cassette

castanets las castañuelas [kastan-ywaylass]

Castile Castilla [kastee-ya]

Castilian castellano [kastay-yano]

castle el castillo [kastee-yo]

casualty department las urgencias [oorHenth-yass]

cat el gato

Catalonia Cataluña [kata-loon-ya]

catch (verb) coger [koHair]

where do we catch the bus to ...? ¿dónde se coge el autobús a ...? [donday say koHay]

cathedral la catedral

Catholic (adj) católico

cauliflower la coliflor

cave la cueva [kwayba]

ceiling el techo [taycho]

celery el apio [ap-yo]

cellar (for wine) la bodega [bodayga]

cemetery el cementerio [thementair-yo]

Centigrade* centígrado [thenteegrado]

centimetre* el centímetro [thenteemetro]

central central [thentral]

central heating la calefacción central [kalayfakth-yon]

centre el centro [thentro]
how do we get to the city centre? ¿cómo se llega al centro? [say yayga]

cereal los cereales [theray-aless]

certainly desde luego [desday lwaygo]
certainly not desde luego que no [kay]

chair la silla [see-ya]

champagne el champán

change (money) el cambio [kamb-yo]
(verb) cambiar [kamb-yar]
can I change this for ...? ¿puedo cambiar esto por ...? [pwaydo]
I don't have any change no tengo nada suelto [swelto]
can you give me change for a 20 euro note? ¿puede cambiarme un billete de viente euros? [pwayday kamb-yarmay oon bee-yaytay day bay-eentay ay-ooross]

dialogue

do we have to change (trains)? ¿tenemos que cambiar de tren? [tenaymoss kay kamb-yar]
yes, change at Córdoba/no it's a direct train sí, cambie en Córdoba/no, es un tren directo [kamb-yay]

changed: to get changed cambiarse [kamb-yarsay]

chapel la capilla [kapee-ya]

charge (verb) cobrar

cheap barato
do you have anything cheaper? tiene algo más barato? [t-yaynay]

check (US) el cheque [chaykay]
(US: bill) la cuenta [kwaynta]
see bill
(verb) revisar [rebeesar]
could you check the ..., please? ¿puede revisar el ..., por favor? [pwayday]

check book el talonario de cheques [chaykess]

check-in la facturación [faktoorath-yon]

check in facturar
where do we have to check in? ¿dónde se factura? [donday say]

cheek la mejilla [meнee-ya]

cheerio! hasta luego [asta lwaygo]

cheers! (toast) ¡salud! [sal**oo**]

cheese el queso [**kay**so]

chemist's la farmacia [farmath-ya]

cheque el cheque [**chay**kay]
  do you take cheques? ¿aceptan cheques? [a**thep**tan]

cheque book el talonario de cheques [day]

cheque card la tarjeta de banco [tar**Hay**ta]

cherry la cereza [thai**ray**tha]

chess el ajedrez [a**Hed**reth]

chest el pecho [**pay**cho]

chewing gum el chicle [**cheek**lay]

chicken el pollo [**po**-yo]

chickenpox la varicela [baree**the**la]

child (male/female) el niño [**neen**-yo]/la niña

  children los niños

child minder la niñera [neen-**yai**ra]

children's pool la piscina infantil [pees**thee**na eenfan**teel**]

children's portion la ración pequeña (para niños) [rath-**yon** pe**kayn**-ya – neen-**yoss**]

chin la barbilla [bar**bee**-ya]

china la porcelana [porthe**la**na]

Chinese (adj) chino [**chee**no]

chips las patatas fritas

chocolate el chocolate [choko**la**tay]
  milk chocolate el chocolate con leche [**le**chay]

plain chocolate el chocolate negro [**nay**gro]
  a hot chocolate la taza de chocolate [**ta**tha]

choose elegir [ele**Heer**]

Christian name el nombre de pila [**nom**bray day **pee**la]

Christmas Navidad [nabee**da**]
  Christmas Eve Nochebuena [nochay-**bway**na]
  merry Christmas! ¡Feliz Navidad! [fe**leeth**]

church la iglesia [eeg**lays**-ya]

cider la sidra [**seed**ra]

cigar el puro [**poo**ro]

cigarette el cigarro [thee**ga**rro], el cigarrillo [theega**rree**-yo]

cigarette lighter el encendedor [enthende**dor**]

cinema el cine [**thee**nay]

circle el círculo [**theer**koolo]
  (in theatre) el anfiteatro [anfeetay-**a**tro]

city la ciudad [thee-oo-**da**]

city centre el centro de la ciudad [**then**tro day]

clean (adj) limpio [**leem**p-yo]
  can you clean these for me? ¿puede limpiarme estos? [**pway**day leemp-**yar**may]

cleaning solution (for contact lenses) el líquido limpiador para las lentillas [**lee**keedo leemp-**ya**dor – lente-**yass**]

cleansing lotion la crema limpiadora [**kray**ma leemp-**ya**dora]

clear claro

clever listo

cliff el acantilado

climbing el alpinismo

cling film el plástico de
envolver [day embolbair]

clinic la clínica

cloakroom el guardarropa
[gwardarropa]

clock el reloj [reloH]

close (verb) cerrar [therrar]

dialogue

what time do you close?
¿a qué hora se cierra? [kay
ora say th-yairra]
we close at 8 p.m. on
weekdays and 1:30 p.m.
on Saturdays cerramos a
las ocho de la tarde entre
semana y a la una y media
los sábados [therramoss – day
la tarday entray]
do you close for lunch?
¿cierra al mediodía?
[th-yairra – med-yodee-a]
yes, between 1 and 3.30
p.m. sí, entre una y tres y
media de la tarde [entray
– day la tarday]

closed cerrado [thairrado]

cloth (fabric) la tela [tayla]
(for cleaning etc) el trapo

clothes la ropa

clothes line la cuerda para
tender [kwairda para tendair]

clothes peg la pinza de la ropa
[peentha day]

cloud la nube [noobay]

cloudy nublado

clutch el embrague [embragay]

coach (bus) el autocar [owtokar]
(on train) el vagón [bagon]

coach station la estación
de autobuses [estath-yon day
owtoboosess]

coach trip la excursión (en
autobús) [eskoorss-yon]

coast la costa

on the coast en la costa

coat (long coat) el abrigo
(jacket) la chaqueta [chakayta]

coathanger la percha [paircha]

cockroach la cucaracha
[kookaracha]

cocoa el cacao [kaka-o]

coconut el coco

code (for phoning) el prefijo
[prefeeHo]

what's the (dialling) code for
Málaga? ¿cuál es el prefijo de
Málaga [kwal]

coffee el café [kafay]

two coffees, please dos cafés,
por favor

coin la moneda [monayda]

Coke® la Coca-Cola

cold frío [free-o]

I'm cold tengo frío

I have a cold tengo catarro

collapse: he's collapsed se ha
desmayado [say a desma-yado]

collar el cuello [kway-yo]

collect recoger [rekoHair]

I've come to collect ... he
venido a recoger ... [ay
beneedo]

collect call la llamada a cobro revertido [yamada – rebairteedo]

college la Universidad [ooneebairseeda]

colour el color

do you have this in other colours? ¿tiene otros colores? [t-yaynay]

colour film la película en color

comb el peine [pay-eenay]

come venir [bayneer]

dialogue

where do you come from? ¿de dónde es? [day donday]
I come from Edinburgh soy de Edimburgo

come back volver [bolbair]
I'll come back tomorrow volveré mañana [bolbairay]

come in entrar

comfortable cómodo

compact disc el compact disc

company (business) la compañía [kompan-yee-a]

compartment (on train) el compartimento

compass la brújula [broo-Hoola]

complain quejarse [kayHarsay]

complaint la queja [kayHa]
I have a complaint tengo una queja

completely completamente [komplaytamentay]

computer el ordenador

concert el concierto [konth-yairto]

concussion la conmoción cerebral [kommoth-yon thairebral]

conditioner (for hair) el acondicionador de pelo [akondeeth-yonador day paylo]

condom el condón

conference el congreso

confirm confirmar

congratulations! ¡enhorabuena! [enorabwayna]

connecting flight el vuelo de conexión [bwaylo day koneks-yon]

connection el enlace [enlathay]

conscious consciente [konth-yentay]

constipation el estreñimiento [estren-yeem-yento]

consulate el consulado [konsoolado]

contact (verb) ponerse en contacto con [ponairsay]

contact lenses las lentes de contacto, las lentillas [lentess – lentee-yass]

contraceptive el anticonceptivo [anteekontheepteebo]

convenient a mano
that's not convenient eso no viene bien [b-yaynay b-yen]

cook (verb) cocinar [kotheenar]
not cooked poco hecho

[echo]

cooker la cocina [kotheena]

cookie la galleta [ga-yayta]

cooking utensils los utensilios de cocina [ootenseel-yoss day kotheena]

cool fresco [fraysko]

cork el corcho

corkscrew el sacacorchos

corner: on the corner en la esquina [eskeena]

in the corner en el rincón

cornflakes los cornflakes

correct (right) correcto

corridor el pasillo [pasee-yo]

cosmetics los cosméticos

cost (verb) costar

how much does it cost? ¿cuánto cuesta? [kwanto kwesta]

cot la cuna

cotton el algodón

cotton wool el algodón

couch (sofa) el sofá

couchette la litera [leetaira]

cough la tos

cough medicine la medicina para la tos [medeetheena]

could: could you ...? ¿podría ...?

could I have ...? quisiera ... [kees-yaira...]

I couldn't ... (wasn't able to) no podía ...

country (nation) el país [pa-eess]

(countryside) el campo

countryside el campo

couple (two people) la pareja

[parayHa]

a couple of ... un par de ...

courgette el calabacín [kalabatheen]

courier el/la guía turístico [gee-a]

course (main course etc) el plato

of course por supuesto [soopwesto]

of course not ¡claro que no! [kay]

cousin (male/female) el primo [preemo]/la prima

cow la vaca [baka]

crab el cangrejo [kangrayHo]

cracker la galleta salada [ga-yayta]

craft shop la tienda de artesanía [t-yenda day artesanee-a]

crash el accidente [aktheedentay]

I've had a crash he tenido un accidente [ay teneedo]

crazy loco

cream (on milk, in cake) la nata (lotion) la crema [krayma] (colour) color crema

creche la guardería infantil [gwardairee-a]

credit card la tarjeta de crédito [tarHayta day]

dialogue

can I pay by credit card? ¿puedo pagar con tarjeta? [pwaydo]

Cr

which card do you want to use? ¿qué tarjeta quiere usar? [kay – k-**yai**ray oo**sar**]
yes, sir sí, señor [sen-**yor**]
what's the number? ¿qué número es? [**noo**mairo]
and the expiry date? ¿y la fecha de caducidad? [**fe**cha day kadoo**thee**da]

crisps las patatas fritas (de bolsa)
crockery la loza [**lo**tha]
crossing (by sea) la travesía [trabe**see**-a]
crossroads el cruce [**kroo**thay]
crowd la muchedumbre [moochay-**doo**mbray]
crowded lleno [**yay**no]
crown (on tooth) la funda [**foo**nda]
cruise el crucero [kroo**thai**ro]
crutches la muleta [moo**lay**ta]
cry (verb) llorar [yo**rar**]
cucumber el pepino
cup la taza [**ta**tha]
a cup of ..., please una taza de ..., por favor
cupboard el armario [ar**mar**-yo]
cure la cura [**koo**ra]
curly rizado [ree**tha**do]
current la corriente [korr-**yen**tay]
curtains las cortinas
cushion el cojín [ko**heen**]
custom la costumbre [kos**too**mbray]
Customs la aduana [ad**wa**na]
cut el corte [**kor**tay]

(verb) cortar
I've cut myself me he cortado [may ay]
cutlery los cubiertos [koob-**yair**toss]
cycling el ciclismo [thee**klee**smo]
cyclist el/la ciclista [thee**klee**sta]

D

dad el papá
daily el periódico [pair-yo**dee**ko]
damage: damaged estropeado [estropay-**a**do]
I'm sorry, I've damaged this lo siento, he estropeado esto [s-**yen**to – ay]
damn! ¡maldita sea! [**say**-a]
damp (adj) húmedo [**oo**maydo]
dance el baile [ba-**ee**lay]
(verb) bailar [ba-ee**lar**]
would you like to dance? ¿quiere bailar? [k-**yai**ray]
dangerous peligroso
Danish el danés [da**nayss**]
dark (adj: colour) oscuro [os**koo**ro]
(hair) moreno [mo**ray**no]
it's getting dark está oscureciendo [oskooreth-**yen**do]
date*: what's the date today? ¿qué día es hoy? [kay – oy]
let's make a date for next Monday vamos a quedar para el lunes que viene [**ba**moss a

Cr

kedar – kay b-**yay**nay]

dates (fruit) los dátiles
[**dat**eeless]

daughter la hija [ee**Ha**]

daughter-in-law la nuera
[**nwai**ra]

dawn el amanecer [amanet**hair**]

at dawn al amanecer

day el día

the day after el día siguiente
[seeg-**yen**tay]

the day after tomorrow
pasado mañana [man-**ya**na]

the day before el día anterior
[antair-**yor**]

the day before yesterday
anteayer [antay-a-**yair**]

every day todos los días

all day todo el día

in two days' time dentro de
dos días

have a nice day! ¡que pase un
buen día! [kay **pa**say oon bwen]

day trip la excursión [exkoors-
yon]

dead muerto [**mwair**to]

deaf sordo

deal (business) la transacción
[transakth-**yon**]

it's a deal trato hecho [**ay**cho]

death la muerte [**mwair**tay]

decaffeinated coffee el café
descafeinado [ka**fay** deskafay-
ee**na**do]

December diciembre [deeth-
yembray]

decide decidir [detheed**eer**]

we haven't decided
yet todavía no hemos

decidido [todab**ee**-a no **ay**moss
detheed**ee**do]

decision la decisión [detheess-
yon]

deck (on ship) la cubierta [koob-
yairta]

deckchair la tumbona

deduct descontar

deep profundo

definitely claramente, ¡desde
luego! [klara**men**tay **des**day
l**way**go]

definitely not desde luego
que no [kay]

degree (qualification) la carrera
[ka**rrai**ra]

delay el retraso

deliberately a propósito

delicatessen la charcutería
[charkootai**ree**-a]

delicious delicioso [deleeth-
yoso]

deliver repartir

delivery (of mail) el reparto

Denmark Dinamarca

dental floss el hilo dental
[**ee**lo]

dentist el/la dentista

dialogue

it's this one here es ésta de
aquí [day a**kee**]
this one? ¿ésta?
no, that one no, esa [**ay**sa]
here? ¿aquí?
yes sí

dentures la dentadura postiza

[posteetha]

deodorant el desodorante
[desodorantay]

department el departamento

department store los
grandes almacenes [grandess
almathayness]

departure la salida

departure lounge la sala de
embarque [day embarkay]

depend: it depends depende
[dependay]

it depends on ... depende
de ... [day]

deposit (as security) la fianza
[fee-antha]

(as part payment) el depósito

description la descripción
[deskreepth-yon]

dessert el postre [postray]

destination el destino

develop (photos) revelar
[rebelar]

dialogue

could you develop these
films? ¿puede revelar
estos carretes? [pwayday
– karraytess]

when will they be ready?
¿cuándo estarán listos?
[kwando]

tomorrow afternoon
mañana por la tarde [man-
yana por la tarday]

how much is the four-hour
service? ¿cuánto es el
servicio de cuatro horas?

[kwanto ess el sairbeeth-yo day
kwatro orass]

diabetic (man/woman) el
diabético [dee-abayteeko]/la
diabética

diabetic foods la comida para
diabéticos

dial marcar

dialling code el prefijo
[prefeeHo]

diamond el diamante
[d-yamantay]

diaper el pañal [pan-yal]

diarrhoea la diarrea
[d-yarray-a]

diary (business etc) la agenda
[aHenda]

(for personal experiences) el
diario [d-yar-yo]

dictionary el diccionario
[deekth-yonar-yo]

didn't
see not

die morir

diesel el gasoil

diet la dieta [d-yayta]

I'm on a diet estoy a dieta

I have to follow a special diet
tengo que seguir una dieta
especial [kay segeer – espeth-yal]

difference la diferencia
[deefairenth-ya]

what's the difference? ¿cuál
es la diferencia? [kwal]

different diferente [deefairentay]

this one is different éste es
diferente [estay]

a different table otra mesa

[**may**sa]

difficult difícil [deef**ee**theel]

difficulty la dificultad
[deefeek**oo**lta]

dinghy el bote [**bo**tay]

dining room el comedor
[komay**dor**]

dinner (evening meal) la cena
[**thay**na]

to have dinner cenar

direct (adj) directo

is there a direct train? ¿hay
un tren directo? [ī]

direction la dirección [deerekth-
yon]

which direction is it? ¿en qué
dirección está? [kay]

is it in this direction? ¿es por
aquí? [a**kee**]

directory enquiries
información [eenformath-
yon]

dirt la suciedad [sooth-**yay**da]

dirty sucio [**sooth**-yo]

disabled minusválido
[meenoosba**lee**do]

is there access for the
disabled? ¿hay acceso
para minusválidos? [ī
akth**ay**so]

disappear desaparecer
[dessapareth**air**]

it's disappeared
ha desaparecido [a
dessapareth**ee**do]

disappointed desilusionado
[deseeloos-yo**na**do]

disappointing decepcionante
[dethepth-yo**nan**tay]

disaster el desastre [des**a**stray]

disco la discoteca

discount el descuento
[desk**wen**to]

is there a discount? ¿hacen
descuento? [**a**then]

disease la enfermedad
[enfairm**ed**a]

disgusting repugnante
[repoogn**an**tay]

dish (meal) el plato [**pla**to]

dishcloth el paño de cocina
[**pan**-yo day koth**ee**na]

disinfectant el desinfectante
[deseenfekt**an**tay]

disk (for computer) diskette
[deesk**ay**tay]

disposable diapers los pañales
(braguita) [pan-**ya**less brag**ee**ta]

disposable nappies los
pañales (braguita)

distance la distancia [deest**anth**-
ya]

in the distance a lo lejos
[**lay**Hoss]

distilled water el agua
destilada [**a**gwa]

district el distrito

disturb molestar

diversion (detour) el desvío
[desb**ee**-o]

diving board el trampolín

divorced divorciado [deeborth-
yado]

dizzy: I feel dizzy estoy
mareado [maray-**a**do]

do hacer [ath**air**]

what shall we do? ¿qué
hacemos? [kay ath**ay**moss]

how do you do it? ¿cómo se hace? [say athay]
will you do it for me? ¿me lo puede hacer usted? [pwayday athair oostay]

dialogues

how do you do? ¿qué tal? [kay]
nice to meet you encantado de conocerle [day konothairlay]
what do you do? (work) ¿a qué se dedica? [say]
I'm a teacher, and you? soy profesor, ¿y usted? [ee oostay]
I'm a student soy estudiante [estood-yantay]
what are you doing this evening? ¿qué hace esta tarde? [athay]
we're going out for a drink; do you want to join us? vamos a salir a tomar una copa; ¿nos acompaña? [bamoss – akompan-ya]

do you want cream? ¿quiere crema? [k-yairay krayma]
I do, but she doesn't yo sí, pero ella no [pairo ay-ya]

doctor el/la médico
we need a doctor necesitamos un médico [naytheseetamoss]
please call a doctor por favor, llame a un médico [yamay]

dialogue

where does it hurt? ¿dónde le duele? [donday lay dwaylay]
right here justo aquí [Hoosto akee]
does that hurt now? ¿le duele ahora? [lay dwaylay a-ora]
yes sí
take this to the chemist's lleve esto a la farmacia [yaybay – farmath-ya]

document el documento [dokoomento]
dog el perro [pairro]
doll la muñeca [moon-yayka]
domestic flight el vuelo nacional [bwaylo nath-yonal]
donkey el burro [boorro]
don't! ¡no lo haga! [aga]
don't do that! ¡no haga eso! [ayso]
see not
door la puerta [pwairta]
doorman el portero [portairo]
double doble [doblay]
double bed la cama de matrimonio [matreemon-yo]
double room la habitación doble [abeetath-yon doblay]
doughnut el dónut [donoot]

down: down here aquí abajo [akee abaнo]

put it down over there póngalo ahí [a-ee]

it's down there on the right está ahí a la derecha [dairecha]

it's further down the road está bajando la calle [baнando la ka-yay]

downhill skiing el esquí alpino [ayskee alpeeno]

downmarket (restaurant etc) barato

downstairs abajo [abaнo]

dozen la docena [dothayna]

half a dozen media docena [mayd-ya]

drain el desagüe [desagway]

draught beer la cerveza de grifo [thairbaytha day]

draughty: it's draughty hay corriente [ī korr-yentay]

drawer el cajón [kaнon]

drawing el dibujo [deebooнo]

dreadful horrible [orreeblay]

dream el sueño [sway-yo]

dress el vestido [besteedo]

dressed: to get dressed vestirse [besteersay]

dressing (for cut) el vendaje [bendaнay]

salad dressing el aliño [aleen-yo]

dressing gown la bata

drink (alcoholic) la copa (non-alcoholic) la bebida (verb) beber [bebair]

a cold drink una bebida fría

can I get you a drink? ¿quiere beber algo? [k-yairay]

what would you like (to drink)? ¿qué le apetece beber? [kay lay apetaythay]

no thanks, I don't drink no gracias, no bebo [grath-yass no baybo]

I'll just have a drink of water voy a beber sólo agua [boy – agwa]

drinking water agua potable [agwa potablay]

is this drinking water? ¿esto es agua potable?

drive (verb) conducir [kondootheer]

we drove here vinimos en coche [beenemoss en kochay]

I'll drive you home te llevaré a casa en el coche [tay yebaray – kochay]

driver (man/woman) el conductor [kondooktor]/la conductora

driving licence el permiso de conducir [pairmeeso day kondootheer]

drop: just a drop, please (of drink) un poquito [pokeeto]

drug la medicina [maydeetheena]

drugs (narcotics) la droga

drunk (adj) borracho

drunken driving conducir

en estado de embriaguez
[kondootheer – embr-yageth]
dry (adj) seco [**sayko**]
(sherry) fino
dry-cleaner la tintorería
[teentorairee-a]
duck el pato
due: he was due to arrive
yesterday tenía que llegar
ayer [tenee-a kay yegar a-**yair**]
when is the train due?
¿cuándo tiene el tren la
llegada? [kwando t-**yay**nay
– ye**ga**da]
dull (pain) sordo
(weather) gris [**greess**]
dummy (baby's) el chupete
[choo**pay**tay]
during durante [doo**ran**tay]
dust el polvo [**po**lbo]
dusty polvoriento [polbor-
yento]
dustbin el cubo de la basura
[**koo**bo day]
duty-free (goods) (los
productos) duty free
duty-free shop la tienda de
duty free [t-**yen**da day]
duvet el edredón

E

each cada
how much are they each?
¿cuánto es cada uno? [**kwan**to]
ear la oreja [o**ray**Ha]
earache: I have earache tengo
dolor de oídos [o-**ee**doss]

early temprano
early in the morning por la
mañana temprano [man-**yan**a]
I called by earlier vine antes
[**bee**nay an**tess**]
earring el pendiente [pend-
yentay]
east este [**es**tay]
in the east en el este
Easter la Semana Santa
easy fácil [**fath**eel]
eat comer [ko**mair**]
we've already eaten, thanks
ya hemos comido, gracias
[**ay**moss]
eau de toilette el agua de
baño [**a**gwa day ban-yo]
EC la CE [thay-ay]
economy class la clase turista
[kla**ssay**]
Edinburgh Edimburgo
[edeem**boo**rgo]
egg el huevo [**way**bo]
eggplant la berenjena
[beren**Hay**na]
either: either ... or ... o ... o ...
either of them cualquiera de
ellos [kwalk-**yai**ra day **ay**-yoss]
elastic el elástico
elastic band la goma elástica
elbow el codo
electric eléctrico
electrical appliances los
electrodomésticos
electric fire la estufa eléctrica
electrician el electricista
[elektree**thee**sta]
electricity la electricidad
[elektreethee**da**]

elevator el ascensor
[asthensor]
else: something else algo más
somewhere else en otra parte
[partay]

dialogue

would you like anything
else? ¿quiere algo más?
[k-yairay]
no, nothing else, thanks
nada más, gracias

email el email
embassy la embajada
[embaHada]
emergency la emergencia
[emairHenth-ya]
this is an emergency! ¡es una
emergencia!
emergency exit la salida de
emergencia
empty vacío [bathee-o]
end el final [feenal]
(verb) terminar [tairmeenar]
at the end of the street al
final de la calle [day la ka-yay]
when does it end? ¿cuándo
termina? [kwando tairmeena]
engaged (toilet) ocupado
(telephone) comunicando
(to be married) prometido
engine (car) el motor
England Inglaterra
[eenglatairra]
English inglés [eenglayss]
I'm English (man/woman) soy
inglés/inglesa

do you speak English? ¿habla
inglés? [abla]
enjoy: to enjoy oneself
divertirse [deebairteersay]

dialogue

how did you like the film?
¿le gustó la película? [lay
goosto]
I enjoyed it very much, did
you enjoy it? me gustó
mucho, ¿le gustó a usted?
[may – moocho – lay – oostay]

enjoyable entretenido
enlargement (of photo) la
ampliación [ampl-yath-yon]
enormous enorme [enormay]
enough suficiente [soofeeth-
yentay]
there's not enough no hay
bastante [ī bastantay]
it's not big enough no es
suficientemente grande
[soofeeth-yentementay]
that's enough es suficiente
entrance la entrada
envelope el sobre [sobray]
epileptic epiléptico
equipment el equipo [ekeepo]
especially especialmente
[espeth-yalmentay]
essential imprescindible
[eemprestheendeeblay]
it is essential that ... es
imprescindible que ... [kay]
EU UE [oo-ay]
euro el euro [ay-ooro]

Eurocheque el eurocheque [ay-oorochekay]

Eurocheque card la tarjeta eurocheque [tarHayta]

Europe Europa [ay-ooropa]

European europeo [ay-ooropay-o]

European Union la Unión Europea [oon-yon]

even (including) incluso [eenklooso]

even if ... incluso si ...

evening (early evening) la tarde [tarday]

(after nightfall) la noche [nochay]

this evening esta tarde/noche

in the evening por la tarde/noche

evening meal la cena [thayna]

eventually finalmente [feenalmentay]

ever alguna vez [beth]

dialogue

have you ever been to Barcelona? ¿ha estado alguna vez en Barcelona? [a]

yes, I was there two years ago sí, estuve allí hace dos años [estoobay a-yee athay – an-yoss]

every cada

every day todos los días

everyone todos

everything todo

everywhere en todas partes

[partess]

exactly! ¡exactamente! [exactamentay]

exam el examen

example el ejemplo [eHaymplo]

for example por ejemplo

excellent excelente [esthelentay]

excellent! ¡estupendo!

except excepto [esthepto]

excess baggage el exceso de equipaje [esthayso day ekeepaHay]

exchange rate el cambio [kamb-yo]

exciting emocionante [emoth-yonantay]

excuse me (to get past) con permiso

(to get attention) ¡por favor! [fabor]

(to say sorry) perdone [pairdonay]

exhaust (pipe) el tubo de escape [toobo day eskapay]

exhausted (tired) agotado

exhibition la exposición [exposeeth-yon]

exit la salida

where's the nearest exit? ¿cuál es la salida más próxima? [kwal]

expect esperar [espairar]

expensive caro

experienced con experiencia [espair-yenth-ya]

explain explicar [espleekar]

can you explain that? ¿puede explicármelo?

[pw**ay**day]

express (mail) urgente
[oorH**ay**tay]

(train) expreso [espr**ay**so]

extension (phone) extensión
[estens-y**on**]

extension 221, please
extensión doscientos
veintiuno, por favor

extension lead el alargador

**extra: can we have an extra
one?** ¿nos puede dar otro?
[pw**ay**day]

do you charge extra for that?
¿esto tiene recargo?
[t-y**ay**nay]

extraordinary
extraordinario [estra-ordeenar-
yo]

extremely extremadamente
[estremadam**en**tay]

eye el ojo [o**ho**]

**will you keep an eye on my
suitcase for me?** ¿puede
cuidarme la maleta? [pw**ay**day
kweed**ar**may la
mal**ay**ta]

eyebrow pencil el lápiz de
cejas [l**a**peeth day th**ay**Hass]

eye drops el colirio
[koleer-yo]

eyeglasses las gafas

eyeliner el lápiz de ojos
[l**a**peeth day o**H**oss]

eye make-up remover el
desmaquillador de ojos
[desmakee-y**a**dor]

eye shadow la sombra de ojos

F

face la cara

factory la fábrica

Fahrenheit* Fahrenheit

faint (verb) desmayarse [desma-
y**ar**say]

she's fainted se ha
desmayado [say a desma-y**a**do]

I feel faint estoy mareado
[maray-**a**do]

fair la feria [f**air**-ya]

(adj) justo [**H**oosto]

fairly bastante [bast**an**tay]

fake la falsificación
[falseefeekath-y**on**]

fall el otoño [ot**on**-yo]
see **autumn**

fall caerse [ka-**air**say]

she's had a fall se ha caído
[say a ka-**ee**do]

false falso [f**al**-so]

family la familia [fam**eel**-ya]

famous famoso

fan (electrical) el ventilador
[bentee**la**dor]

(hand held) el abanico

(sports) el/la hincha [**een**cha]

fan belt la correa del
ventilador [korr**ay**-a del
bentee**la**dor]

fantastic fantástico

far lejos [l**ay**Hoss]

dialogue

is it far from here? ¿está
lejos de aquí? [day ak**ee**]

no, not very far no, no muy lejos [mwee]
well how far? bueno, ¿cuánto? [bwayno kwanto]
it's about 20 kilometres unos veinte kilómetros

fare el precio [prayth-yo]
farm la granja [granHa]
fashionable de moda
fast rápido
fat (person) gordo
  (on meat) la grasa
father el padre [padray]
father-in-law el suegro [swaygro]
faucet el grifo [greefo]
fault el defecto
  sorry, it was my fault lo siento, fue culpa mía [s-yento fway koolpa mee-a]
  it's not my fault no es culpa mía
faulty defectuoso [dayfektwoso]
favourite favorito [faboreeto]
fax el fax
  (verb: person) mandar un fax a (document) mandar por fax
February febrero [febrairo]
feel sentir
  I feel hot tengo calor
  I feel unwell no me siento bien [may s-yento b-yen]
  I feel like going for a walk me apetece dar un paseo [apetaythay – pasay-o]
  how are you feeling today? ¿qué tal se encuentra hoy? [kay tal say enkwentra oy]

I'm feeling better me siento mejor [mayHor]
felt-tip (pen) el rotulador
fence la valla [ba-ya]
fender el parachoques [parachokess]
ferry el ferry
festival el festival [festeebal]
fetch: I'll fetch him yo iré a recogerle [eeray a raykoHairlay]
  will you come and fetch me later? ¿quiere venir a buscarme más tarde? [k-yairay beneer a booskarmay mass tarday]
feverish con fiebre [f-yaybray]
few: a few unos pocos
  a few days unos pocos días
fiancé el novio [nob-yo]
fiancée la novia [nob-ya]
field el campo
fight la pelea [pelay-a]
figs los higos [eegoss]
fill (verb) llenar [yenar]
fill in rellenar [ray-yenar]
  do I have to fill this in? ¿tengo que rellenar esto? [kay]
fill up llenar [yenar]
  fill it up, please lleno, por favor [yayno]
filling (in cake, sandwich) el relleno [ray-yeno]
  (in tooth) el empaste [empastay]
film (movie, for camera) la película

dialogue

do you have this kind of film? ¿tiene películas de este tipo? [t-**yay**nay – day e**stay**]

yes, how many exposures? sí, ¿de cuántas fotos? [**kwan**tass]

36 treinta y seis

film processing el revelado [rebe**la**do]

filter coffee el café de filtro [ka**fay** day fee**ltro**]

filter papers los filtros

filthy sucísimo [soothee**seemo**]

find (verb) encontrar

I can't find it no lo encuentro [en**kwen**tro]

I've found it lo he encontrado [ay]

find out enterarse [entera**rsay**]

could you find out for me? ¿me lo puede preguntar? [may lo **pway**day pregoon**tar**]

fine (weather) bueno [**bway**no] (noun) la multa [**mool**ta]

dialogues

how are you? ¿cómo estás?

I'm fine, thanks, gracias bien, [b-yen **grath**-yass]

is that OK? ¿va bien así? [ba]

that's fine, thanks está bien, gracias

finger el dedo [**day**do]

finish (verb) terminar [tairmee**nar**], acabar

I haven't finished yet no he terminado todavía [ay tairmee**na**do todabee-a]

when does it finish? ¿cuándo termina? [**kwan**do ter**mee**na]

fire: fire! ¡fuego! [**fway**go]

can we light a fire here? ¿se puede encender fuego aquí? [say **pway**day enthen**dair** – ake**e**]

it's on fire está ardiendo [ard-**yen**do]

fire alarm la alarma de incendios [day eenthend-yoss]

fire brigade los bomberos [bomba**iross**]

fire escape la salida de incendios [day eenthend-yoss]

fire extinguisher el extintor [estee**ntor**]

first primero [pree**mairo**]

I was first fui el primero [**fwoo-ee**]

at first al principio [preenth**ee**p-yo]

the first time la primera vez [beth]

first on the left la primera a la izquierda [eethk-**yairda**]

first aid primeros auxilios [owk**seel**-yoss]

first aid kit el botiquín [botee**keen**]

first class (travel etc) de primera

(clase) [preemaira klasay]

first floor la primera planta

(US) la planta baja [baHa]

first name el nombre de pila
[nombray day]

fish el pez [peth]

(food) el pescado

fishing village el pueblo
de pescadores [pweblo day
peskadoress]

fishmonger's la pescadería
[peskadairee-a]

fit (attack) el ataque [atakay]

fit: it doesn't fit me no me
viene bien [b-yaynay b-yen]

fitting room el probador

fix (verb) arreglar

(arrange) fijar [feeHar]

can you fix this? ¿puede
arreglar esto? [pwayday]

fizzy con gas

flag la bandera [bandaira]

flannel la manopla

flash (for camera) el flash

flat (noun: apartment) el piso

(adj) llano [yano]

I've got a flat tyre tengo un
pinchazo [peenchatho]

flavour el sabor

flea la pulga

flight el vuelo [bwaylo]

flight number el número de
vuelo [noomairo day]

flippers las aletas [alaytass]

flood la inundación
[eenoondath-yon]

floor (of room) el suelo [swaylo]

(of building) el piso

on the floor en el suelo

florist la floristería
[floreestairee-a]

flour la harina [areena]

flower la flor

flu la gripe [greepay]

**fluent: he speaks fluent
Spanish** domina el castellano
[kastay-yano]

fly la mosca

(verb) volar [bolar]

can we fly there? ¿podemos
ir en avión allí? [podaymoss eer
en ab-yon a-yee]

fly in llegar en avión [yegar]

fly out irse en avión [eersay]

fog la niebla [n-yebla]

foggy: it's foggy hay niebla [ī]

folk dancing el baile
tradicional [ba-eelay tradeeth-
yonal]

folk music la música popular
[mooseeka popoolar]

follow seguir [segeer]

follow me sígame [seegamay]

food la comida

food poisoning la intoxicación
alimenticia [eentoxeekath-yon
aleementeeth-ya]

food shop/store la tienda
de comestibles [t-yenda day
komesteebless]

foot* el pie [p-yay]

on foot a pie

football (game) el fútbol

(ball) el balón

football match el partido de
fútbol

for para, por

do you have something

for ...? (headache/diarrhoea etc)
¿tiene algo para ...?
[t-**yay**nay]

dialogues

who's the chicken paella for? ¿para quién es la paella con pollo? [k-**yen** ess la pa-**ay**-ya con **po**-yo]
that's for me es para mí
and this one? ¿y ésta? [ee]
that's for her ésa es para ella [**ay**sa – **ay**-ya]

where do I get the bus for Granada? ¿dónde se coge el autobús para Granada? [**don**day say ko**Hay**]
the bus for Granada leaves from Plaza de España el autobús para Granada sale de la Plaza de España [**sa**lay day]

how long have you been here for? ¿cuánto tiempo lleva aquí? [**kwan**to t-**yem**po **yay**ba a**kee**]
I've been here for two days, how about you? llevo aquí dos días, ¿y usted? [**yay**bo – ee oos**tay**]
I've been here for a week llevo aquí una semana

forehead la frente [**fren**tay]
foreign extranjero [estran**Hai**ro]
foreigner (man/woman) el

extranjero/la extranjera
forest el bosque [**bos**kay]
forget olvidar [olbee**dar**]
I forget no me acuerdo [no may ak**wair**do]
I've forgotten me he olvidado [ay olbee**da**do]
fork el tenedor
(in road) la bifurcación [beefoorkath-**yon**]
form (document) el impreso [eem**pray**so]
formal (dress) de etiqueta [day eteek**ay**ta]
fortnight quince días [**keen**thay]
fortunately afortunadamente [afortoonada**men**tay]
forward: could you forward my mail? ¿puede enviarme el correo? [**pway**day emb-**yar**may el kor**ray**-o]
forwarding address la nueva dirección [n**way**ba deerekth-**yon**]
foundation (make-up) la crema base [**kray**ma **ba**say]
fountain la fuente [**fwen**tay]
foyer (of hotel, theatre) el hall [Hol]
fracture la fractura [frak**too**ra]
France Francia [**franth**-ya]
free libre [**lee**bray]
(no charge) gratuito [grat**wee**to]
is it free (of charge)? ¿es gratis?
freeway la autopista [owtop**ee**sta]
freezer el congelador [konHayla**dor**]
French francés [fran**thess**]

French fries las patatas fritas

frequent frecuente [frekwentay]

how frequent is the bus to Seville? ¿cada cuánto tiempo hay autobús a Sevilla? [kwanto t-yempo ī]

fresh fresco

fresh orange el zumo de naranja natural [thoomo de naranHa natooral]

Friday viernes [b-yairness]

fridge el frigorífico

fried frito

fried egg el huevo frito [waybo]

friend (male/female) el amigo/la amiga

friendly simpático

from de, desde [day, desday]

when does the next train from Tarragona arrive? ¿cuándo llega el próximo tren de Tarragona? [kwando yayga]

from Monday to Friday de lunes a viernes [day]

from next Thursday desde el próximo jueves

dialogue

where are you from? ¿de dónde es usted? [day donday ess oostay]

I'm from Slough soy de Slough [soy day]

front la parte delantera [partay delantaira]

in front delante [delantay]

in front of the hotel delante del hotel

at the front delante

frost la escarcha

frozen congelado [konHaylado]

frozen food los congelados

fruit la fruta

fruit juice el zumo de frutas [thoomo]

fry freír [fray-eer]

frying pan la sartén

full lleno [yayno]

it's full of ... está lleno de ... [day]

I'm full estoy lleno/llena

full board pensión completa [pens-yon komplayta]

fun: it was fun fue muy divertido [fway mwee deebairteedo]

funeral el funeral [foonairal]

funny (strange) raro

(amusing) gracioso [grath-yoso]

furniture los muebles [mwaybless]

further más allá [a-ya]

it's further down the road está más adelante [adelantay]

dialogue

how much further is it to Cáceres? ¿cuánto queda para Cáceres? [kwanto kayda]

about 5 kilometres unos cinco kilómetros

fuse el fusible [fooseeblay]
 the lights have fused se han
 fundido los plomos [say an]
fuse box la caja de fusibles
 [kaHa day fooseebless]
fuse wire el plomo [footooro]
future el futuro [footooro]
 in the future en lo sucesivo
 [sootheseebo]

G

gallon* el galón
game (cards etc) el juego
 [Hwaygo]
 (match) el partido
 (meat) la caza [catha]
garage (for fuel) la gasolinera
 [gasoleenaira]
 (for repairs) el taller (de
 reparaciones) [ta-yair day
 reparath-yoness]
 (for parking) el garaje [garaHay]
garden el jardín [Hardeen]
garlic el ajo [aHo]
gas el gas
 (US) la gasolina
gas cylinder (camping gas) la
 bombona de gas
gasoline la gasolina
gas permeable lenses las
 lentillas porosas
 [lentee-yass]
gas station la gasolinera
 [gasoleenaira]
gate la puerta [pwairta]
 (at airport) la puerta de
 embarque [embarkay]

gay el gay
gay bar el bar gay
gears la marcha
gearbox la caja de cambios
 [kaHa day kamb-yoss]
gear lever la palanca de
 velocidades [belotheedadess]
general general [Heneral]
gents (toilet) el aseo de
 caballeros [asay-o day kaba-
 yaiross]
genuine (antique etc) genuino
 [Henweeno]
German alemán
German measles la rubéola
 [roobay-ola]
Germany Alemania
 [aleman-ya]
Gerona Gerona [Herona]
get (fetch) traer [tra-air]
 will you get me another one,
 please? me quiere traer otro,
 por favor [may keeairay]
 how do I get to ...? ¿cómo se
 va a ...? [say ba]
 do you know where I can get
 them? ¿sabe dónde las puedo
 comprar? [sabay donday lass
 pwaydo]

dialogue

can I get you a drink?
¿puedo ofrecerle algo de
beber? [pwaydo ofrethair-lay
– day bebair]
no, I'll get this one; what
would you like? no, ésta la
pago yo; ¿qué le apetece?

[kay lay apay**tay**thay]
a glass of red wine un vaso
de vino tinto [**b**aso day
beeno **tee**nto]

get back (return) volver
[bol**b**air]
get in (arrive) llegar [yegar]
get off bajarse [ba**H**arsay]
where do I get off? ¿dónde
tengo que bajarme? [**d**onday
– kay ba**H**armay]
get on (to train etc) subirse
[soo**bee**rsay]
get out (of car etc) bajarse
[ba**H**arsay]
get up (in the morning)
levantarse [le**b**antarsay]
gift el regalo
gift shop la tienda de regalos
[t-yenda]
gin la ginebra
[**H**ee**nay**bra]
a gin and tonic, please
un gintónic, por favor
[**H**een**t**oneek]
girl la chica [**ch**eeka]
girlfriend la novia [n**ob**-ya]
give dar
**can you give me some
change?** ¿me puede dar
cambio? [may p**w**ayday –
kamb-yo]
I gave it to him se lo dí a él
[say]
will you give this to ...?
¿podría entregarle esto a ...?
[entregarlay]

dialogue

**how much do you want for
this?** ¿cuánto quiere por
esto? [**k**wanto k-yairay]
10 euros diez euros [d-yeth
ay-ooross]
I'll give you 8 euros le doy
ocho euros [lay]

give back devolver
[de**b**ol**b**air]
glad alegre [alegray]
glass (material) el cristal
[kreestal]
(tumbler) el vaso [**b**aso]
(wine glass) la copa
glasses las gafas
gloves los guantes
[**g**wantess]
glue el pegamento
go (verb) ir [eer]
**we'd like to go to the
swimming-pool** nos gustaría
ir a la piscina [pees**thee**na]
where are you going?
¿adónde va? [a**d**onday ba]
where does this bus go?
¿adónde va este autobús?
[estay]
let's go! ¡vamos! [**b**amoss]
she's gone (left) se ha
marchado [say a]
where has he gone? ¿dónde
se ha ido? [**d**onday – **ee**do]
I went there last week fui allí
la semana pasada
[fwee a-**yee**]
go away irse [**ee**rsay]

go away! ¡váyase!
[bayasay]

go back (return) volver [bolbair]

go down (the stairs etc) bajar
[baHar]

go in entrar

go out salir

do you want to go out
tonight? ¿quiere salir esta
noche? [k-yairay – nochay]

go through pasar por

go up (the stairs etc) subir

goat la cabra

God Dios [d-yoss]

goggles las gafas protectoras

gold el oro

golf el golf

golf course el campo de golf

good bueno [bwayno]

good! ¡muy bien! [mwee
b-yen]

it's no good es inútil
[eenooteel]

goodbye adiós [ad-yoss]

good evening buenas tardes
[bwenass tardess]

Good Friday el Viernes Santo
[b-yairness]

good morning buenos días
[bwaynoss]

good night buenas noches
[nochess]

goose el ganso

got: we've got to ... tenemos
que ... [taynaymoss kay]

have you got any apples?
¿tiene manzanas? [t-yaynay]

government el gobierno [gob-
yairno]

gradually gradualmente
[gradwalmentay]

grammar la gramática

gram(me) el gramo

granddaughter la nieta
[n-yayta]

grandfather el abuelo [abwaylo]

grandmother la abuela

grandson el nieto [n-yayto]

grapefruit el pomelo [pomaylo]

grapefruit juice el zumo de
pomelo [thoomo]

grapes las uvas [oobass]

grass la hierba [yairba]

grateful agradecido
[agradetheedo]

gravy la salsa

great (excellent) muy bueno
[mwee bwayno]

that's great! ¡estupendo!
[estoopendo]

a great success un gran
éxito

Great Britain Gran Bretaña
[bretanya]

Greece Grecia [grayth-ya]

greedy comilón

Greek (adj) griego [gr-yaygo]

green verde [bairday]

green card (car insurance) la
carta verde

greengrocer's la frutería
[frootairee-a]

grey gris

grill la parrilla [parree-ya]

grilled a la parrilla

grocer's (la tienda de)
comestibles [t-yenda day
komesteebless]

ground el suelo [swaylo]
  on the ground en el suelo
ground floor la planta baja
  [baHa]
group el grupo
guarantee la garantía
  is it guaranteed? ¿está
  garantizado? [garanteethado]
guest (man/woman) el invitado
  [eembeetado]/la invitada
guesthouse la casa de
  huéspedes [day wespedess]
guide el/la guía [gee-a]
guidebook la guía
guided tour la visita con guía
  [beeseeta]
guitar la guitarra [geetarra]
gum (in mouth) la encía
  [enthee-a]
gun la pistola
gym el gimnasio [Heemnas-yo]

H

hair el pelo [paylo]
hairbrush el cepillo para el
  pelo [thepee-yo]
haircut el corte de pelo [kortay]
hairdresser's (men's) la barbería
  (women's) la peluquería
  [pelookairee-a]
hairdryer el secador de pelo
  [day paylo]
hair gel el fijador (para el
  pelo) [feehador]
hairgrips la horquilla [orkee-ya]
hair spray la laca
half* la mitad [la meeta]

half an hour media hora
  [mayd-ya ora]
half a litre medio litro
  about half that
  aproximadamente la mitad
  de eso [aproximadamentay – day
  ayso]
half board la media pensión
  [pens-yon]
half-bottle la botella pequeña
  [botay-ya pekayn-ya]
half fare el medio billete
  [mayd-yo bee-yaytay]
half price la mitad del precio
  [meeta del preth-yo]
ham el jamón [Hamon]
hamburger la hamburguesa
  [amboorgaysa]
hammer el martillo [martee-yo]
hand la mano
handbag el bolso
handbrake el freno de mano
  [frayno day]
handkerchief el pañuelo [pan-
  ywaylo]
handle (on door) la manilla
  [manee-ya]
  (on suitcase etc) el asa
hand luggage el equipaje de
  mano [ekeepahay]
hang-gliding el ala delta
hangover la resaca
  I've got a hangover tengo
  resaca
happen suceder [soothedair]
  what's happening? ¿qué
  pasa? [kay]
  what has happened? ¿qué ha
  pasado? [a]

happy contento
I'm not happy about this esto
no me agrada [may]
harbour el puerto [pwairto]
hard duro [dooro]
(difficult) difícil [deefeetheel]
hard-boiled egg el huevo
duro [waybo]
hard lenses las lentillas duras
[lentee-yass]
hardly apenas [apaynass]
hardly ever casi nunca
hardware shop la ferretería
[fairretairee-a]
hat el sombrero
hate (verb) odiar
have* tener [tenair]
can I have a ...? ¿me da ...?
[may]
do you have ...? ¿tiene ...?
[t-yaynay]
what'll you have? ¿qué va a
tomar? [kay ba]
I have to leave now tengo
que dejarle ahora [dayHarlay
a-ora]
do I have to ...? ¿tengo
que ...?
can we have some ...? ¿nos
pone ...? [ponay]
hayfever la alergia al polen
[alairHee-a al polayn]
hazelnut la avellana [abay-yana]
he* él
head la cabeza [kabaytha]
headache el dolor de cabeza
headlights el faro
headphones los auriculares
[owreekoolaress]

health food shop la tienda
naturista [t-yenda natooreesta]
healthy sano
hear oir [o-eer]

dialogue

can you hear me? ¿me
oye? [may oy-ay]
I can't hear you, could you
repeat that? no le oigo,
podría repetirlo [lay oygo
podree-a]

hearing aid el aparato del
oído [o-eedo]
heart el corazón [korathon]
heart attack el infarto
heat el calor
heater (in room) el calefactor
(in car) la calefacción
[kalayfakth-yon]
heating la calefacción
heavy pesado
heel (of foot) el talón
(of shoe) el tacón
could you heel these?
¿podría cambiarles los
tacones? [kamb-yarless
– takoness]
heelbar el zapatero [thapatairo]
height la altura
helicopter el helicóptero
hello ¡hola! [ola]
(answer on phone) ¡dígame!
[deegamay]
helmet el casco
help la ayuda [a-yooda]
(verb) ayudar [a-yoodar]

help! ¡socorro!
can you help me? ¿puede ayudarme? [pwayday a-yoodarmay]
thank you very much for your help gracias por su ayuda
helpful amable [amablay]
hepatitis la hepatitis [epateeteess]
her*: I haven't seen her no la he visto [ay]
to her a ella [ay-ya]
with her con ella
for her para ella
that's her ésa es (ella) [aysa]
that's her towel ésa es su toalla
herbal tea el té de hierbas [tay day yairbass]
herbs las hierbas
here aquí [akee]
here is/are ... aquí está/están ...
here you are (offering) tenga
hers* (el) suyo [soo-yo], (la) suya
that's hers es de ella [day ay-ya], es suyo/suya
hey! ¡oiga!
hi! (hello) ¡hola! [ola]
hide (verb) esconder [eskondair]
high alto
highchair la silla alta para bebés [see-ya – baybayss]
highway (US) la autopista [owtopeesta]
hill la colina
him*: I haven't seen him no le he visto [lay ay]

to him a él
with him con él
for him para él
that's him ése es (él) [aysay]
hip la cadera [kadaira]
hire: (verb) alquilar [alkeelar]
for hire de alquiler [alkeelair]
where can I hire a bike? ¿dónde puedo alquilar una bicicleta? [donday pwaydo]
his*: it's his car es su coche
that's his eso de él [ayso day], eso es suyo [soo-yo]
hit (verb) golpear [golpay-ar]
hitch-hike hacer autostop [athair owtostop]
hobby el pasatiempo [pasat-yempo]
hold (verb) sostener [sostaynair]
hole el agujero [agooнairo]
holiday las vacaciones [bakath-yoness]
on holiday de vacaciones
home la casa
at home (in my house) en casa (in my country) en mi país [pa-eess]
we go home tomorrow volvemos a casa mañana [bolbaymoss]
honest honrado [onrado]
honey la miel [m-yel]
honeymoon la luna de miel [loona day]
hood (US) el capó
hope la esperanza [espairantha]

I hope so espero que sí
[espairo kay]

I hope not espero que no

hopefully it won't rain no
lloverá, eso espero [no yobaira
ayso]

horn (of car) la bocina
[botheena]

horrible horrible [orreeblay]

horse el caballo [kaba-yo]

horse riding la equitación
[ekeetath-yon]

hospital el hospital
[ospeetal]

hospitality la hospitalidad
[ospeetaleeda]

thank you for your hospitality
gracias por su hospitalidad
[soo]

hot caliente [kal-yentay]
(spicy) picante [peekantay]

I'm hot tengo calor

it's hot today hoy hace calor
[oy athay]

hotel el hotel [otel]

hotel room: in my hotel room
en mi habitación del hotel
[abeetath-yon]

hour la hora [ora]

house la casa

house wine el vino de la casa
[beeno day]

hovercraft el aerodeslizador
[a-airodesleethador]

how como

how many? ¿cuántos?
[kwantoss]

how do you do? ¡mucho
gusto! [moocho]

dialogues

how are you? ¿cómo está?
fine, thanks, and you? bien
gracias, y usted
[b-yen – ee oostay]

how much is it? ¿cuánto
es? [kwanto]
10 euros diez euros [d-yeth
ay-ooross]
I'll take it me lo quedo
[may lo kaydo]

humid húmedo [oomedo]

humour el humor [oomor]

hungry hambriento [ambr-
yento]

I'm hungry tengo hambre
[ambray]

are you hungry? ¿tiene
hambre? [t-yaynay]

hurry (verb) darse prisa [darsay
preesa]

I'm in a hurry tengo prisa

there's no hurry no hay prisa
[ī]

hurry up! ¡dese prisa! [daysay]

hurt doler [dolair]

it really hurts me duele
mucho [may dwaylay moocho]

husband mi marido

hydrofoil la hidroala [eedro-ala]

hypermarket el hipermercado
[eepairmairkado]

I

I yo
ice el hielo [yaylo]
  with ice con hielo
  no ice, thanks sin hielo,
  gracias [seen]
ice cream el helado [elado]
ice-cream cone el cucurucho
  de helado [kookooroochoo]
iced coffee el café helado
ice lolly el polo
idea la idea [eeday-a]
idiot el/la idiota [eed-yota]
if si
ignition el encendido
  [enthendeedo]
ill enfermo [enfairmo]
  I feel ill me encuentro mal
  [may enkwentro]
illness la enfermedad
  [enfairmayda]
imitation (leather etc) de
  imitación [day eemeetath-yon]
immediately ahora mismo
  [a-ora meesmo]
important importante
  [eemportantay]
  it's very important es muy
  importante [mwee]
  it's not important no tiene
  importancia [t-yaynay
  eemportanth-ya]
impossible imposible
  [eemposeeblay]
impressive impresionante
  [eempres-yonantay]
improve mejorar [mayHorar]

I want to improve my Spanish
  quiero mejorar mi español
  [k-yairo – espan-yol]
in: it's in the centre está en el
  centro
  in my car en mi coche
  in Córdoba en Córdoba
  in two days from now dentro
  de dos días [day]
  in five minutes dentro de
  cinco minutos
  in May en mayo
  in English en inglés
  in Spanish en español?
  is he in? ¿está?
inch* la pulgada [poolgada]
include incluir [eenklweer]
  does that include meals?
  ¿eso incluye las comidas?
  [ayso eenkloo-yay]
  is that included? ¿está eso
  incluido en el precio?
  [eenklweedo en el prayth-yo]
inconvenient inoportuno
  [eenoportoono]
incredible increíble [eenkray-
  eeblay]
Indian (adj) indio [eend-yo]
indicator el intermitente
  [eentairmeetentay]
indigestion la indigestión
  [eendeeHest-yon]
indoor pool la piscina
  cubierta [peestheena koob-
  yairta]
indoors dentro
inexpensive barato
infection la infección [eenfekth-
  yon]

70

infectious infeccioso [eenfekth-yoso]

inflammation la inflamación [eenflamath-yon]

informal (occasion, meeting) informal [eenformal] (dress) de sport [day]

information la información [eenformath-yon]

do you have any information about ...? ¿tiene información sobre ... ? [t-yaynay – sobray]

information desk la información

injection la inyección [een-yekth-yon]

injured herido [ereedo]

she's been injured está herida

in-laws mi familia política [fameel-ya]

inner tube (for tyre) la cámara de aire [a-eeray]

innocent inocente [eenothentay]

insect el insecto

insect bite la picadura de insecto [day]

do you have anything for insect bites? ¿tiene algo para la picadura de insectos? [t-yaynay]

insect repellent el repelente de insectos [repelentay day]

inside dentro de [day]

inside the hotel dentro del hotel

let's sit inside vamos a sentarnos adentro [bamoss]

insist insistir [eenseesteer]

I insist insisto

insomnia el insomnio [eensomn-yo]

instant coffee el café instantáneo [kafay eenstantanay-o]

instead: give me that one instead deme ese otro [daymay aysay]

instead of ... en lugar de ... [day]

intersection el cruce [kroothay]

insulin la insulina [eensooleena]

insurance el seguro [segooro]

intelligent inteligente [eenteleeнentay]

interested: I'm interested in ... estoy interesado en ...

interesting interesante [eenteresantay]

that's very interesting eso es muy interesante [ayso ess mwee]

international internacional [internath-yonal]

Internet el Internet [eentairnet]

interpret actuar de intérprete [actoo-ar day eentairpretay]

interpreter el/la intérprete

interval (at theatre) el descanso

into en

I'm not into ... no me gusta ... [may goosta]

introduce presentar

may I introduce ...? le presento a ...

invitation la invitación [eembeetath-yon]

invite invitar [eembeetar]
Ireland Irlanda [eerlanda]
Irish irlandés [eerlandayss]
 I'm Irish (man/woman) soy irlandés/irlandesa
iron (for ironing) la plancha
 can you iron these for me? ¿puede planchármelos? [pwayday]
is* es, está
island la isla [eessla]
it ello, lo [ay-yo]
 it is ... es ...; está ...
 is it ...? ¿es ...?; ¿está ... ?
 where is it? ¿dónde está? [donday]
 it's him es él
 it was ... era ...; estaba ... [aira]
Italian (adj) italiano [eetal-yano]
Italy Italia
itch: it itches me pica [may]

J

jack (for car) el gato
jacket la chaqueta [chakayta]
jar el tarro
jam la mermelada [mairmaylada]
jammed: it's jammed está atascado
January enero [enairo]
jaw la mandíbula [mandeeboola]
jazz el jazz
jealous celoso [theloso]
jeans los vaqueros [bakaiross]
jellyfish la medusa [medoosa]

jersey el jersey [Hairsay]
jetty el muelle [mway-yay]
Jewish judío [Hoodee-o]
jeweller's la joyería [Ho-yeree-a]
jewellery las joyas [Hoyass]
job el trabajo [trabaHo]
jogging el footing
 to go jogging hacer footing [athair]
joke el chiste [cheesstay]
journey el viaje [b-yaHay]
 have a good journey! ¡buen viaje! [bwen b-yaHay]
jug la jarra [Harra]
 a jug of water una jarra de agua [agwa]
juice el zumo [thoomo]
July julio [Hool-yo]
jump (verb) saltar
jumper el jersey [Hairsay]
jump leads las pinzas (para la batería) [peenthass – bataree-a]
junction el cruce [kroothay]
June junio [Hoon-yo]
just (only) solamente [solamentay]
 just two sólo dos
 just for me sólo para mí
 just here aquí mismo [akee meesmo]
 not just now ahora no [a-ora]
 we've just arrived acabamos de llegar [yegar]

K

keep quedarse [kedarsay]
 keep the change quédese con

el cambio [kay-daysay – kamb-yo]

can I keep it? ¿puedo quedármelo? [pwaydo kedarmelo]

please keep it por favor, quédeselo [kaydayselo]

ketchup el ketchup

kettle el hervidor [airbeedor]

key la llave [yabay]

the key for room 201, please la llave de la habitacion doscientos uno, por favor [day la abeetath-yon]

key ring el llavero [yabairo]

kidneys los riñones [reen-yoness]

kill matar

kilo* el kilo

kilometre* el kilómetro

how many kilometres is it to ...? ¿cuántos kilómetros hay a ...? [kwantoss – ī]

kind (nice) amable [amablay]

that's very kind es muy amable [mwee]

dialogue

which kind do you want? ¿qué tipo quiere? [kay teepo k-yairay]

I want this/that kind quiero este/aquel tipo [k-yairo estay/akel]

king el rey [ray]

kiosk el quiosco [kee-osko]

kiss el beso [bayso]

(verb) besarse [baysarsay]

kitchen la cocina [kotheena]

kitchenette la cocina pequeña [pekwayn-ya]

Kleenex® el kleenex®

knee la rodilla [rodee-ya]

knickers las bragas

knife el cuchillo [koochee-yo]

knitwear los géneros de punto [Henaiross]

knock (verb: on door) llamar [yamar]

knock down atropellar [atropay-yar]

he's been knocked down le han atropellado [lay an atropay-yado]

knock over (object) volcar [bolkar]

(pedestrian) atropellar [atropay-yar]

know (somebody, a place) conocer [konothair]

(something) saber [sabair]

I don't know no sé [say]

I didn't know that no lo sabía

do you know where I can find ...? ¿sabe dónde puedo encontrar ...? [sabay donday pwaydo]

dialogue

do you know how this works? ¿sabe cómo funciona esto? [foonth-yona]

sorry, I don't know lo siento, no sé [s-yento – say]

L

label la etiqueta [eteekayta]
ladies' (toilets) el aseo de señoras [asay-o day sen-yorass]
ladies' wear la ropa de señoras
lady la señora [sen-yora]
lager la cerveza [thairbaytha]
lake el lago
lamb (meat) el cordero [kordairo]
lamp la lámpara
lane (motorway) el carril [karreel]
(small road) la callejuela [ka-yay-Hwayla]
language el idioma [eed-yoma]
language course el curso de idiomas [koorso day eed-yomass]
large grande [granday]
last último [oolteemo]
 last week la semana pasada
 last Friday el viernes pasado
 last night anoche [anochay]
 what time is the last train to Toledo? ¿a qué hora es el último tren a Toledo? [kay ora]
late tarde [tarday]
 sorry I'm late siento llegar tarde [s-yaynto yegar]
 the train was late el tren llegó con retraso [yaygo]
 we must go – we'll be late debemos irnos – llegaremos tarde [debaymoss eernoss – yegaraymoss]
 it's getting late se hace tarde

[say athay]
later más tarde
 I'll come back later volveré más tarde [bolbairay]
 see you later hasta luego [asta lwaygo]
 later on más tarde
latest lo último [oolteemo]
 by Wednesday at the latest para el miércoles lo más tarde
laugh (verb) reirse [ray-eersay]
launderette/laundromat la lavandería [labandairee-a]
laundry (clothes) la ropa sucia [sooth-ya]
 (place) la lavandería
lavatory el lavabo [lababo]
law la ley [lay]
lawn el césped [thesped]
lawyer (man/woman) el abogado/la abogada
laxative el laxante [laxantay]
lazy perezoso [pairethoso]
lead (electrical) el cable [kablay]
lead (verb) conducir [kondootheer]
 where does this lead to? ¿adónde va esta carretera? [adonday ba – karraytaira]
leaf la hoja [oHa]
leaflet el folleto [fo-yayto]
leak (in roof) la gotera [gotaira]
 (gas, water) el escape [eskapay]
 (verb) filtrar [feeltrar]
 the roof leaks el tejado tiene goteras [teHado t-yaynay gotairass]
learn aprender [aprendair]

least: not in the least de
ninguna manera [day
neengoona manaira]

at least por lo menos
[maynoss]

leather (fine) la piel [p-yel]
(heavy) el cuero [kwairo]

leave (verb) irse [eersay]

I am leaving tomorrow me
marcho mañana [may]

he left yesterday se marchó
ayer [say]

may I leave this here? ¿puedo
dejar esto aquí? [pwaydo dayHar
– akee]

I left my coat in the bar me he
dejado el abrigo en el bar [ay
dayHado]

dialogue

when does the bus for
Montoro leave? ¿cuándo
sale el autobús para
Montoro? [kwando salay]
it leaves at 9 o'clock sale a
las nueve

leek el puerro [pwairro]
left izquierda [eethk-yairda]
on the left a la izquierda
to the left a la izquierda
turn left gire a la izquierda
[Heeray]
there's none left no queda
ninguno [kayda]
left-handed zurdo [thoordo]
left luggage (office) la
consigna [konseegna]

leg la pierna [p-yairna]
lemon el limón [leemon]
lemonade la limonada
lemon tea el té con limón [tay]
lend prestar
will you lend me your ... ?
¿podría prestarme su ...?
[prestarmay]
lens (of camera) el objetivo
[obHeteebo]
lesbian la lesbiana
less menos [maynoss]
less expensive menos caro
less than 10 menos de diez
less than you menos que tú
[kay too]
lesson la lección [lekth-yon]
let (allow) dejar [dayHar]
will you let me know? ¿me lo
dirá? [may]
I'll let you know se lo diré [say
lo deeray]
let's go for something to eat
vamos a comer algo [bamoss a
komair]
let off: will you let me off at ...?
¿me para en ...? [may]
letter la carta
do you have any letters for
me? ¿tiene cartas para mí?
[t-yaynay]
letterbox el buzón [boothon]
lettuce la lechuga [lechooga]
lever la palanca
library la biblioteca [beebl-
yotayka]
licence el permiso
lid la tapa
lie (verb: tell untruth) mentir

lie down acostarse [akostarsay], echarse [aycharsay]

life la vida [beeda]

lifebelt el salvavidas [salbabeedass]

lifeguard el/la socorrista

life jacket el chaleco salvavidas [chalayko salbabeedass]

lift (in building) el ascensor [asthensor]

could you give me a lift? ¿podría llevarme en su coche? [yebarmay – kochay]

would you like a lift? ¿quiere que le lleve? [k-yairay kay lay yaybay]

lift pass el forfait [forfa-ee]

a daily/weekly lift pass un forfait de un día/una semana

light la luz [looth]

(not heavy) ligero [leeHairo]

do you have a light? (for cigarette) ¿tiene fuego? [t-yaynay fwaygo]

light green verde claro [bairday]

light bulb la bombilla [bombee-ya]

I need a new light bulb necesito una bombilla nueva [netheseeto – nwayba]

lighter (cigarette) el encendedor [enthendedor]

lightning el relámpago

like (verb) gustar [goostar]

I like it me gusta [may]

I like going for walks me gusta pasear [pasay-ar]

I like you me gustas

I don't like it no me gusta

do you like ...? ¿le gusta ...? [lay]

I'd like a beer quisiera una cerveza [kees-yaira oona thairbaytha]

I'd like to go swimming me gustaría ir a nadar

would you like a drink? ¿le apetece beber algo? [apaytaythay bebair]

would you like to go for a walk? ¿le apetece dar un paseo? [lay – pasay-o]

what's it like? ¿cómo es?

I want one like this quiero uno como éste [k-yairo – estay]

lime la lima [leema]

lime cordial el zumo de lima [thoomo day]

line la línea [leenay-a]

could you give me an outside line? ¿puede darme línea? [pwayday darmay]

lips el labio [lab-yo]

lip salve la crema de labios [krayma]

lipstick el lápiz de labios [lapeeth]

liqueur el licor

listen escuchar [eskoochar]

litre* el litro

a litre of white wine un litro de vino blanco [day beeno]

little pequeño [paykayn-yo]

just a little, thanks sólo un poco, gracias

a little milk un poco de leche

[lechay]

a little bit more un poquito
más [pokeeto]

live (verb) vivir [beebeer]

we live together vivimos
juntos [beebeemoss Hoontoss]

dialogue

where do you live? ¿dónde
vive? [donday beebay]
I live in London vivo en
Londres [beebo]

lively alegre [alaygray]

liver el hígado [eegado]

loaf el pan

lobby (in hotel) el vestíbulo
[besteeboolo]

lobster la langosta

local local

**can you recommend a local
wine/restaurant?** puede
recomendarme un vino/un
restaurante local [pwayday
rekomendarmay oon beeno/oon
restowrantay]

lock la cerradura [thairradoora]
(verb) cerrar [thairrar]
it's locked está cerrado con
llave [thairrado kon yabay]

lock in dejar encerrado [day-
Har enthairrado]

**lock out: I've locked myself
out** he cerrado la puerta con
las llaves dentro [ay – la pwairta
– yabayss]

locker (for luggage etc) la
consigna automática

[konseegna owtomateeka]

lollipop el chupa-chups®
[choopa-choopss]

London Londres [londress]

long largo
**how long will it take to fix
it?** ¿cuánto tiempo llevará
arreglarlo? [kwanto t-yempo
yaybara]
how long does it take?
¿cuánto tiempo se tarda?
[say]
a long time mucho tiempo
[moocho]
one day/two days longer un
día/dos días más
long distance call la
conferencia [konfairenth-ya]

look: I'm just looking, thanks
sólo estoy mirando, gracias
you don't look well no tienes
buen aspecto [t-yayness bwen]
look out! ¡cuidado! [kweedado]
can I have a look? ¿puedo
mirar? [pwaydo]

look after cuidar [kweedar]

look at mirar

look for buscar
I'm looking for ... estoy
buscando ...

**look forward to: I'm looking
forward to it:** tengo muchas
ganas [moochass]

loose (handle etc) suelto [swelto]

lorry el camión [kam-yon]

lose perder [pairdair]
I've lost my way me he
perdido [may ay pairdeedo]
I'm lost, I want to get to ...

estoy perdido/perdida,
quiero ir a … [k-yairo]
I've lost my bag he perdido
el bolso [ay]
lost property (office) (la
oficina de) objetos perdidos
[ofeetheena day obHaytoss
pairdeedoss]
lot: a lot, lots mucho, muchos
[moocho]
not a lot no mucho
a lot of people mucha gente
[Hentay]
a lot bigger mucho mayor
I like it a lot me gusta mucho
[may goosta]
lotion la loción [loth-yon]
loud fuerte [fwairtay]
lounge (in house, hotel) el salón
(in airport) la sala de espera [day
espaira]
love el amor
(verb) querer [kairair]
I love Spain me encanta
España [may]
lovely encantador
low bajo [baHo]
luck la suerte [swairtay]
good luck! ¡buena suerte!
[bwayna]
luggage el equipaje [ekeepaHay]
luggage trolley el carrito
portaequipaje [porta-
ekeepaHay]
lump (on body) la hinchazón
[eenchathon]
lunch el almuerzo [almwairtho]
lungs los pulmones
[poolmoness]

luxurious (hotel, furnishings) de
lujo [looHo]
luxury el lujo

M

machine la máquina
[makeena]
mad (insane) loco
(angry) furioso [foor-yoso]
Madrid Madrid [madree]
magazine la revista [rebeesta]
maid (in hotel) la camarera
[kamaraira]
maiden name el nombre de
soltera [nombray day soltaira]
mail el correo [korray-o]
is there any mail for me? ¿hay
correspondencia para mí?
[ī korrespondenth-ya]
see post
mailbox el buzón [boothon]
main principal [preentheepal]
main course el plato principal
main post office la oficina
central de correos [ofeetheena
thentral day korray-oss]
main road (in town) la calle
principal [ka-yay preentheepal]
(in country) la carretera
principal [karretaira]
mains (for water) la llave de
paso [yabay day]
mains switch (for electricity)
el interruptor de la red
eléctrica [eentairrooptor day]
Majorca Mallorca [ma-yorka]
make (brand name) la marca

(verb) hacer [ath**ai**r]

I make it 50 euros creo que son cincuenta euros [kr**ay**o kay – theenk**wen**ta **ay**-ooross]

what is it made of? ¿de qué está hecho? [day kay – **ay**cho]

make-up el maquillaje [makee-ya**Hay**]

man el hombre [**om**bray]

manager el gerente [Hair**en**tay]

can I see the manager? ¿puedo ver al gerente? [pw**ay**do bair]

manageress la gerente

manual (car with manual gears) el coche de marchas [**ko**chay]

many muchos [**moo**choss]

not many no muchos

map (city plan) el plano (road map, geographical) el mapa

March marzo [**mar**tho]

margarine la margarina

market el mercado [mair**ka**do]

marmalade la mermelada de naranja [mairmel**a**da day nara**n**Ha]

married: I'm married (said by a man/woman) est**oy** casado/ casada

are you married? (said to a man/ woman) ¿est**á** casado/casada?

mascara el rímel

match (football etc) el partido

matches las cerillas [thair**ee**-yass]

material (fabric) el tejido [te**Hee**do]

matter: it doesn't matter no importa

what's the matter? ¿qué pasa? [kay]

mattress el colchón

May mayo [**ma**-yo]

may: may I have another one? ¿me da otro? [may]

may I come in? ¿se puede entrar? [say pw**ay**day]

may I see it? ¿puedo verlo? [pw**ay**do b**ai**rlo]

may I sit here? ¿puedo sentarme aqui? [sent**ar**may ak**ee**]

maybe tal vez [beth]

mayonnaise la mayonesa [ma-yon**ay**sa]

me*: that's for me eso es para mí [**ay**so]

send it to me envíemelo [embee-**ay**melo]

me too yo también [tamb-**yen**]

meal la comida

dialogue

did you enjoy your meal? ¿te ha gustado la comida? [tay a goost**a**do]

it was excellent, thank you estaba riquísima, gracias [reek**ee**seema]

mean (verb) querer decir [kair**ai**r deth**ee**r]

what do you mean? ¿qué quiere decir? [kay k-y**ai**ray]

dialogue

what does this word mean? ¿qué significa esta palabra? [kay]
it means ... in English significa ... en inglés [eenglayss]

measles el sarampión [sarampyon]
meat la carne [karnay]
mechanic el mecánico
medicine la medicina [medeetheena]
Mediterranean el Mediterráneo [medeetairranay-o]
medium (adj: size) medio [mayd-yo]
medium-dry semi-seco [sayko] (sherry) amontillado [amontee-yado]
medium-rare poco hecho [aycho]
medium-sized de tamaño medio [taman-yo mayd-yo]
meet encontrar
(for the first time) conocer [konothair]
nice to meet you encantado de conocerle [day konothairlay]
where shall I meet you? ¿dónde nos vemos? [donday noss baymoss]
meeting la reunión [ray-oon-yon]
meeting place el lugar de reunión [loogar]

melon el melón
men los hombres [ombress]
mend arreglar
could you mend this for me? ¿puede arreglarme esto? [pwayday arreglarmay]
men's room el servicio de caballeros [sairbeeth-yo day kaba-yaiross]
menswear la ropa de caballero
mention (verb) mencionar [menth-yonar]
don't mention it de nada [day]
menu el menú [menoo]
may I see the menu, please? ¿puede traerme el menú? [pwayday tra-airmay]
see menu reader page 202
message: are there any messages for me? ¿hay algún recado para mí? [ī]
I want to leave a message for ... quisiera dejar un recado para ... [kees-yaira day-Har]
metal el metal
metre* el metro
microwave (oven) el (horno) microondas [orno meekro-ondass]
midday el mediodía [mayd-yodee-a]
at midday al mediodía
middle: in the middle en el medio [mayd-yo]
in the middle of the night a mitad de la noche [meeta day la nochay]
the middle one el del medio

midnight la medianoche
[mayd-ya-nochay]

at midnight a medianoche

might: I might es posible
[poseeblay]

I might not puede que no
[pwayday kay]

I might want to stay another
day quizás decida quedarme
otro día [keethass detheeda
kedarmay]

migraine la jaqueca [Hakayka]

mild (taste) suave [swabay]
(weather) templado

mile* la milla [mee-ya]

milk la leche [lechay]

milkshake el batido

millimetre* el milímetro

minced meat la carne picada
[karnay]

mind: never mind ¡qué más
da! [kay]

I've changed my mind he
cambiado de idea [ay kamb-
yado day eeday-a]

dialogue

do you mind if I open the
window? ¿le importa
si abro la ventana? [lay
eemporta – bentana]
no, I don't mind no, no me
importa [may]

mine*: it's mine es mío

mineral water el agua mineral
[agwa meenairal]

mint-flavoured con sabor a
menta

mints los caramelos de menta
[karamayloss day]

minute el minuto [meenooto]

in a minute en seguida
[segeeda]

just a minute un momento

mirror el espejo [espayHo]

Miss Señorita [sen-yoreeta]

miss: I missed the bus he
perdido el autobús [ay
pairdeedo]

missing: one of my ... is
missing me falta uno de
mis ... [may — day]

there's a suitcase missing
falta una maleta

mist la niebla [n-yaybla]

mistake el error

I think there's a mistake
me parece que hay una
equivocación [may parethay kay
ī oona ekeebokath-yon]

sorry, I've made a mistake
perdón, me he equivocado
[may ay ekeebokado]

misunderstanding el
malentendido

mix-up: sorry, there's been
a mix-up perdón ha habido
una confusión [a abeedo oona
konfoos-yon]

mobile phone el teléfono
móvil [telayfono mobeel]

modern moderno [modairno]

modern art gallery la galería
de arte moderno [galairee-a
day artay]

moisturizer la crema

hidratante [krayma eedratantay]
moment: I won't be a moment
vuelvo enseguida [bwelbo
ensegeeeda]
monastery el monasterio
[monastair-yo]
Monday lunes [looness]
money el dinero [deenairo]
month el mes
monument el monumento
[monoomento]
(statue) la estatua [estatwa]
moon la luna
moped el ciclomotor
[theeklomotor]
more* más
can I have some more water,
please? más agua, por favor
more expensive/interesting
más caro/interesante
more than 50 más de
cincuenta
more than that más que eso
[kay ayso]
a lot more mucho más
[moocho]

dialogue

would you like some
more? ¿quiere más?
[k-yairay]
no, no more for me, thanks
no, para mí no, gracias
how about you? ¿y usted?
[ee oostay]
I don't want any more,
thanks no quiero más,
gracias [k-yairo]

morning la mañana [man-yana]
this morning esta mañana
in the morning por la mañana
Morocco Marruecos
[marrwaykoss]
mosquito el mosquito
mosquito repellent el
repelente de mosquitos
[repelentay]
most: I like this one most of all
éste es el que más me gusta
[estay – kay mass may goosta]
most of the time la mayor
parte del tiempo [ma-yor
partay del t-yempo]
most tourists la mayoría de
los turistas [ma-yoree-a day]
mostly generalmente
[Haynairalmentay]
mother la madre [madray]
motorbike la moto
motorboat la (lancha) motora
motorway la autopista
[owtopeesta]
mountain la montaña [montan-
ya]
in the mountains en las
montañas
mountaineering el
montañismo [montan-yeesmo]
mouse el ratón
moustache el bigote [beegotay]
mouth la boca
mouth ulcer la llaga [yaga]
move: he's moved to another
room se ha cambiado a otra
habitación [say a kamb-yado
– abeetath-yon]
could you move your car?

¿podría cambiar de sitio su coche? [podree-a kamb-yar day seet-yo]

could you move up a little? ¿puede correrse un poco? [pwayday corrairsay]

where has it moved to? ¿adónde se ha trasladado? [adonday say a]

movie la película [peleekoola]

movie theater el cine [theenay]

Mr Señor [sen-yor]

Mrs Señora [sen-yora]

Ms Señorita [sen-yoreeta]

much mucho [moocho]

much better/worse mucho mejor/peor [ma-yor/pay-or]

much hotter mucho más caliente [kal-yentay]

not (very) much no mucho

I don't want very much no quiero mucho [k-yairo]

mud el barro

mug (for drinking) la taza [tatha]

I've been mugged me han asaltado [may an]

mum la mamá

mumps las paperas [papairass]

museum el museo [moosay-o]

mushrooms los champiñones [champeen-yoness]

music la música [mooseeka]

musician el/la músico

Muslim (adj) musulmán [moosoolman]

mussels los mejillones [meHeeyoness]

must*: I must tengo que [kay]

I mustn't drink alcohol no

debo beber alcohol [daybo bebair alko-ol]

mustard la mostaza [mostatha]

my* mi; (pl) mis

myself: I'll do it myself lo haré yo mismo [aray yo meesmo]

by myself yo solo

N

nail (finger) la uña [oon-ya]

(metal) el clavo [klabo]

nailbrush el cepillo para las uñas [thepee-yo –oon-yass]

nail varnish el esmalte para uñas [esmaltay]

name el nombre [nombray]

my name's John me llamo John [may yamo]

what's your name? ¿cómo se llama usted? [say – oostay]

what is the name of this street? ¿cómo se llama esta calle?

napkin la servilleta [sairbee-yayta]

nappy el pañal [pan-yal]

narrow (street) estrecho [estraycho]

nasty (person) desagradable [desagradablay]

(weather, accident) malo

national nacional [nath-yonal]

nationality la nacionalidad [nath-yonaleeda]

natural natural [natooral]

nausea la nausea [nowsay-a]

navy (blue) azul marino [at**hool** mar**ee**no]

near cerca [th**air**ka]

is it near the city centre? ¿está cerca del centro? [th**entro**]

do you go near Las Ramblas? ¿pasa usted cerca de Las Ramblas? [oost**ay** – day]

where is the nearest ...? ¿dónde está el ... más cercano? [**don**day – th**air**kano]

nearby por aquí cerca [ak**ee**]

nearly casi

necessary necesario [nethesar-yo]

neck el cuello [kw**ay**-yo]

necklace el collar [ko-yar]

necktie la corbata

need: I need ... necesito un ... [nethes**ee**to]

do I need to pay? ¿necesito pagar?

needle la aguja [ag**oo**Ha]

negative (film) el negativo [negat**ee**bo]

neither: neither (one) of them ninguno (de ellos) [neeng**oo**no day **ay**-yoss]

neither ... nor ... ni ... ni ...

nephew el sobrino

Nerja Nerja [**nair**Ha]

net (in sport) la red

Netherlands Los Países Bajos [pa-**ee**sess ba**Hoss**]

network map el mapa

never nunca [**noo**nka]

dialogue

have you ever been to Seville? ¿ha estado alguna vez en Sevilla? [a – beth]

no, never, I've never been there no, nunca, nunca he estado allí [ay – a-**yee**]

new nuevo [nw**ay**bo]

news (radio, TV etc) las noticias [not**ee**th-yass]

newsagent's el kiosko de prensa [day]

newspaper el periódico [pair-yo**dee**ko]

newspaper kiosk el kiosko de prensa [day]

New Year el Año Nuevo [**an**-yo nw**ay**bo]

Happy New Year! ¡Feliz Año Nuevo [fel**eeth**]

New Year's Eve Nochevieja [**no**chay-b-**yay**Ha]

New Zealand Nueva Zelanda [nw**ay**ba thel**a**nda]

New Zealander: I'm a New Zealander (man/woman) soy neozelandés/neozelandesa [nayo-thelanda**yss**]

next próximo

the next turning/street on the left la siguiente calle a la izquierda [seeg-y**en**tay ka-yay a la eethk-y**air**da]

at the next stop en la siguiente parada

next week la próxima semana

next to al lado de [day]

nice (food) bueno [bwayno]
(looks, view etc) bonito
(person) simpático
niece la sobrina
night la noche [nochay]
at night por la noche
good night buenas noches
[bwaynass]

dialogue

do you have a single room
for one night? ¿tiene una
habitación individual para
una noche? [t-yaynay oona
abeetath-yon eendeebeedwal]
yes, madam sí, señora
[sen-yora]
how much is it per night?
¿cuánto es la noche?
[kwanto]
it's 35 euros for one night
son treinta y cinco euros
la noche [tray-eenti theenko
ay-ooross]
thank you, I'll take it
gracias, me la quedo [may
la kaydo]

nightclub la discoteca
[deeskotayka]
nightdress el camisón
night porter el portero
[portairo]
no no
I've no change no tengo
cambio [kamb-yo]
there's no ... left no queda ...
[kayda]

no way! ¡ni hablar! [ablar]
oh no! (upset, annoyed) ¡Dios
mío!
nobody nadie [nad-yay]
there's nobody there no hay
nadie ahí [ī – a-ee]
noise el ruido [rweedo]
noisy: it's too noisy hay
demasiado ruido [ī daymas-
yado]
non-alcoholic sin alcohol
[alko-ol]
none ninguno
non-smoking compartment no
fumadores [foomadoress]
noon el mediodía [mayd-yo-
dee-a]
no-one nadie [nad-yay]
nor: nor do I yo tampoco
normal normal
north norte [nortay]
in the north en el norte
north of Girona al norte de
Girona
northeast nordeste [nordestay]
northern del norte [nortay]
northwest noroeste [noro-estay]
Northern Ireland Irlanda del
Norte [eerlanda del nortay]
Norway Noruega [norwayga]
Norwegian (adj) noruego
nose la nariz [nareeth]
nosebleed la hemorragia
nasal [emorraH-ya]
not* no
no, I'm not hungry no, no
tengo hambre [ambray]
I don't want any, thank you
no quiero ninguno, gracias

85

[k-yairo]

it's not necessary no es necesario [naythesar-yo]

I didn't know that no lo sabía

not that one – this one ése no – éste [aysay – estay]

note (banknote) el billete [bee-yaytay]

notebook el cuaderno [kwadairno]

notepaper (for letters) el papel de carta

nothing nada

nothing for me, thanks para mí nada, gracias

nothing else nada más

novel la novela [nobayla]

November noviembre [nob-yembray]

now ahora [a-ora]

number el número [noomairo]

I've got the wrong number me he equivocado de número [may ay ekeebokado day]

what is your phone number? ¿cuál es su número de teléfono? [kwal – telayfono]

number plate la matrícula

nurse (man/woman) el enfermero [enfairmairo]/la enfermera

nursery slope la pista de principiantes [day preentheep-yantess]

nut (for bolt) la tuerca [twairka]

nuts los frutos secos

O

o'clock* en punto [poonto]

occupied (toilet) ocupado [okoopado]

October octubre [oktoobray]

odd (strange) raro

of* de [day]

off (lights) apagado

it's just off calle Corredera está cerca de calle Corredera [thairka day ka-yay]

we're off tomorrow nos vamos mañana [bamoss]

offensive (language, behaviour) insultante [eensooltantay]

office (place of work) la oficina [ofeetheena]

officer (said to policeman) señor [sen-yor]

often a menudo

not often pocas veces [baythess]

how often are the buses? ¿cada cuánto son los autobuses? [kwanto]

oil el aceite [athay-eetay]

ointment la pomada

OK vale [balay]

are you OK? ¿está bien? [b-yen]

is that OK with you? ¿le parece bien? [lay paraythay]

is it OK to ...? ¿se puede ...? [say pwayday]

that's OK thanks (it doesn't matter) está bien, gracias

I'm OK (nothing for me) yo no

quiero [k-yairo]
(I feel OK) me siento bien [may s-yento]
is this train OK for ...? ¿este tren va a...? [estay – ba]
I said I'm sorry, OK? he dicho que lo siento, ¿vale? [ay – kay – balay]
old viejo [b-yayHo]

dialogue

how old are you? ¿cuántos años tiene? [kwantoss an-yoss t-yaynay]
I'm twenty-five tengo veinticinco
and you? ¿y usted? [ee oostay]

old-fashioned pasado de moda [day]
old town (old part of town) el casco antiguo [anteegwo]
  in the old town en el casco antiguo
olive la aceituna [athay-eetoona], la oliva
  black/green olives las aceitunas negras/verdes [bairdess]
olive oil el aceite de oliva [athay-eetay day oleeba]
omelette la tortilla [tortee-ya]
on* en
  on the street/beach en la calle/la playa
  is it on this road? ¿está en esta calle?

on the plane en el avión [ab-yon]
on Saturday el sábado
on television en la tele [taylay]
I haven't got it on me no lo llevo encima [yaybo entheema]
this one's on me (drink) ésta va de mi cuenta [ba day mee kwenta]
the light wasn't on la luz no estaba encendida [looth – enthendeeda]
what's on tonight? ¿qué ponen esta noche? [kay]
once (one time) una vez [oona beth]
  at once (immediately) en seguida [segeeda]
one* uno [oono], una
  the white one el blanco, la blanca
one-way: a one-way ticket to ... un billete de ida para ... [bee-yaytay day eeda]
onion la cebolla [thebo-ya]
only sólo
  only one sólo uno
  it's only 6 o'clock son sólo las seis
  I've only just got here acabo de llegar [yegar]
on/off switch el interruptor [eentairrooptor]
open (adjective) abierto [ab-yairto]
  (verb) abrir [abreer]
  when do you open? ¿a qué hora abre? [kay ora abray]
  I can't get it open no puedo

87

abrirlo [pwaydo]
in the open air al aire libre [a-eeray leebray]
opening times el horario [orar-yo]
open ticket el billete abierto [bee-yaytay ab-yairto]
opera la ópera
operation (medical) la operación [opairath-yon]
operator (telephone: man/woman) el operador/la operadora
opposite: the opposite direction la dirección contraria [deerekth-yon kontrar-ya]
the bar opposite el bar de enfrente [day enfrentay]
opposite my hotel enfrente de mi hotel
optician el óptico
or o
orange (fruit) la naranja [naranHa]
(colour) (color) naranja
orange juice (fresh) el zumo de naranja [thoomo day]
(fizzy, diluted) la naranjada [naranHada]
orchestra la orquesta [orkesta]
order: can we order now? (in restaurant) ¿podemos pedir ya? [podaymoss]
I've already ordered, thanks ya he pedido, gracias [ay]
I didn't order this no he pedido eso [ayso]
out of order averiado, fuera

de servicio [abair-yado, fwaira day sairbeeth-yo]
ordinary corriente [korr-yentay]
other otro
the other one el otro
the other day el otro día
I'm waiting for the others estoy esperando a los demás
do you have any others? ¿tiene usted otros? [t-yaynay oostay]
otherwise de otra manera [manaira]
our* nuestro [nwestro], nuestra; (pl) nuestros, nuestras
ours* (el) nuestro, (la) nuestra
out: he's out no está
three kilometres out of town a tres kilómetros de la ciudad
outdoors fuera de casa [fwaira day]
outside ... fuera de ...
can we sit outside? ¿podemos sentarnos fuera? [podaymoss]
oven el horno [orno]
over: over here por aquí [akee]
over there por allí [a-yee]
over 500 más de quinientos
it's over se acabó [say]
overcharge: you've overcharged me me ha cobrado de más [may a – day]
overcoat el abrigo
overlook: I'd like a room overlooking the courtyard querría una habitación que

dé al patio [kairree-a oona
abeetath-yon kay day]

overnight (travel) de noche [day
nochay]

overtake adelantar

owe: how much do I owe you?
¿cuánto le debo? [kwanto lay
daybo]

own: my own ... mi propio ...
[prop-yo]

are you on your own? (to a
man/woman) ¿está solo/sola?

I'm on my own (man/woman)
estoy solo/sola

owner (man/woman) el
propietario [prop-yetar-yo]/la
propietaria

P

pack: a pack of ... un paquete
de ... [pakaytay day]
(verb) hacer las maletas
[malaytass]

package el paquete
[pakaytay]

package holiday el viaje
organizado [b-yaHay
organeethado]

packed lunch la bolsa con la
comida

packet: a packet of
cigarettes un paquete de
cigarrillos [pakaytay day
theegaree-yoss]

padlock el candado

page (of book) la página
[paHeena]

could you page Mr ...?
¿podría llamar al Señor (por
altavoz) ...? [yamar]

pain el dolor

I have a pain here me duele
aquí [may dwaylay akee]

painful doloroso

painkillers los analgésicos
[analHayseekoss]

paint la pintura

painting el cuadro [kwadro]

pair: a pair of ... un par de ...
[day]

Pakistani (adj) paquistaní
[pakeestanee]

palace el palacio [palath-yo]

pale pálido

pale blue azul claro [athool]

pan la cazuela [kathwayla]

panties las bragas

pants (underwear: men's) los
calzoncillos
[kalthonthee-yoss]
(women's) las bragas
(US: trousers) los pantalones
[pantaloness]

pantyhose los pantis

paper el papel
(newspaper) el periódico [pair-
yodeeko]

a piece of paper un trozo de
papel [trotho day]

paper handkerchiefs los
kleenex®

parcel el paquete [pakaytay]

pardon (me)? (didn't understand/
hear) ¿cómo?

parents: my parents mis
padres [padress]

parents-in-law los suegros
[swegross]
park el parque [parkay]
(verb) aparcar
  can I park here? ¿puedo
  aparcar aquí? [pwaydo –
  akee]
parking lot el aparcamiento
[aparcam-yento]
part la parte [partay]
partner (boyfriend, girlfriend etc) el
compañero [kompan-yairo]
party (group) el grupo
(celebration) la fiesta
pass (in mountains) el puerto
[pwairto]
passenger (man/woman)
el pasajero [pasaHairo]/la
pasajera
passport el pasaporte
[pasaportay]
past*: in the past
antiguamente
[anteegwamentay]
  just past the information
  office justo después de la
  oficina de información
  [Hoosto despwayss day]
path el camino
pattern el dibujo [deebooHo]
pavement la acera [athaira]
  on the pavement en la acera
pavement café el café terraza
[terratha]
pay (verb) pagar
  can I pay, please? la cuenta,
  por favor [kwenta]
  it's already paid for ya está
  pagado

dialogue

who's paying? ¿quién
paga? [k-yen]
I'll pay pago yo
no, you paid last time,
I'll pay no, usted pagó
la última vez, yo pago
[oostay – oolteema beth]

pay phone el teléfono público
[telayfono poobleeko]
peaceful tranquilo [trankeelo]
peach el melocotón
peanuts los cacahuetes
[kakawaytess]
pear la pera [paira]
peas los guisantes [geesantess]
peculiar (taste, custom) raro
pedestrian crossing el paso de
peatones [pay-atoness]
pedestrian precinct la calle
peatonal [ka-yay pay-atonal]
peg (for washing) la pinza
[peentha]
  (for tent) la estaca
pen la pluma [plooma]
pencil el lápiz [lapeeth]
penfriend (male/female)
el amigo/la amiga
por correspondencia
[korrespondenth-ya]
penicillin la penicilina
[peneetheeleena]
penknife la navaja [nabaHa]
pensioner el/la pensionista
[pens-yoneesta]
people la gente [Hentay]
  the other people in the hotel

los otros huéspedes del hotel [wespedess]

too many people demasiada gente [daymas-yada]

pepper (spice) la pimienta [peem-yenta]

(vegetable) el pimiento

peppermint (sweet) el caramelo de menta [karamaylo day]

per: per night por noche [nochay]

how much per day? ¿cuánto es por noche? [kwanto]

per cent por ciento [th-yento]

perfect perfecto [pairfekto]

perfume el perfume [pairfoomay]

perhaps quizás [keethass]

perhaps not quizás no

period (of time, menstruation) el período [pairee-odo]

perm la permanente [pairmanentay]

permit el permiso [pairmeeso]

person la persona [pairsona]

personal stereo el walkman® [wolman]

petrol la gasolina

petrol can la lata de gasolina [day]

petrol station la gasolinera [gasoleenaira]

pharmacy la farmacia [farmath-ya]

phone el teléfono [telayfono]

(verb) llamar por teléfono [yamar]

phone book la guía telefónica [gee-a]

phone box la cabina telefónica [kabeena]

phonecard la tarjeta de teléfono [tarHayta day taylayfono]

phone number el número de teléfono [noomairo]

photo la foto

excuse me, could you take a photo of us? ¿le importaría hacernos una foto? [lay – athairnoss]

phrasebook el libro de frases [day frasess]

piano el piano [p-yano]

pickpocket el/la carterista

pick up: will you be there to pick me up? ¿va a ir a recogerme? [ba – rekoHairmay]

picnic el picnic

picture el cuadro [kwadro]

pie (meat) la empanada

(fruit) la tarta

piece el pedazo [pedatho]

a piece of ... un pedazo de ... [day]

pill la píldora

I'm on the pill estoy tomando la píldora

pillow la almohada [almo-ada]

pillow case la funda (de almohada) [foonda]

pin el alfiler [alfeelair]

pineapple la piña [peen-ya]

pineapple juice el zumo de piña [thoomo]

pink rosa
pipe (for smoking) la pipa [peepa]
  (for water) el tubo [toobo]
pipe cleaners los limpiapipas
  [leemp-yapeepass]
pity: it's a pity es una lástima
pizza la pizza
place el sitio [seet-yo]
  is this place taken? ¿está
  ocupado este sitio? [estay]
  at your place en tu casa
  at his place en su casa
plain (not patterned) liso
plane el avión [ab-yon]
  by plane en avión
plant la planta
plaster cast la escayola [eska-
  yola]
plasters las tiritas
plastic plástico
  (credit cards) las tarjetas
  de crédito [tarHaytass day
  kraydeeto]
plastic bag la bolsa de plástico
plate el plato
platform el andén
  which platform is it for
  Saragossa, please? ¿qué
  andén para Zaragoza, por
  favor? [kay]
play (in theatre) la obra
  (verb) jugar [Hoogar]
playground el patio de recreo
  [pat-yo day rekray-o]
pleasant agradable [agradablay]
please por favor [fabor]
  yes please sí, por favor
  could you please ...? ¿podría
  hacer el favor de ...? [athair

  – day]
please don't no, por favor
pleased to meet you
  encantado de conocerle [day
  konothairlay]
pleasure: my pleasure es un
  placer [plathair]
plenty: plenty of ... mucho ...
  [moocho]
  there's plenty of time
  tenemos mucho tiempo
  [taynaymoss – t-yempo]
  that's plenty, thanks es
  suficiente, gracias [soofeeth-
  yentay]
pliers los alicates [aleekatess]
plug (electrical) el enchufe
  [enchoofay]
  (for car) la bujía [booHee-a]
  (in sink) el tapón
plumber el fontanero
  [fontanairo]
p.m.* de la tarde [day la tarday]
poached egg el huevo
  escalfado [waybo]
pocket el bolsillo [bolsee-yo]
point: two point five dos coma
  cinco
  there's no point no merece la
  pena [mairaythay la payna]
points (in car) los platinos
poisonous venenoso
  [benenoso]
police la policía [poleethee-a]
  call the police! ¡llame a la
  policía! [yamay]
policeman el (agente de)
  policía [aHentay day]
police station la comisaría de

policía
policewoman la policía
polish el betún [betoon]
polite educado [edookado]
polluted contaminado
pony el poney
pool (for swimming) la piscina [peestheena]
poor (not rich) pobre [pobray]
(quality) de baja calidad [day baHa kaleeda]
pop music la música pop [mooseeka]
pop singer el/la cantante de música pop [kantantay]
population la población [poblath-yon]
pork la carne de cerdo [karnay day thairdo]
port (for boats) el puerto [pwairto]
(drink) el Oporto
porter (in hotel) el conserje [konsairHay]
portrait el retrato
Portugal Portugal
Portuguese (adj) portugués [portoogayss]
posh (restaurant) de lujo [looHo]
(people) pijo [peeHo]
possible posible [poseeblay]
is it possible to ...? ¿es posible ...?
as ... as possible tan ... como sea posible [say-a]
post (mail) el correo [korray-o]
(verb) echar al correo
could you post this for me? ¿podría enviarme esto por

correo? [emb-yarmay]
postbox el buzón [boothon]
postcard la postal
poster el poster [postair], el cartel
post office Correos [korray-oss]
poste restante la lista de Correos [leesta]
potato la patata
potato chips las patatas fritas (de bolsa)
pots and pans (ie cooking implements) los cacharros de cocina [day kotheena]
pottery (objects) la cerámica [thairameeka]
pound* (money, weight) la libra
power cut el apagón
power point la toma de corriente [day korr-yentay]
practise: I want to practise my Spanish quiero practicar el español [k-yairo – espan-yol]
prawns las gambas
prefer: I prefer ... prefiero ... [pref-yairo]
pregnant embarazada [embarathada]
prescription (for chemist) la receta [rethayta]
present (gift) el regalo
president (of country) el/la presidente [preseedentay]
pretty mono
it's pretty expensive es bastante caro [bastantay]
price el precio [preth-yo]
priest el sacerdote [sathairdotay]
prime minister (man/woman) el

primer ministro [preemair]/la primera ministra
printed matter los impresos [eempraysoss]
priority (in driving) la preferencia [prefairenth-ya]
prison la cárcel [karthel]
private privado [preebado]
private bathroom el baño privado [ban-yo]
probably probablemente [probablementay]
problem el problema [problayma]
no problem! ¡con mucho gusto! [moocho goosto]
program(me) el programa
promise: I promise lo prometo [promayto]
pronounce: how is this pronounced? ¿cómo se pronuncia esto? [say pronoonth-ya]
properly (repaired, locked etc) bien [b-yen]
protection factor (of suntan lotion) el factor de protección [protekth-yon]
Protestant (adj) protestante [protestantay]
public convenience los aseos públicos [asay-oss poobleekoss]
public holiday el día de fiesta [day]
pudding (dessert) el postre [postray]
pull tirar
pullover el jersey [Hairsay]
puncture el pinchazo

[peenchatho]
purple morado
purse (for money) el monedero [monedairo]
(US: handbag) el bolso
push empujar [empooHar]
pushchair la sillita de ruedas [see-yeeta day rwaydass]
put poner [ponair]
where can I put ...? ¿dónde puedo poner ...? [donday pwaydo]
could you put us up for the night? ¿podría alojarnos esta noche? [aloHarnoss – nochay]
pyjamas el pijama [peeHama]
Pyrenees los Pirineos [peereenay-oss]

Q

quality la calidad [kaleeda]
quarantine la cuarentena [kwarentayna]
quarter la cuarta parte [kwarta partay]
quayside: on the quayside en el muelle [mway-yay]
question la pregunta [pregoonta]
queue la cola
quick rápido
that was quick sí que ha sido rápido [kay a]
what's the quickest way there? ¿cuál es el camino más rápido? [kwal]
fancy a quick drink? ¿te

apetece **a**lgo rápido de beber? **[**tay apet**ay**thay – day beb**air]**

quickly rápidamente **[**rapeedamentay**]**

quiet (place, hotel) tranquilo **[**trank**ee**lo**]**

quiet! ¡cállese! **[**ka-yaysay**]**

quite (fairly) bastante **[**bast**a**ntay**]**
(very) muy **[**mwee**]**

that's quite right **e**so es cierto **[**th-y**ai**rto**]**

quite a lot bastante

R

rabbit el conejo **[**kon**ay**Ho**]**

race (for runners, cars) la carrera **[**karr**ai**ra**]**

racket (tennis etc) la raqueta **[**rak**ay**ta**]**

radiator (of car, in room) el radiador **[**rad-yador**]**

radio la radio **[**rad-yo**]**
on the radio por la radio

rail: by rail en tren

railway el ferrocarril

rain la lluvia **[**y**oo**b-ya**]**
in the rain bajo la lluvia **[**ba**H**o**]**

it's raining está lloviendo **[**yob-yendo**]**

raincoat el impermeable **[**eempairmay-ablay**]**

rape la violación **[**b-yolath-yon**]**

rare (steak) (muy) p**o**co hecho **[**mwee – **ay**cho**]**

rash (on skin) la erupción cutánea **[**airoopth-y**o**n kootanay-a**]**

raspberry la frambuesa **[**frambw**ay**sa**]**

rat la r**a**ta

rate (for changing money) el cambio **[**kamb-yo**]**

rather: it's rather good es bast**a**nte bueno **[**bast**a**ntay bw**ay**no**]**

I'd rather ... prefiero … **[**pref-y**ai**ro**]**

razor la maquinilla de afeitar **[**makeen**ee**-ya day afay-eetar**]**
(electric) la máquina de afeitar el**é**ctrica **[**mak**ee**na**]**

razor blades las hojas de afeitar **[o**Hass**]**

read leer **[**lay-**air]**

ready preparado
are you ready? ¿est**á**s listo? **[l**eesto**]**

I'm not ready yet aún no est**oy** listo **[**a-**oo**n**]**

dialogue

when will it be ready?
¿cuándo estar**á** listo?
[kwando**]**

it should be ready in a couple of days estar**á** listo d**e**ntro de un par de d**í**as **[**day**]**

real verdadero **[**bairdad**ai**ro**]**

really realmente **[**ray-alm**e**ntay**]**
that's really great **e**so es estup**e**ndo **[**ayso**]**

really? (doubt) ¿de verdad?
[day bairda]

(polite interest) ¿sí?

rearview mirror el (espejo) retrovisor [espayHo retrobeesor]

reasonable (prices etc) razonable [rathonablay]

receipt el recibo [retheebo]

recently recientemente [rethyentementay]

reception la recepción [rethepth-yon]

at reception en recepción

reception desk la recepción

receptionist el/la recepcionista [rethepth-yoneesta]

recognize reconocer [rekonothair]

recommend: could you recommend ...? ¿puede usted recomendar ...? [pwayday oostay]

record (music) el disco [deesko]

red rojo [roHo]

red wine el vino tinto [beeno teento]

refund el reembolso [rayembolso]

can I have a refund? ¿puede devolverme el dinero? [pwayday debolbairmay el deenairo]

region la zona [thona], la región [reH-yon]

registered: by registered mail por correo certificado [korray-o thairteefeekado]

registration number el número

de la matrícula [noomairo day]

relatives los parientes [paryentess]

religion la religión [releeH-yon]

remember: I don't remember no recuerdo [rekwairdo]

I remember recuerdo

do you remember? ¿recuerda? [rekwairda]

rent (for apartment etc) el alquiler [alkeelair]

(verb) alquilar

to/for rent de alquiler

rented car el coche alquilado [kochay alkeelado]

repair (verb) reparar

can you repair it? ¿puede arreglarlo? [pwayday]

repeat repetir

could you repeat that? ¿puede repetir eso? [pwayday – ayso]

reservation la reserva [resairba]

I'd like to make a reservation quisiera hacer una reserva [kees-yaira athair]

dialogue

I have a reservation tengo una reserva

yes sir, what name please? sí, señor, ¿a qué nombre, por favor? [sen-yor a kay nombray]

reserve reservar [resairbar]

dialogue

can I reserve a table for
tonight? ¿puedo reservar
una mesa para esta noche?
[pwaydo – maysa – nochay]
yes madam, for how
many people? sí, señora,
¿para cuántos? [sen-yora
– kwantoss]
for two para dos
and for what time? ¿y para
qué hora? [kay ora]
for eight o'clock para las
ocho
and could I have your
name please? ¿me dice su
nombre, por favor? [may
deethay soo nombray]
see alphabet for spelling

rest: I need a rest necesito un
descanso [netheseeto]
the rest of the group el resto
del grupo [groopo]
restaurant el restaurante
[restowrantay]
restaurant car el vagón-
cafetería [bagon kafetairee-a]
rest room los servicios
[sairbeeth-yoss]
see toilet
retired: I'm retired estoy
jubilado/jubilada
[Hoobeelado]
return (ticket) el billete de ida
y vuelta [bee-yaytay day eeda
ee bwelta]
reverse charge call la llamada

a cobro revertido [yamada
– reberteedo]
reverse gear la marcha atrás
revolting asqueroso [askairoso]
rib la costilla [kostee-ya]
rice arroz [arroth]
rich (person) rico [reeko]
(food) sustancial [soostanth-yal]
ridiculous ridículo [reedeekoolo]
right (correct) correcto
(not left) derecho
you were right tenía razón
[rathon]
that's right eso es [ayso]
this can't be right esto no
puede ser así [pwayday sair]
right! ¡bien! [b-yen]
is this the right road for ...?
¿por aquí se va bien a ...?
[akee say ba b-yen]
on the right a la derecha
turn right gire a la derecha
[Heeray]
right-hand drive con el
volante a la derecha [bolantay]
ring (on finger) la sortija
[sorteeHa]
I'll ring you te llamaré [tay
yamaray]
ring back volver a llamar
[bolbair a yamar]
ripe (fruit) maduro
rip-off: it's a rip-off es un timo
rip-off prices los precios
altísimos [prayth-yoss]
risky arriesgado [arr-yesgado]
river el río
road la carretera [karretaira]
is this the road for ...? ¿es ésta

la carretera que va a ...? [kay ba]

down the road en esta calle [ka-yay]

road accident el accidente automovilístico [aktheedentay owtomobeeleesteeko]

road map el mapa de carreteras

roadsign la señal de tráfico [sen-yal day]

rob: I've been robbed ¡me han robado! [may an]

rock la roca
(music) el rock

on the rocks (with ice) con hielo [yaylo]

roll (bread) el bollo [bo-yo]

roof el tejado [teHado]

roof rack la baca

room la habitación [abeetath-yon]

in my room en mi habitación

room service el servicio de habitaciones [sairbeeth-yo day]

rope la cuerda [kwairda]

rosé (wine) vino rosado [beeno]

roughly (approximately) aproximadamente [–mentay]

round: it's my round es mi turno [toorno]

roundabout (for traffic) la rotonda

round trip ticket el billete de ida y vuelta [bee-yaytay day eeda ee bwelta]

route la ruta [roota]

what's the best route? ¿cuál

es la mejor ruta? [kwal ess la mayHor]

rubber (material) la goma
(eraser) la goma de borrar

rubber band la goma elástica

rubbish (waste) la basura
(poor quality goods) las porquerías [porkairee-ass]

rubbish! (nonsense) ¡tonterías! [tontairee-ass]

rucksack la mochila

rude grosero [grosairo]

ruins las ruinas [rweenass]

rum el ron

rum and coke el ron con coca-cola®

run (verb: person) correr [korrair]

how often do the buses run? ¿cada cuánto pasan los autobuses? [kwanto]

I've run out of money se me ha acabado el dinero [say may a – deenairo]

rush hour la hora punta [ora poonta]

S

sad triste [treestay]

saddle (for horse) la silla de montar [see-ya day]
(on bike) el sillín [see-yeen]

safe seguro [segooro]

safety pin el imperdible [eempairdeeblay]

sail la vela [bayla]

sailboard el windsurf

sailboarding el windsurf

salad la ensalada

salad dressing el aliño para la ensalada [aleen-yo]

sale: for sale en venta [em baynta]

salmon el salmón [sal-mon]

salt la sal

same: the same mismo [meesmo]

the same as this igual que éste [eegwal kay estay]

the same again, please lo mismo otra vez, por favor [beth]

it's all the same to me me es igual [may – eegwal]

sand la arena [arayna]

sandals las sandalias [sandal-yass]

sandwich el sandwich

sanitary napkin la compresa [kompraysa]

sanitary towel la compresa

Saragossa Zaragoza [tharagotha]

sardines las sardinas

Saturday sábado

sauce la salsa

saucepan el cazo [katho]

saucer el platillo [platee-yo]

sauna la sauna [sowna]

sausage la salchicha

say: how do you say ... in Spanish? ¿cómo se dice ... en español? [say deethay en espan-yol]

what did he say? ¿que ha dicho? [kay a]

I said ... he dicho ... [ay]

he said ... ha dicho ...

could you say that again? ¿podría repetirlo?

scarf (for neck) la bufanda (for head) el pañuelo [pan-ywaylo]

scenery el paisaje [pa-eesaHay]

schedule (US) el horario [orar-yo]

scheduled flight el vuelo regular [bwaylo regoolar]

school la escuela [eskwayla]

scissors: a pair of scissors las tijeras [teeHairass]

scotch el whisky

Scotch tape® la cinta adhesiva [theenta adeseeba]

Scotland Escocia [eskoth-ya]

Scottish escocés [eskothayss]

I'm Scottish (man/woman) soy escocés/escocesa

scrambled eggs los huevos revueltos [wayboss rebwayltoss]

scratch el rasguño [rasgoon-yo]

screw el tornillo [tornee-yo]

screwdriver el destornillador [destornee-yador]

sea el mar

by the sea junto al mar [Hoonto]

seafood los mariscos

seafood restaurant la marisquería [mareeskairee-a]

seafront el paseo marítimo [pasay-o maree̱teemo]

on the seafront en línea de playa [leenay-a day pla-ya]

seagull la gaviota [gab-yota]

search (verb) buscar

seashell la concha marina

seasick: I feel seasick estoy mareado [maray-**ado**]

I get seasick me mareo [may mar**ay**-o]

seaside: by the seaside en la playa [**pla**-ya]

seat el asiento [as-**yen**to]

is this anyone's seat? ¿es de alguien este asiento? [day **alg**-yen est**ay**]

seat belt el cinturón de seguridad [theentoor**on** day segooreed**a**]

sea urchin el erizo de mar [air**ee**tho]

seaweed el alga

secluded apartado

second (adjective) segundo [seg**oo**ndo]

(of time) el segundo

just a second! ¡un momento!

second class (travel) en segunda clase [kl**a**ssay]

secondhand de segunda mano [day]

see ver [bair]

can I see? ¿puedo ver? [p**way**do]

have you seen ...? ¿ha visto ...? [a b**ee**sto]

I saw him this morning le vi esta mañana [lay bee]

see you! ¡hasta luego! [**a**sta lw**ay**go]

I see (I understand) ya comprendo

self-catering apartment el apartamento

self-service autoservicio [owtosairb**ee**th-yo]

sell vender [bend**air**]

do you sell ...? ¿vende ...? [bend**ay**]

Sellotape® la cinta adhesiva [th**een**ta adese**ee**ba]

send enviar [emb-y**ar**]

I want to send this to England quiero enviar esto a Inglaterra [k-y**ai**ro emb-y**ar**]

senior citizen el/la pensionista [pens-yon**ee**sta]

separate separado

separated: I'm separated estoy separado/separada

separately (pay, travel) por separado

September septiembre [sept-y**em**bray]

septic séptico

serious serio [**sair**-yo]

service charge el servicio [sairb**eeth**-yo]

service station la estacion de servicio [estath-yon day]

serviette la servilleta [sairbee-**yay**ta]

set menu el menu del día [men**oo**]

several varios [**bar**-yoss]

Seville Sevilla [sebee-ya]

sew coser [kos**air**]

could you sew this back on? ¿podría coserme esto? [kos**air**may]

sex el sexo

sexy sexy

shade: in the shade a la sombra

shake: let's shake hands choque esa mano [chokay **ay**sa]

shallow (water) poco profundo [prof**oo**ndo]

shame: what a shame! ¡que lástima! [kay]

shampoo el champú

a shampoo and set un lavado y marcado [labado ee]

share (verb: room, table etc) compartir

sharp (knife) afilado

(taste) ácido [a**thee**do]

(pain) agudo

shattered (very tired) agotado

shaver la máquina de afeitar [mak**ee**na day afay-e**e**tar]

shaving foam la espuma de afeitar

shaving point el enchufe (para la máquina de afeitar) [ench**oo**fay – mak**ee**na]

she* ella [**ay**-ya]

is she here? ¿está (ella) aquí? [ak**ee**]

sheet (for bed) la sábana

shelf la estantería [estant**ee**ree-a]

shellfish los mariscos

sherry el jerez [Hereth]

ship el barco

by ship en barco

shirt el camisa

shit! ¡mierda! [m-**ya**irda]

shock el susto [**soo**sto]

I got an electric shock me ha dado calambre [may a – kalambray]

shock-absorber el amortiguador [amorteeg**wa**dor]

shocking escandaloso

shoes los zapatos [thap**a**toss]

a pair of shoes un par de zapatos

shoelaces los cordones para zapatos [kord**o**ness]

shoe polish la crema para los zapatos [**kray**ma]

shoe repairer's la zapatería [thapatair**ee**-a]

shop la tienda [t-**ye**nda]

shopping: I'm going shopping voy de compras [boy]

shopping centre el centro comercial [**the**ntro komairth-**ya**l]

shop window el escaparate [eskapar**a**tay]

shore la orilla [or**ee**-ya]

short (time, journey) corto

(person) bajo [b**a**Ho]

it's only a short distance queda bastante cerca [**kay**da bastantay th**ai**rka]

shortcut el atajo [at**a**Ho]

shorts los pantalones cortos [pantal**o**ness]

should: what should I do? ¿que hago? [kay **a**go]

he shouldn't be long no tardará mucho [m**oo**cho]

you should have told me debiste habérmelo dicho [deb**ee**stay ab**ai**rmelo]

shoulder el hombro [**o**mbro]

shout (verb) gritar

show (in theatre) el espectáculo
[espektakoolo]

could you show me? ¿me lo
enseña? [may lo ensen-ya]

shower (in bathroom) la ducha
[doocha]

with shower con ducha

shower gel el gel de ducha
[Hel]

shut (verb) cerrar [thairrar]

when do you shut? ¿a qué
hora cierran? [a kay ora
th-yairran]

when do they shut? ¿a qué
hora cierran?

they're shut está cerrado
[thairrado]

I've shut myself out he
cerrado y he dejado la llave
dentro [ay – ee ay dayHado la
yabay]

shut up! ¡cállese! [ka-yesay]

shutter (on camera) el
obturador
(on window) la contraventana
[kontrabentana]

shy tímido [teemeedo]

sick (ill) enfermo [enfairmo]

I'm going to be sick (vomit)
voy a vomitar [boy a bomeetar]

side el lado

the other side of town al otro
lado de la ciudad [day la th-
yooda]

side lights las luces de
posición [loothess day poseeth-
yon]

side salad la ensalada aparte
[apartay]

side street la callejuela
[ka-yay-Hwayla]

sidewalk la acera [athaira]

sight: the sights of ... los
lugares de interés de ...
[loogaress day eentairess]

sightseeing: we're going
sightseeing vamos a hacer un
recorrido turístico [bamoss
a athair]

sightseeing tour el recorrido
turístico

sign (notice) el letrero [letrairo]
(roadsign) la señal de tráfico
[sen-yal day]

signal: he didn't give a signal
no hizo ninguna señal [no
eetho]

signature la firma [feerma]

signpost el letrero [letrairo]

silence el silencio
[seelenth-yo]

silk la seda [sayda]

silly tonto

silver la plata

silver foil el papel de aluminio
[aloomeen-yo]

similar parecido
[paretheedo]

simple (easy) sencillo
[senthee-yo]

since: since yesterday desde
ayer [desday a-yair]

since I got here desde que
llegué aquí [kay yegay akee]

sing cantar

singer el/la cantante
[kantantay]

single: a single to ... un billete

para … [bee-yaytay]

I'm single soy soltero [soltairo]

single bed la cama individual [eendeebeedwal]

single room la habitación individual [abeetath-yon]

sink (in kitchen) el fregadero [fregadairo]

sister la hermana [airmana]

sister-in-law la cuñada [koon-yada]

sit: can I sit here? ¿puedo sentarme aquí? [pwaydo sentarmay akee]

sit down sentarse [sentarsay]

sit down! ¡siéntese! [s-yentaysay]

is anyone sitting here? ¿está ocupado este asiento? [estay as-yento]

size el tamaño [taman-yo] (of clothes) la talla [ta-ya]

ski el esquí [eskee] (verb) esquiar [esk-yar] a pair of skis un par de esquís [day]

ski boots las botas de esquiar

skiing el esquí [eskee] we're going skiing vamos a esquiar [bamoss – esk-yar]

ski instructor (man/woman) el monitor/la monitora de esquí

ski-lift el telesquí [teleskee]

skin la piel [p-yel]

skin-diving el buceo [boothay-o]

skinny flaco

ski-pants los pantalones de

esquí [pantaloness day eskee]

ski-pass el abono

ski pole el bastón de esquí [day]

skirt la falda

ski run la pista de esquí [eskee]

ski slope la pista de esquí

ski wax la cera de esquís [thaira]

sky el cielo [th-yaylo]

sleep (verb) dormir

did you sleep well? ¿ha dormido bien? [a – b-yen]

I need a good sleep necesito dormir bien [netheseeto]

sleeper (on train) el coche-cama [kochay-kama]

sleeping bag el saco de dormir [day]

sleeping car el coche-cama [kochay-kama]

sleeping pill la pastilla para dormir [pastee-ya]

sleepy: I'm feeling sleepy tengo sueño [swayn-yo]

sleeve la manga

slide (photographic) la diapositiva [d-yaposeeteeba]

slip (under dress) la combinación [kombeenath-yon]

slippery resbaladizo [resbaladeetho]

slow lento

slow down! ¡más despacio! [despath-yo]

slowly despacio

could you say it slowly? ¿podría decirlo despacio? [detheerlo]

very slowly muy despacio
[mwee]

small pequeño [peken-yo]

smell: it smells! (smells bad)
¡apesta!

smile (verb) sonreír [sonray-eer]

smoke el humo [oomo]

do you mind if I smoke? ¿le
importa si fumo? [lay – foomo]

I don't smoke no fumo

do you smoke? ¿fuma?

snack: I'd just like a snack
quisiera una tapa solamente
[kees-yaira – solamentay]

sneeze el estornudo

snorkel el tubo de buceo
[toobo day boothay-o]

snow la nieve [n-yaybay]

it's snowing está nevando

so: it's so good es tan bueno
[bwayno]

not so fast no tan de prisa
[preesa]

so am I yo también [tamb-yen]

so do I yo también

so-so más o menos [maynoss]

soaking solution (for contact
lenses) el líquido preservador
[leekeedo]

soap el jabón [Habon]

soap powder el jabón en
polvo [em polbo]

sober sobrio [sobr-yo]

sock el calcetín [kaltheteen]

socket (electrical) el enchufe
[enchoofay]

soda (water) la soda

sofa el sofá

soft (material etc) suave [swabay]

soft-boiled egg el huevo
pasado por agua [waybo
– agwa]

soft drink el refresco

soft lenses las lentes blandas
[lentess]

sole (of shoe, of foot) la suela
[swayla]

could you put new soles on
these? ¿podría cambiarles las
suelas? [kamb-yarless]

some: can I have some water?
¿me da un poco de agua?
[may – day]

can I have some rolls? ¿me
da unos bollos? [bo-yoss]

can I have some? ¿me da un
poco?

somebody, someone alguien
[alg-yen]

something algo

something to drink algo de
beber [bebair]

sometimes a veces [baythess]

somewhere en alguna parte
[partay]

son el hijo [eeHo]

song la canción [kanth-yon]

son-in-law el yerno [yairno]

soon pronto

I'll be back soon volveré
pronto [bolbairay]

as soon as possible lo antes
posible [antess poseeblay]

sore: it's sore me duele [may
dwaylay]

sore throat el dolor de
garganta

sorry: (I'm) sorry perdone

[pairdonay]
 sorry? (didn't understand)
 ¿cómo?
sort: what sort of ...? ¿qué
 clase de ...? [kay klassay day]
soup la sopa
sour (taste) ácido [atheedo]
south el sur [soor]
 in the south en el sur
South Africa Sudáfrica
South African (adj)
 sudafricano
 I'm South African (man/woman)
 soy sudafricano/sudafricana
southeast el sudeste [sood-
 estay]
southwest el sudoeste [soodo-
 estay]
souvenir el recuerdo
 [rekwairdo]
Spain España [espan-ya]
Spaniard (man/woman) el
 español [espan-yol]/la española
Spanish español
 the Spanish los españoles
 [espan-yoless]
spanner la llave inglesa [yabay
 eenglaysa]
spare part el repuesto
 [repwesto]
spare tyre la rueda de
 repuesto [rwayda day]
spark plug la bujía
 [booHee-a]
speak: do you speak English?
 ¿habla inglés? [abla]
 I don't speak ... no hablo ...
 [ablo]

dialogue

can I speak to Pablo?
¿puedo hablar con Pablo?
[pwaydo]
who's calling ¿quién
llama? [k-yen yama]
it's Patricia soy Patricia
I'm sorry, he's not in, can I
take a message? lo siento,
no está, ¿quiere dejar
algún recado?
[s-yento – k-yairay dayHar]
no thanks, I'll call back
later no gracias, llamaré
más tarde [yamaray mass
tarday]
please tell him I called
por favor, dígale que he
llamado [deegalay kay ay
yamado]

speciality la especialidad
 [espeth-yaleeda]
spectacles las gafas
speed la velocidad [belotheeda]
speed limit el límite de
 velocidad [leemeetay day]
speedometer el velocímetro
 [belotheemetro]
spell: how do you spell
 it? ¿cómo se escribe? [say
 eskreebay]
 see alphabet
spend gastar
spider la araña [aran-ya]
spin-dryer la secadora
splinter la astilla [astee-ya]
spoke (in wheel) el radio [rad-yo]

spoon la cuchara
sport el deporte [dayportay]
sprain: I've sprained my ...
me he torcido el ... [may ay
torth**ee**do]
spring (season) la primavera
[preemab**air**a]
(of car, seat) el muelle [mway-
yay]
square (in town) la plaza
[platha]
stairs las escaleras [eskal**air**ass]
stale (bread, taste) pasado
stall: the engine keeps stalling
el motor se para a cada rato
[say]
stamp el sello [say-yo]

dialogue

a stamp for England,
please un sello para
Inglaterra, por favor
what are you sending?
¿qué es lo que envía? [kay
– embee-a]
this postcard esta postal

standby el vuelo standby
[bwaylo]
star la estrella [estray-ya]
(in film) el/la protagonista
start el principio [preentheep-
yo]
(verb) comenzar [komenthar]
when does it start? ¿cuándo
empieza? [kwando emp-yaytha]
the car won't start el coche
no arranca [kochay]

starter (of car) el motor de
arranque [arrankay]
(food) la entrada
starving: I'm starving me
muero de hambre [may
mwairo day ambray]
state (in country) el estado
the States (USA) los Estados
Unidos [ooneedoss]
station la estación del
ferrocarril [estath-yon]
statue la estatua [estatwa]
stay: where are you staying?
¿dónde se hospedan? [donday
say ospaydan]
I'm staying at ... me hospedo
en ... [may ospaydo]
I'd like to stay another two
nights me gustaría quedarme
otras dos noches [may
– kedarmay – nochess]
steak el filete [feelaytay]
steal robar
my bag has been stolen me
han robado el bolso [may an]
steep (hill) empinado
steering la dirección [deerekth-
yon]
step: on the steps en las
escaleras [eskal**air**ass]
stereo el estéreo [estairay-o]
sterling las libras esterlinas
[estairleenass]
steward (on plane) el auxiliar
de vuelo [owkseel-yar day
bwelo]
stewardess la azafata [athafata]
sticking plaster la tirita
still: I'm still waiting todavía

est**oy** esperando [todabee-a]

is he still there? ¿est**á** todavía ahí? [a-**ee**]

keep still! ¡qu**é**dese quieto! [**kay**daysay k-y**e**to]

sting: I've been stung **a**lgo me ha picado [may a]

stockings las medias [**mayd**-yass]

stomach el est**ó**mago

stomach ache el dol**or** de est**ó**mago [day]

stone (rock) la piedra [p-y**e**dra]

stop (verb) par**a**r

please, stop here (to taxi driver etc) pare aquí, por fav**or** [**pa**ray a**kee**]

do you stop near ...? ¿para cerca de …? [th**ai**rka day]

stop doing that! ¡deje de hacer eso! [**day**Hay day ath**ai**r **ay**so]

stopover la escala, la parada

storm la torm**e**nta

straight: it's straight ahead **t**odo derecho [d**ai**recho]

a straight whisky un whisky solo

straightaway en seguida [seg**ee**da]

strange (odd) extr**a**ño [estr**a**n-yo]

stranger (man/woman) el forastero [forast**ai**ro]/la forast**e**ra

I'm a stranger here no s**oy** de aquí [day a**kee**]

strap la correa [korr**ay**-a]

strawberry la fresa [fr**ay**sa]

stream el arroyo [arr**o**-yo]

street la calle [ka-**ya**y]

on the street en la calle

streetmap el m**a**pa de la ci**u**dad [thyo**o**da]

string la cuerda [kw**ai**rda]

strong fuerte [fw**ai**rtay]

stuck atasc**a**do

the key's stuck la llave se ha atasc**a**do [ya**ba**y say a]

student el/la estudi**a**nte [estood-y**a**ntay]

stupid est**ú**pido [esto**o**peedo]

subway (US) el metro

suburb el sub**u**rbio [soob**oo**rb-yo]

suddenly de rep**e**nte [rep**e**ntay]

suede el **a**nte [**a**ntay]

sugar el az**ú**car [ath**oo**kar]

suit el tr**a**je [tr**a**Hay]

it doesn't suit me (jacket etc) no me sienta bien [no may s-y**e**nta b-yen]

it suits you te sienta muy bien [tay – mw**ee**]

suitcase la maleta [mal**ay**ta]

summer el verano [b**ai**rano]

in the summer en el verano

sun el sol

in the sun en el sol

out of the sun en la sombra

sunbathe tomar el sol

sunblock (cream) la crema protect**o**ra [**kray**ma]

sunburn la quemadura de sol [kemad**oo**ra]

sunburnt quem**a**do [kem**a**do]

Sunday domingo

sunglasses las gafas de sol

sun lounger la tumbona

sunny: it's sunny hace sol [athay]

sun roof (in car) el techo corredizo [korraydeetho]

sunset la puesta de sol [pwesta day]

sunshade la sombrilla [sombree-ya]

sunshine la luz del sol [looth]

sunstroke la insolación [eensolath-yon]

suntan el bronceado [bronthay-ado]

suntan lotion la loción bronceadora [loth-yon bronthay-adora]

suntanned bronceado

suntan oil el aceite bronceador [athay-eetay]

super fabuloso

supermarket el supermercado [soopairmairkado]

supper la cena [thayna]

supplement (extra charge) el suplemento

sure: are you sure? ¿está seguro?

sure! ¡por supuesto¡ [soopwesto]

surname el apellido [apay-yeedo]

swearword la palabrota

sweater el suéter [swetair]

sweatshirt la sudadera [soodadaira]

Sweden Suecia [swayth-ya]

Swedish (adj) sueco [swayko]

sweet (dessert) el postre [postray]

(adj: taste) dulce [doolthay]

(sherry) oloroso

sweets los caramelos [karamayloss]

swelling la hinchazón [eenchathon]

swim (verb) nadar

I'm going for a swim voy a nadar [boy]

let's go for a swim vamos a nadar [bamoss]

swimming costume el bañador [ban-yador]

swimming pool la piscina [peestheena]

swimming trunks el traje de baño [traHay day banyo]

switch el interruptor [eentairrooptor]

switch off apagar

switch on encender [enthendair]

swollen inflamado

T

table la mesa [maysa]

a table for two una mesa para dos

tablecloth el mantel

table tennis el ping-pong

table wine el vino de mesa [beeno day maysa]

tailback (of traffic) la caravana de coches [karabana day kochess]

tailor el sastre [sastray]

take (lead) coger [koHair]

(accept) aceptar [atheptar]

can you take me to the airport? ¿me lleva al aeropuerto? [may yayba al a-airopwairto]

do you take credit cards? ¿acepta tarjetas de crédito? [athepta tarHaytass day kraydeeto]

fine, I'll take it está bien, lo compro [b-yen]

can I take this? (leaflet etc) ¿puedo llevarme esto? [pwaydo yebarmay]

how long does it take? ¿cuánto se tarda? [kwanto say]

it takes three hours se tarda tres horas [orass]

is this seat taken? ¿está ocupado este asiento? [estay as-yento]

a hamburger to take away una hamburguesa para llevar [yebar]

can you take a little off here? (to hairdresser) ¿puede quitarme un poco de aquí? [pwayday keetarmay – day akee]

talcum powder el talco

talk (verb) hablar [ablar]

tall alto

tampons los tampones [tamponess]

tan el bronceado [bronthay-ado]

to get a tan broncearse [bronthay-arsay]

tank (of car) el depósito [deposeeto]

tap el grifo

tape (for cassette) la cinta [theenta]

(sticky) la cinta adhesiva [adeseeba]

tape measure la cinta métrica

tape recorder el casete [kaset]

taste el sabor

can I taste it? ¿puedo probarlo? [pwaydo]

taxi el taxi

will you get me a taxi? ¿podría conseguirme un taxi? [konsegeermay]

where can I find a taxi? ¿dónde puedo coger un taxi? [donday pwaydo koHair]

dialogue

to the airport/to Hotel Sol please al aeropuerto/al hotel Sol, por favor [a-airopwairto/otel]

how much will it be? ¿cuánto costará? [kwanto]

20 euros viente euros [bay-eentay ay-ooross]

that's fine, right here, thanks está bien, aquí mismo, gracias [b-yen akee meesmo]

taxi-driver el/la taxista

taxi rank la parada de taxis [day]

tea (drink) el té [tay]

tea for one/two please un té/dos tés, por favor

teabags las bolsas de té

teach: could you teach me?
¿podría enseñarme? [ensen-
yarmay]

teacher (primary: man/woman) el
maestro [ma-estro]/la maestra
(secondary: man/woman) el
profesor/la profesora

team el equipo [ekeepo]

teaspoon la cuchara de té
[day tay]

tea towel el paño de cocina
[pan-yo day kotheena]

teenager el/la adolescente
[adolesthentay]

telephone el teléfono [telayfono]
see phone

television la televisión
[telebees-yon]

tell: could you tell him ...?
¿podría decirle ...?
[detheerlay]

temperature (weather) la
temperatura [temperatoora]
(fever) la fiebre [f-yebray]

tennis el tenis

tennis ball la pelota de tenis
[day]

tennis court la pista de tenis

tennis racket la raqueta de
tenis [rakayta]

tent la tienda de campaña
[t-yenda day kampan-ya]

term (at university, school) el
trimestre [treemestray]

terminus (rail) la estación
terminal [estath-yon tairmeenal]

terrible terrible [terreeblay]

terrific fabuloso [fabooloso]

text (message) el mensaje (de

texto) [mensaHay]

than* que [kay]

smaller than más pequeño
que [pekayn-yo]

thanks, thank you gracias
[grath-yass]

thank you very much muchas
gracias [moochass]

thanks for the lift gracias por
traerme [tra-airmay]

no thanks no gracias

dialogue

thanks gracias
that's OK, don't mention it
no hay de qué [ī day kay]

that: that man ese hombre
[aysay ombray]

that woman esa mujer
[mooHair]

that one ése

I hope that ... espero que ...
[espairo kay]

that's nice (clothes, souvenir etc)
es bonito

is that ...? ¿es ése ...? [aysay]

that's it (that's right) eso es

the* el, la; (pl) los, las

theatre el teatro [tay-atro]

their* su; (pl) sus [sooss]

theirs* su, sus; (pl) suyos [soo-
yoss], suyas; de ellos [day ay-
yoss], de ellas

them* (things) los, las
(people) les

for them para ellos [ay-yoss]/
ellas

with them con ellos/ellas
I gave it to them se lo di a
ellos/ellas [say]
who? – them ¿quién? – ellos/
ellas [k-yen]
then entonces [entonthess]
there allí [a-yee]
over there allí
up there allí arriba
is/are there ...? ¿hay ...? [ī]
there is/are ... hay ...
there you are (giving something)
aquí tiene [akee t-yaynay]
thermometer el termómetro
[tairmometro]
thermos flask el termo [tairmo]
these: these men estos
hombres
these women estas mujeres
can I have these? ¿me puedo
llevar éstos? [may pwaydo
yebar]
they* (male) ellos [ay-yoss]
(female) ellas [ay-yass]
thick grueso [grwayso]
(stupid) estúpido [estoopeedo]
thief (man/woman) el ladrón/la
ladrona
thigh el muslo [mooslo]
thin delgado
thing la cosa
my things mis cosas [meess]
think pensar
I think so creo que sí [kray-o
kay]
I don't think so no lo creo
I'll think about it lo pensaré
[pensaray]
third party insurance el seguro

contra terceros [tairthaiross]
thirsty: I'm thirsty tengo sed
[seth]
this: this man este hombre
[estay]
this woman esta mujer
this one éste/ésta
this is my wife ésta es mi
mujer
is this ...? ¿es éste/ésta ...?
those: those men aquellos
hombres [akay-yoss]
those women aquellas
mujeres [akay-yass]
which ones? – those ¿cuáles?
– aquéllos/aquéllas
[kwaless]
thread el hilo [eelo]
throat la garganta
throat pastilles las pastillas
para la garganta [pastee-
yass]
through a través de [day]
does it go through ...? (train,
bus) ¿pasa por...?
throw (verb) tirar
throw away (verb) tirar
thumb el dedo pulgar
[daydo]
thunderstorm la tormenta
Thursday jueves [Hwaybess]
ticket el billete [bee-yaytay]

dialogue

a return to Salamanca un
billete de ida y vuelta
a Salamanca [day eeda ee
bwelta]

coming back when?
¿cuándo piensa volver?
[kwando p-yensa bolbair]
today/next Tuesday hoy/el
martes que viene [oy/el
martess kay b-yaynay]
that will be 12 euros son
doce euros [dothay ay-
ooross]

ticket office (bus, rail) la taquilla
[takee-ya]
tide la marea [maray-a]
tie (necktie) la corbata
tight (clothes etc) ajustado
[aHoostado]
  it's too tight es demasiado
  estrecho [daymas-yado]
tights los panties
till la caja [kaHa]
time* el tiempo [t-yempo]
  what's the time? ¿qué hora
  es? [kay ora]
  this time esta vez [beth]
  last time la última vez
  [oolteema]
  next time la próxima vez
  four times cuatro veces
  [bethess]
timetable el horario [orar-yo]
tin (can) la lata
tinfoil el papel de aluminio
[aloomeen-yo]
tin opener el abrelatas
tiny diminuto
tip (to waiter etc) la propina
tired cansado
  I'm tired estoy cansado/
  cansada

tissues los Kleenex®
to: to Barcelona/London a
Barcelona/Londres
to Spain/England a España/
Inglaterra
to the post office a la oficina
de Correos
toast (bread) la tostada
today hoy [oy]
toe el dedo del pie [daydo del
p-yay]
together junto [Hoonto]
  we're together (in shop etc)
  venimos juntos [beneemoss]
  can we pay together?
  ¿podemos pagar todo junto,
  por favor? [podaymoss]
toilet los servicios [sairbeeth-
yoss]
  where is the toilet? ¿dónde
  están los servicios? [donday]
  I have to go to the toilet
  tengo que ir al servicio [kay]
toilet paper el papel higiénico
[eeH-yayneeko]
tomato el tomate [tomatay]
tomato juice el zumo de
tomate [thoomo]
tomato ketchup el ketchup
tomorrow mañana [man-yana]
  tomorrow morning mañana
  por la mañana
  the day after tomorrow
  pasado mañana
toner (for skin) el tonificador
facial [fath-yal]
tongue la lengua [lengwa]
tonic (water) la tónica
tonight esta noche [nochay]

tonsillitis las anginas
[anHeenass]
too (excessively) demasiado
[demass-yado]
(also) también [tamb-yen]
too hot demasiado caliente
[kal-yentay]
too much demasiado
me too yo también
tooth el diente [d-yentay]
toothache el dolor de muelas
[day mwaylass]
toothbrush el cepillo de
dientes [thepee-yo day
d-yentess]
toothpaste la pasta de dientes
top: on top of ... encima de ...
[entheema day]
at the top en lo alto
top floor el último piso
[oolteemo]
topless topless
torch la linterna [leentairna]
total el total
tour el viaje [b-yaHay]
is there a tour of ...? ¿hay una
gira por ...? [ī oona Heera]
tour guide el/la guía turístico
[gee-a]
tourist el/la turista
tourist information office
la oficina de información
turística [ofeetheena day
eenformath-yon]
tour operator la agencia de
viajes [aHenth-ya day b-yaHess]
towards hacia [ath-ya]
towel la toalla [to-a-ya]
town la ciudad [th-yooda]

in town en el centro
[thentro]
just out of town en las afueras
de la ciudad [afwairass]
town centre el centro de la
ciudad
town hall el ayuntamiento
[a-yoontam-yento]
toy el juguete [Hoogaytay]
track (US) el andén
tracksuit el chándal
traditional tradicional [tradeeth-
yonal]
traffic el tráfico
traffic jam el embotellamiento
de tráfico [embotayam-yento
day]
traffic lights los semáforos
trailer (for carrying tent etc) el
remolque [remolkay]
(US: caravan) la caravana
[karabana]
trailer park el camping
train el tren
by train en tren

dialogue

is this the train for ...? ¿es
éste el tren para ...? [estay]
sure exacto
no, you want that platform
there no, tiene que ir a
aquel andén de allí
[t-yaynay kay eer a akayl – day
a-yee]

trainers (shoes) las zapatillas
de deporte [thapatee-yass day

113

deportay]

train station la estación de
trenes [estath-yon day trayness]

tram el tranvía [trambee-a]

translate traducir [tradootheer]
could you translate that?
¿podría traducir eso? [ayso]

translation la traducción
[tradookth-yon]

translator (man/woman) el
traductor/la traductora

trashcan el cubo de la basura
[koobo day la basoora]

travel (verb) viajar [b-yaHar]
we're travelling around
estamos viajando [b-yaHando]

travel agent's la agencia de
viajes [aHenth-ya day b-yaHess]

traveller's cheque el cheque
de viaje [chaykay day b-yaHay]

tray la bandeja [bandayHa]

tree el árbol

tremendous tremendo

trendy moderno [modairno]

trim: just a trim please (to
hairdresser) córtemelo sólo un
poco, por favor [kortaymelo]

trip (excursion) la excursión
[eskoors-yon]
I'd like to go on a trip to ...
me gustaría hacer una
excursión a ... [may – athair]

trolley el carrito

trouble problemas
[problaymass]
I'm having trouble with ...
tengo problemas con ...
sorry to trouble you perdone
que le moleste [pairdonay kay

lay molestay]

trousers los pantalones
[pantaloness]

true verdadero [bairdadairo]
that's not true no es verdad
[bairda]

trunk (US) el maletero
[maletairo]

trunks (swimming) el bañador
[ban-yador]

try (verb) intentar
can I have a try? ¿puedo
probarlo? [pwaydo]

try on: can I try it on? ¿puedo
probármelo?

T-shirt la camiseta [kameesayta]

Tuesday martes [martess]

tuna el atún [atoon]

tunnel el túnel [toonel]

turn: turn left/right gire a la
izquierda/derecha [Heeray]

turn off: where do I turn off?
¿dónde me desvío? [donday
may desbee-o]
can you turn the heating off?
¿puede apagar la calefacción?
[pwayday – kalefakth-yon]

turn on: can you turn the
heating on? ¿puede encender
la calefacción? [enthendair]

turning (in road) el desvío
[desbee-o]

TV la tele [taylay]

tweezers las pinzas [peenthass]

twice dos veces [baythess]
twice as much el doble
[doblay]

twin beds las camas gemelas
[Haymaylass]

twin room la habitación doble
[abeetath-yon doblay]

twist: I've twisted my ankle
me he torcido el tobillo [may
ay tortheedo el tobee-yo]

type el tipo

a different type of ... un tipo
diferente de ... [deefairayntay
day]

typical típico

tyre la rueda [rwayda]

U

ugly (person, building) feo [fay-o]

UK el Reino Unido [ray-eeno
ooneedo]

ulcer la úlcera [oolthaira]

umbrella el paraguas
[paragwass]

uncle el tío

unconscious inconsciente
[eenkonsth-yentay]

under (in position) debajo de
[debaHo day]

(less than) menos de [maynoss]

underdone (meat) poco hecha
[aycha]

underground (railway) el metro

underpants los calzoncillos
[kalthonthee-yoss]

understand: I understand lo
entiendo [ent-yendo]

I don't understand no
entiendo

do you understand?
¿entiende usted? [ent-yenday
oostay]

unemployed desempleado
[desemplay-ado]

United States los Estados
Unidos [ooneedoss]

university la universidad
[ooneebairseeda]

unleaded petrol la gasolina sin
plomo [gasoleena seen]

unlimited mileage sin límite
de kilometraje [seen leemeetay
day keelometraHay]

unlock abrir [abreer]

unpack deshacer las maletas
[desathair lass malaytass]

until hasta que [asta kay]

unusual poco común
[komoon]

up arriba

up there allí arriba [a-yee]

he's not up yet (not out of bed)
todavía no se ha levantado
[todabee-a no say a laybantado]

what's up? (what's wrong?) ¿qué
pasa? [kay]

upmarket (restaurant, hotel, goods
etc) de lujo [day looHo]

upset stomach el malestar de
estómago

upside down al revés
[rebayss]

upstairs arriba

urgent urgente [oorHentay]

us*: with us con nosotros

for us para nosotros

USA EE. UU., Estados
Unidos [ooneedoss]

use (verb) usar [oosar]

may I use ...? ¿podría usar ...?

useful útil [ooteel]

usual habitual [abeetwal]
the usual (drink etc) lo de siempre [day s-yempray]

V

vacancy: do you have any vacancies? (hotel) ¿tiene habitaciones libres? [t-yaynay abeetath-yoness leebress]
vacation las vacaciones [bakath-yoness]
see **holiday**
vaccination la vacuna [bakoona]
vacuum cleaner la aspiradora
valid (ticket etc) válido [baleedo]
how long is it valid for? ¿hasta cuándo tiene validez? [asta kwando t-yaynay baleedeth]
valley el valle [ba-yay]
valuable (adjective) valioso [bal-yoso]
can I leave my valuables here? ¿puedo dejar aquí mis objetos de valor? [pwaydo dayHar akee meess obHaytoss day balor]
value el valor
van la furgoneta [foorgonayta]
vanilla vainilla [ba-eenee-ya]
a vanilla ice cream un helado de vainilla [elado]
vary: it varies depende [daypenday]
vase el florero [florairo]

veal la ternera [tairnaira]
vegetables las verduras [bairdoorass]
vegetarian (man/woman) el vegetariano [beHetar-yano]/la vegetariana
vending machine la máquina [makeena]
very muy [mwee]
very little for me un poquito para mí [pokeeto]
I like it very much me gusta mucho [may goosta moocho]
vest (under shirt) la camiseta [kameesayta]
via por
video el video [beeday-o]
view la vista [beesta]
villa el chalet [chalay]
village el pueblo [pwayblo]
vinegar el vinagre [beenagray]
vineyard el viñedo [been-yaydo]
visa la visa
visit (verb) visitar [beeseetar]
I'd like to visit Valencia ... me gustaría ir a Valencia [may]
vital: it's vital that ... es de vital importancia que ... [day beetal eemportanth-ya kay]
vodka el vodka [bodka]
voice la voz [both]
voltage el voltaje [boltaHay]
vomit vomitar [bomeetar]

W

waist la cintura [theentoora]
waistcoat el chaleco [chalayko]

wait esperar [espairar]

wait for me espéreme [espairaymay]

don't wait for me no me espere [may]

can I wait until my wife/partner gets here? ¿puedo esperar hasta que llegue mi mujer/compañero? [pwaydo – asta kay yaygay]

can you do it while I wait? ¿puede hacerlo mientras espero? [pwayday athairlo m-yentrass]

could you wait here for me? ¿puede esperarme aquí? [espairarmay akee]

waiter el camarero [kamarairo]

waiter! ¡camarero!

waitress la camarera [kamaraira]

waitress! ¡señorita! [sen-yoreeta]

wake: can you wake me up at 5.30? ¿podría despertarme a las cinco y media? [despertarmay]

wake-up call la llamada para despertar [yamada]

Wales Gales [galess]

walk: is it a long walk? ¿se tarda mucho en llegar andando? [say – moocho en yegar]

it's only a short walk está cerca [thairka]

I'll walk iré andando [eeray]

I'm going for a walk voy a dar una vuelta [boy – bwelta]

Walkman® el walkman [wolman]

wall (inside) la pared [paray] (outside) la tapia

wallet la billetera [bee-yetaira]

wander: I like just wandering around me gusta caminar por ahí [may goosta – a-ee]

want: I want a ... quiero un/una ... [k-yairo]

I don't want ... no quiero ...

I want to go home quiero irme a casa [eermay]

I don't want to no quiero

he wants to ... quiere ... [k-yairay]

what do you want? ¿qué quiere? [kay]

ward (in hospital) la habitación [abeetath-yon]

warm caliente [kal-yentay]

I'm so warm tengo mucho calor [moocho]

was*: it was ... era ... [aira]; estaba ...

wash (verb) lavar [labar]

can you wash these? ¿puede lavarlos? [pwayday labarloss]

washer (for bolt etc) la arandela [arandayla]

washhand basin el lavabo [lababo]

washing (clothes) la ropa sucia [sooth-ya]

washing machine la lavadora [labadora]

washing powder el detergente [detairhentay]

washing-up liquid el
(detergente) lavavajillas
[daytairhentay lababaHee-yass]

wasp la avispa [abeespa]

watch (wristwatch) el reloj
[rayloH]

will you watch my things for
me? ¿puede cuidarme mis
cosas? [pwayday kweedarmay
meess]

watch out! ¡cuidado!
[kweedado]

watch strap la correa
[korray-a]

water el agua [agwa]

may I have some water? ¿me
da un poco de agua? [may
– day]

waterproof (adjective)
impermeable [eempairmay-
ablay]

waterskiing el esquí acuático
[eskee akwateeko]

wave (in sea) la ola

way: it's this way es por aquí
[akee]

it's that way es por allí
[a-yee]

is it a long way to ...? ¿queda
lejos...? [kayda layHoss]

no way! ¡de ninguna manera!
[day – manaira]

dialogue

could you tell me the way
to ...? podría indicarme el
camino a ...? [eendeekarmay]
go straight on until you

reach the traffic lights
siga recto hasta llegar al
semáforo [asta yegar]
turn left gire a la izquierda
[Heeray]
take the first on the right
tome la primera a la
derecha [tomay]
see where

we* nosotros, nosotras

weak (person, drink) débil
[daybeel]

weather el tiempo [t-yempo]

dialogue

what's the weather going
to be like? ¿qué tiempo va
a hacer? [kay – ba a athair]
it's going to be fine va a
hacer bueno [bwayno]
it's going to rain va a llover
[yobair]
it'll brighten up later
despejará más tarde
[despayHara – tarday]

wedding la boda

wedding ring el anillo de
casado [anee-yo]

Wednesday miércoles
[m-yairkoless]

week la semana

a week (from) today dentro
de una semana [day]

a week (from) tomorrow
dentro de una semana a
partir de mañana [man-yana]

weekend el fin de semana [feen]

at the weekend el fin de semana

weight el peso [payso]

weird extraño [extran-yo]

weirdo: he's a weirdo es un tipo raro

welcome: welcome to ... bienvenido(s) a ... [b-yenbeneedo(ss)]

you're welcome (don't mention it) de nada [day]

well: I don't feel well no me siento bien [may s-yento b-yen]

she's not well no se siente bien [say]

you speak English very well habla inglés muy bien [abla – mwee]

well done! ¡bravo! [brabo]

this one as well éste también [estay tamb-yen]

well well! (surprise) ¡vaya, vaya! [ba-ya]

dialogue

> how are you? ¿cómo está?
> very well, thanks muy bien, gracias [mwee b-yen]
> – and you? – ¿y usted? [ee oostay]

well-done (meat) muy hecho [mwee aycho]

Welsh galés [galayss]

I'm Welsh (man/woman) soy galés/galesa

were*: we were estábamos; éramos [airamoss]

you were estabais [estaba-eess]; erais [aira-eess]

they were estaban; eran [airan]

west el oeste [o-estay]

in the west en el oeste

West Indian (adj) antillano [antee-yano]

wet mojado [moHado]

what? ¿qué? [kay]

what's that? ¿qué es eso? [ayso]

what should I do? ¿qué hago? [a-go]

what a view! ¡qué vista! [beesta]

what number bus is it? ¿qué autobús es ese? [aysay]

wheel la rueda [rwayda]

wheelchair la silla de ruedas [see-ya day rwaydass]

when? ¿cuándo? [kwando]

when we get back cuando volvamos [bolbamoss]

when's the train/ferry? ¿cuándo es el tren/ferry?

where? ¿dónde? [donday]

I don't know where it is no sé dónde está [say]

dialogue

> where is the cathedral? ¿dónde está la catedral?
> it's over there está por ahí [a-ee]
> could you show me where

it is on the map? ¿puede enseñarme en el mapa dónde está? [pwayday ensenyarmay]

it's just here está justo ahí [Hoosto a-ee]

see way

which: which bus? ¿qué autobús? [kay]

dialogue

which one? ¿cuál? [kwal]
that one ese [aysay]
this one? éste [estay]
no, that one no, aquél [akel]

while: while I'm here mientras esté aquí [m-yentrass estay akee]

whisky el whisky

white blanco

white wine el vino blanco [beeno]

who? ¿quién? [k-yen]

who is it? ¿quién es?

the man who ... el hombre que... [kay]

whole: the whole week toda la semana

the whole lot todo

whose: whose is this? ¿de quién es esto? [day k-yen]

why? ¿por qué? [kay]

why not? ¿por qué no?

wide ancho

wife: my wife mi mujer [mee mooHair]

will*: will you do it for me? ¿puede hacer esto por mí? [pwayday athair]

wind el viento [b-yento]

window (of house) la ventana [bentana]

(of ticket office, vehicle) la ventanilla [bentanee-ya]

near the window cerca de la ventana [thairka day]

in the window (of shop) en el escaparate [escaparatay]

window seat el asiento junto a la ventana [as-yento Hoonto a la bentana]

windscreen el parabrisas

windscreen wiper el limpiaparabrisas [leemp-ya-parabreesass]

windsurfing el windsurf

windy: it's so windy hace mucho viento [athay moocho b-yento]

wine el vino [beeno]

can we have some more wine? ¿podría traernos más vino? [tra-airnoss]

wine list la lista de vinos [leesta day beenoss]

winter el invierno [eemb-yairno]

in the winter en el invierno

winter holiday las vacaciones de invierno [bakath-yonayss day]

wire el alambre [alambray]

(electric) el cable eléctrico [kablay]

wish: best wishes saludos [sal**oo**doss]

with con

I'm staying with ... est**oy** en casa de ... [day]

without sin [seen]

witness el/la testigo [test**ee**go]

will you be a witness for me? ¿acepta ser mi testigo? [ath**e**pta sair]

woman la mujer [moo**H**air]

wonderful estupendo [estoop**e**ndo]

won't*: it won't start no arr**a**nca

wood (material) la madera [mad**ai**ra]

woods (forest) el bosque [b**o**skay]

wool la lana

word la palabra

work el trabajo [trab**a**Ho]

it's not working no funciona [foonth-y**o**na]

I work in ... trabajo en ...

world el mundo [m**oo**ndo]

worry: I'm worried est**oy** preocupado/preocupada [pray-okoop**a**do]

worse: it's worse es peor [pay-**o**r]

worst el peor

worth: is it worth a visit? ¿vale la pena visitarlo? [b**a**lay la p**ay**na bees**ee**tarlo]

would: would you give this to ...? ¿le puede dar esto a ...? [lay pw**ay**day]

wrap: could you wrap it up? ¿me lo envuelve? [may lo embw**e**lbay]

wrapping paper el papel de envolver [day embolb**ai**r]

wrist la muñeca [moon-y**ay**ka]

write escribir [eskreeb**ee**r]

could you write it down? ¿puede escribírmelo? [pw**ay**day]

how do you write it? ¿cómo se escribe? [say eskr**ee**bay]

writing paper el papel de escribrir

wrong: it's the wrong key no es ésa la llave [**ay**sa la y**a**bay]

this is the wrong train éste no es el tren [**e**stay]

the bill's wrong la cuenta está equivocada [kw**e**nta – ekeebok**a**da]

sorry, wrong number perdone, me he equivocado de número [pairdonay, may ay – day n**oo**mairo]

there's something wrong with ... le pasa algo a ... [lay]

what's wrong? ¿qué pasa? [kay]

X

X-ray la radiografía [radyograf**ee**-a]

Y

yacht el yate [**ya**tay]
yard* (courtyard) el patio
year el año [**an**-yo]
yellow amarillo [amar**ee**-yo]
yes sí
yesterday ayer [a-**yair**]
  yesterday morning ayer por
  la mañana [man-**ya**na]
  the day before yesterday
  anteayer [antay-a**yair**]
yet

dialogue

  is it here yet? ¿está aquí
  ya? [a**kee**]
  no, not yet no, todavía no
  [toda**bee**-a]
  you'll have to wait a little
  longer yet todavía tendrá
  que esperar un poquito
  más [kay espai**rar** oon pok**ee**to]

yobbo el gamberro [gam**bai**rro]
yoghurt el yogur [yo**goor**]
you* (fam, sing) tú [too]
  (pol, sing) usted [oos**tay**]
  (fam, pl) vosotros [bos**o**tross]
  (pol, pl) ustedes [oos**tay**dess]
  this is for you esto es para
  tí/usted
  with you contigo/con usted
young joven [**Ho**ben]
your* (fam, sing) tu; (pl) tus
  [tooss]
  (fam, pl) vuestro [**bwe**stro],

vuestra; (pl) vuestros,
vuestras
(polite, sing) su; (pl) sus
[sooss]
yours* (fam, sing) tuyo [**too**-yo],
tuya
(fam pl) vuestro [**bwe**stro],
vuestra
(polite, sing) suyo [**soo**-yo],
suya; de usted [day oos**tay**]
youth hostel el albergue
juvenil [al**bai**rgay Hoobayn**eel**]

Z

zero cero [**thai**ro]
zip la cremallera [krema-**ya**ira]
  could you put a new zip
  in? ¿podría cambiar la
  cremallera? [kamb-**yar**]
zoo el zoo(lógico) [tho(**lo**Heeko)]

Spanish

→

English

Colloquialisms

The following are words you might well hear. You shouldn't be tempted to use any of the stronger ones unless you are sure of your audience.

burro **m** [**boo**rro] thickhead
cabrón! [kab**ron**] bastard!
¡capullo! [kap**oo**yo] dickhead!
cojones [ko**Ho**nayss] balls
es pan comido [ess pan kom**ee**do] it's a piece of cake
estar borracho como una cuba [estar borracho komo **oo**na **koo**ba] to be drunk as a skunk
estar como una cabra [estar komo **oo**na kabra] to be as mad as a hatter
estar de broma [estar de br**o**ma] to be joking
!de puta madre! [day p**oo**ta madray] fucking great!
!Dios mío! [**dee**-oss m**ee**o] my God!
gilipollas [Heeleep**o**yass] dickhead
guay [gwī] cool
¡hijo de puta! [**ee**Ho de p**oo**ta] son of a bitch!
!joder! [Hod**air**] fuck!
¡largo! [**l**argo] beat it!
mamón [mam**on**] idiot
!maricón! [mareek**on**] poof!
!me cago en la puta! [may kago en la p**oo**ta] fucking hell!
!me importa un bledo! [may eemp**o**rta oon bl**ay**do] I don't give a damn!
mierda! [m-y**air**da] shit!
!ni hablar! [nee ablar] no way!
¡no digas tonterías! [no d**ee**gass tontair**ee**ass] don't talk nonsense
!no me digas! [no may d**ee**gass] you don't say!
!no me jodas! [no may H**o**dass] you must be bloody joking!
¡qué coñazo! [kay kon-ya**THo**] what a drag!
!qué va! [kay ba] not at all!
tío **m** [t**ee**o] bloke
tía **f** [t**ee**a] woman
tonto [t**o**nto] silly
!venga ya! [**ba**ynga ya] come on!
¡vete al carajo! [**ba**ytay al kara**Ho**] sod off!
!vete al infierno! [**ba**ytay al eenfy-a**ir**no] go to hell!
¡vete a tomar por culo! [**ba**ytay a tomar por k**oo**lo] fuck off!

A

a to; at; per; from

abajo [abaно] downstairs

abierto [ab-yairto] open

abierto de ... a ... open from ... to

abierto las 24 horas del día open 24 hours

abogado m/f lawyer

abonos mpl season tickets

aborrezco [aborethko] I hate

ábrase aquí open here

ábrase en caso de emergencia open in case of emergency

abrebotellas m [abray-botay-yass] bottle-opener

abrelatas m tin opener

abrigo m coat

abrigo de pieles [p-yayless] fur coat

abril m April

abrir to open

abróchense los cinturones fasten your seatbelts

abstenerse de fumar no smoking

abuela f [abwayla] grandmother

abuelo m grandfather

abuelos mpl grandparents

aburrido boring; bored

aburrirse [aboorreersay] to be bored; to get bored

acabar to finish

acabo de ... I have just ...

acantilado m cliff

acceso a ... access to ...

acceso a los andenes to the trains

acceso playa to the beach

acceso prohibido no admittance

accidente m [aktheedentay] accident

tener un accidente to have an accident

accidente de coche [kochay] car accident

accidente de montaña [montan-ya] mountaineering accident

accidente de tráfico road accident

accidente en cadena [kadayna] pile-up

acelerador m [athelairador] accelerator, gas pedal

acelerar [athelairar] to accelerate

acento m [athento] accent

aceptar [atheptar] to accept

acera f [athaira] pavement, sidewalk

acerca de [athairka day] about, concerning

acero m [athairo] steel

acetona f [athaytona] nail polish remover

ácido (m) [atheedo] sour; acid

acompañar [akompan-yar] to accompany

le acompaño en el sentimiento condolences

acondicionador de pelo m [akondeeth-yonador day paylo] hair conditioner aconsejar [akonsay-Har] to advise

acordarse [akordarsay] to remember

acostar: irse a acostar [eersay] to go to bed

acostarse [akostarsay] to lie down; to go to bed
al acostarse when you go to bed

actriz f [aktreeth] actress

acuerdo m [akwairdo] agreement
estoy de acuerdo I agree
de acuerdo OK

adaptador m adaptor

adelantado: por adelantado [adelantado] in advance

adelantar to overtake

adelante [adelantay] come in

además de [ademass day] besides, as well as

adentro inside

adiós [ad-yoss] goodbye

admitir to admit, to confess

adolescente m/f [adoleshentay] teenager

aduana f [ad-wana] customs

aduanero m [adwanairo] customs officer

aerobús m [a-airobooss] local train

aerodeslizador m [a-airo-desleethador] hovercraft

aerolínea f [a-airoleenay-a] airline

aeropuerto m [a-airopwairto] airport

afeitarse [afay-eetarsay] to shave

aficionado a [afeeth-yonado] keen on

afortunadamente [-mentay] fortunately

afueras fpl [afwairass] suburbs

agarrar un colocón to get sozzled

agárrese aquí hold on here

agencia f [a-Henth-ya] agency

agencia de viajes [b-yaHess] travel agency

agenda f [a-Henda] diary

agítese antes de usar(se) shake before use

agosto m August

agradable [agradablay] pleasant

agradar to please

agradecer [agradethair] to thank

agradecido [agradetheedo] grateful

agradezco [agradethko] I thank

agresivo aggressive

agricultor m farmer

agua f [agwa] water

agua de colonia [kolon-ya] eau de toilette

aguantar: no aguanto ... [agwanto] I can't stand ...

aguja f [agooHa] needle

agujero m [agooHairo] hole

ahora [a-ora] now

aire m [a-eeray] air

aire acondicionado [akondeeth-yonado] air-conditioning

ajedrez m [a-Hedreth] chess

ajustado [a-Hoostado] tight

ala f wing

alambre m [alambray] wire

alarma f alarm

dar la señal de alarma [sen-yal] to raise the alarm

albergue m [albairgay] country hotel; hostel

albergue juvenil [Hoobeneel] youth hostel

albornoz m [albornoth] bathrobe

alcohómetro m Breathalyzer®

alegre [alegray] happy

alegro: ¡me alegro de verte! [bairtay] nice to see you!

alemán [alay-man] German

Alemania f [aleman-ya] Germany

alérgico a [alair-Heeko] allergic to

aletas fpl [alay-tass] flippers

alfarería f [alfarairee-a] pottery

alfiler m [alfeelair] pin

alfombra f rug, carpet

algo something

algo más something else

algodón m cotton; cotton wool, (US) absorbent cotton

alguien [alg-yen] somebody; anybody

algún some; any

alguno some; any

alianza f [al-yantha] wedding ring

alicates mpl pliers

alimentación f [aleementath-yon] groceries, foodstuffs

allá: más allá [a-ya] further

allí [a-yee] there

almacén m [almathen]

department store; warehouse

almohada f [almo-ada] pillow

almuerzo m [almwairtho] lunch

alojamiento m [aloHam-yento] accommodation

alojamiento y desayuno [desa-yoono] bed and breakfast

alpinismo m mountaineering

alquilar [alkeelar] to rent; to hire

alquiler m [alkeelair] rental

alquiler de barcos boat hire

alquiler de bicicletas [beetheeklaytass] bike hire

alquiler de coches [kochess] car rental

alquiler de esquís [eskeess] (water-)ski hire

alquiler de sombrillas [sombree-yass] sunshade hire

alquiler de tablas surfboard hire

alquiler de tumbonas deckchair hire

alquileres rentals

alrededor (de) [alray-day-dor] around

alta costura f haute couture, high fashion

alto high; tall

¡alto! stop!

en lo alto at the top

altura f altitude; height

altura máxima maximum headroom

aluminio m aluminium

amable [amablay] kind

amamantar to breastfeed

amanecer m [amanethair] sunrise, daybreak

amargo bitter

amarillo [amaree-yo] yellow

ambos both

ambulancia f [amboolanth-ya] ambulance

ambulatorio national health clinic

América del Norte f [nortay] North America

América del Sur [soor] South America

americano American

amiga f friend

amigo m friend

aminorar la marcha to slow down

amor m love

hacer el amor to make love

amortiguador m [amorteegwador] shock-absorber

amperio m [ampair-yo] amp

ampliación f [amplee-ath-yon] enlargement

amplio loose-fitting

ampolla f [ampo-ya] blister

analgésico m [anal-Hayseeko] painkiller

análisis clínicos mpl clinical tests

anaranjado [anaran-Hado] orange

ancho wide

ancho m width, breadth

anchura f width, breadth

¡anda ya! get away!, come off it!

andaluz [andalooth] Andalusian

andar to walk

andén m platform, (US) track

a los andenes to the trains

anduve [andoobay] I walked

anémico anaemic

anestesia f [anestays-ya] anaesthetic

anfiteatro m [anfeetay-atro] amphitheatre

angina (de pecho) f [an-Heena] angina

anginas fpl tonsillitis

anillo m [anee-yo] ring

anoche last night

anochecer m [anochethair] nightfall, dusk

ante m suede

anteayer [antay-a-yair] the day before yesterday

antepasado m ancestor

antes de before

antes de que before

antes de ayer [a-yair] the day before yesterday

antes de entrar dejen salir let passengers off first

anticonceptivo m [anteekonthepteebo] contraceptive

anticongelante m [anteekon-Helantay] antifreeze

anticuado [anteek-wado] out of date

anticuario m antiques dealer

antigüedad: una tienda de antigüedades [t-yenda day anteegway-dadess] an antique shop

antiguo [anteegwo] ancient

antihistamínico m [antee-eestameeneeko] antihistamine

anulado cancelled

anular to cancel

añadir [an-yadeer] to add

año m [an-yo] year

Año Nuevo m [nwaybo] New Year

  día de Año Nuevo m [dee-a] New Year's Day

  ¡feliz Año Nuevo! [feleeth] Happy New Year!

apagar to switch off

apagar los faros to switch off one's lights

apagar luces de cruce headlights off

apagón m power cut

apague el motor switch off your engine

apague las luces switch off your lights

aparato m device

aparatos electrodomésticos electrical appliances

aparcamiento m [aparkam-yento] car park, (US) parking lot

aparcamiento privado private parking

aparcamiento reservado this parking place reserved

aparcamiento subterráneo underground parking

aparcamiento vigilado supervised parking

aparcar to park

aparecer [aparethair] to appear

aparezco [aparethko] I appear

apartamento m apartment

apasionante [apass-yonantay] thrilling

apearse de [apay-arsay] to get off

apellido m [apay-yeedo] surname

apenado distressed, sorry

apenas [apaynass] scarcely

  apenas ... (cuando) [k-wando] hardly ... when

apetecer: me apetece [may apetaythay] I feel like

apetito m appetite

apodo m nickname

apoplejía f [apoplay-нee-a] stroke

aprender [aprendair] to learn

aprensivo fearful, apprehensive

apresurarse [-arsay] to rush

aproveche: ¡que aproveche! [aprobay-chay] enjoy your meal!

aproximadamente [-mentay] about

aquel [akel] that

aquél that (one)

aquella [akay-ya] that

aquélla that (one)

aquellas [akay-yass] those

aquéllas those (ones)

aquellos [akay-yoss] those

aquéllos those (ones)

aquí [akee] here

aquí tiene [t-yaynay] here you are

árabe [arabay] Arabic

aragonés Aragonese

araña f [aran-ya] spider

arañazo m [aran-yatho] scratch
árbol m tree
arcén m [arthen] lay-by
ardor de estómago m
  heartburn
área de servicios m service
  area, motorway services
arena f [arayna] sand
Argelia f [arHaylee-a] Algeria
armario m cupboard
armería f [armairee-a]
  gunsmith's
arqueología f [arkay-oloHee-a]
  archaeology
arrancar to start up
arreglar to mend; to sort out,
  to arrange
arrepentido sorry
arriba up; upstairs; on top
arroyo m stream
arte m [artay] art
artesanía f crafts
artículos de artesanía mpl arts
  and crafts
artículos de baño [ban-yo]
  swimwear
artículos de boda wedding
  presents
artículos de deporte sports
  goods
artículos de limpieza
  household cleaning products
artículos de ocasión bargains;
  second hand goods
artículos de piel leather goods
artículos de playa beachwear
artículos de regalo gifts
artículos de viaje travel goods
artículos para el bebé

babywear
artículos para el colegio
  schoolwear
artista m/f artist
artritis f [-treeteess] arthritis
asador m restaurant
  specializing in roast meats
  and/or fish
ascensor m [asthensor] lift,
  elevator
asegurar to insure
aseos mpl [asay-oss] toilets,
  rest room
así like this; like that
así que so (that)
asiático Asian
asiento m [ass-yento] seat
asma m asthma
aspiradora f hoover®
asqueroso [askairoso]
  disgusting
astigmático long-sighted
asturiano [astoor-yano]
  Asturian
asustado afraid
asustar to frighten
atacar to attack
atajo m [ataHo] shortcut
ataque m [atakay] attack
ataque al corazón [korathon]
  heart attack
atascado stuck
atasco (de tráfico) m traffic
  jam
atención [atenth-yon] please
  note
¡atención! take care!,
  caution!
atención al tren beware of

trains

ateo [at**ay**-o] atheist

aterrizaje m [atairreetha**Hay**] landing

aterrizaje forzoso [forth**o**so] emergency landing

aterrizar [atairreeth**ar**] to land

atestado m report

atletismo m athletics

atracar to assault, to hold up

atracciones turísticas fpl [atrakth-y**o**ness] tourist attractions

atraco a mano armada m hold-up

atractivo attractive

atrás at the back; behind

¡atrás! get back!

la parte de atrás [**par**tay] the back

está más atrás it's further back

años atrás years ago

atravesar to go through

atravieso [atrab-y**ay**so] I go through

atreverse [atreb**air**say] to dare

atropellar [atropay-y**ar**] to knock over

atroz [atr**o**th] dreadful

audífono m [owd**ee**fono] hearing aid

aun [a-**oo**n] even

aún [a-**oo**n] still; yet

aunque [a-**oo**nkay] although

autobús m [owtob**oo**ss] bus

autobús sólamente buses only

autocar m coach, bus

auto-estopista m/f [-estop**ee**sta] hitch-hiker

automotor m local short-distance train

automóvil m car

automovilista m/f car driver

autopista f motorway, (US) highway

autopista (de peaje) [pay-a**Hay**] (toll) motorway/highway

auto-servicio m [owto-sairb**ee**th-yo] self-service

autorizada para mayores de 18 años for adults only

autorizada para mayores de 14 años y menores acompañados authorized for those over 14 and young people accompanied by an adult

autorizada para todos los públicos suitable for all

autostop m hitchhiking

hacer autostop to hitchhike

autovía f [-bee-a] dual carriageway, (US) divided highway

AVE m high-speed train on the Madrid-Seville line

avenida f avenue

avergonzado [abairgonth**a**do] embarrassed

avería f [abair**ee**-a] breakdown

averiado out of order

averiarse [abairee-**ar**say] to break down

avión m [ab-y**on**] aeroplane

por avión by air

avisar to inform

aviso m information

aviso a los señores pasajeros
  passenger information
avispa f wasp
ayer [a-yair] yesterday
ayer por la mañana [man-yana]
  yesterday morning
ayer por la tarde [tarday]
  yesterday afternoon
ayuda f [a-yooda] help
ayudar to help
ayuntamiento m [ayoontam-
  yento] town hall
azafata f [athafata] air hostess
azul (m) [athool] blue
azul claro light blue
azul marino navy blue

B

baca f roof rack
bahía f [ba-ee-a] bay
bailar [ba-eelar] to dance
  ir a bailar to go dancing
baile m [ba-eelay] dance;
  dancing
bajar [baHar] to go down
  bajar de to get off
bajarse [baHarsay] to get off
bajo [baHo] low; short;
  under(neath)
balcón m balcony
Baleares [balay-aress]
  Balearics
balón m ball
balón volea [bolay-a]
  volleyball
baloncesto m [balonthesto]
  basketball
balonmano m handball

banco m bank; bench
bandeja f [bandayHa] tray
bandera f [bandaira] flag
bañador m [ban-yador]
  swimming costume
bañarse [ban-yarsay] to go
  swimming; to have a bath
bañera f [ban-yaira] bathtub
baño m [ban-yo] bathroom;
  bath
baraja f [baraHa] pack of cards
barato cheap, inexpensive
barba f beard
barbacoa f [barbako-a]
  barbecue
barbería f [barbairee-a] barber's
barbero m barber
barbilla f [barbee-ya] chin
barca de remos f rowing boat
barcas para alquilar boats to
  rent
barco m boat
barco de vela sailing boat
barra de labios f [lab-yoss]
  lipstick
barrio m [barr-yo] district, area
bastante [bastantay] enough
bastante más quite a lot
  more
bastante menos [maynoss]
  quite a lot less
basura f litter
bata f dressing gown
bate m [batay] bat
batería f [batairee-a] battery
batería de cocina [kotheena]
  pots and pans
batín m dressing gown
bautismo m [bowteesmo]

132

christening

bebé m baby

beber [bebair] to drink

bello [bay-yo] beautiful

benvengut [benvengoot] welcome (in Catalan)

besar to kiss

beso m kiss

betún m [betoon] shoe polish

biblioteca f [beebl-yotayka] library; bookcase

bici: ir a dar una vuelta en bici [bwelta en beethee] to go for a cycle

bicicleta f [beetheeklayta] bicycle

bien [b-yen] well

¡bien! good!

bien ... bien either ... or ...

o bien ... o bien either ... or ...

bienes mpl [b-yayness] possessions

¡bienvenido! welcome!

bifurcación f [beefoorkath-yon] fork

bigote m [beegotay] moustache

billete m [bee-yaytay] ticket

billete de andén platform ticket

billete de banco banknote, (US) bill

billete de ida single ticket, one-way ticket

billete de ida y vuelta [bwelta] return ticket, round trip ticket

blanco (m) white

blusa f blouse

boca f mouth

bocina f [botheena] horn

boda f wedding

bodega f [bodayga] wine cellar; wine bar

boite f [bwat] night club

bolígrafo m biro®

bolsa f bag; stock exchange

bolsa de plástico plastic bag

bolsa de viaje [b-yaHay] travel bag

bolsillo m [bolsee-yo] pocket

bolso m handbag, (US) purse

bomba f bomb

bomberos mpl [bombaiross] fire brigade

bombilla f [bombee-ya] light bulb

bombona de gas f camping gas cylinder

bonito (m) nice; tuna fish

bonobús book of 10 reduced-price bus tickets

bordado embroidered

borracho drunk

bosque m [boskay] forest

bota f boot

botas de agua [agwa] wellingtons

botas de esquiar [eskee-ar] ski boots

botella f [botay-ya] bottle

botiquín m [boteekeen] first aid kit

botón m button

botón desatascador coin return button

boxeo m [boksay-o] boxing

boya f buoy
bragas fpl panties
brazo m [bratho] arm
bricolaje m [breekolaHay] DIY
brillar [bree-yar] to shine
brisa f breeze
británico British
brocha de afeitar f [afay-eetar] shaving brush
broche m [brochay] brooch
bronce m [bronthay] bronze
bronceado m [bronthay-ado] suntan
bronceador m [bronthay-ador] suntan oil/lotion
bronquitis f [bronkeeteess] bronchitis
brújula f [brooHoola] compass
Bruselas Brussels
bucear [boothay-ar] to (skin-)dive
buceo m [boothay-o] skin-diving
¡buenas! [bwaynass] hello!
bueno [bwayno] good; good-natured
buenas noches goodnight
buenas tardes good evening
buenos días [dee-ass] good morning
bufanda f scarf
bujía f [booHee-a] spark plug
bulto m piece of luggage
burro m donkey
buscar to look for
busqué [booskay] I looked for
butacas stalls
buzón [boothon] letter box, mail box

C

c/ (calle) street
c/c (cuenta corriente) current account
caballeros mpl [kaba-yaiross] gents, men's rest room
caballo m [kaba-yo] horse
cabello m [kabay-yo] hair
cabeza f [kabetha] head
cabida ... personas capacity ... people
cabina telefónica f telephone booth, phone box
cable alargador m [kablay] extension lead
cabra f goat
cabrón m bastard
cacahuetes [kakawaytess] peanuts
cachondeo m [kachonday-o] laugh
  lo digo de cachondeo I'm only joking
cada every
cadena f [kadayna] chain
cadera f [kadaira] hip
caduca ... expires ...
caer [ka-air] to fall
caerse [ka-airsay] to fall
cafetera f [kafetaira] coffee pot
cafetería f cafe, bar-type restaurant
caída f [ka-eeda] fall
cago: ¡me cago en diez! [d-yayth] for heaven's sake!
caja de cambios f [kaHa] gearbox

caja f [kaHa] cash desk; cashier

caja de ahorros [a-orross] savings bank

cajera f [kaHaira], **cajero m** cashier

cajero automático [owtomateeko] cash dispenser, (US) automatic teller

calambre m [kalambray] cramp

calcetines mpl [kaltheteeness] socks

calcetines de algodón cotton socks

calcetines de lana woollen socks

calculadora f calculator

calefacción f [kalefakth-yon] heating

calefacción central [thentral] central heating

calendario m [-dar-yo] calendar

calidad f quality

caliente [kal-yentay] hot

calle f [ka-yay] street

calle comercial [komairth-yal] shopping street

calle de dirección única [deerekth-yon] one-way street

calle peatonal [pay-atonal] pedestrianized street

calle principal [preentheepal] main street

callejón sin salida m cul-de-sac, dead end

callo m [ka-yo] corn (on foot)

calmante m tranquillizer

calor m heat

  hace calor it's warm/hot

calvo bald

calzada deteriorada poor road surface

calzada irregular uneven surface

calzados shoe shop

calzoncillos mpl [kalthontheeyoss] underpants

cama f bed

cama de campaña [kampan-ya] campbed

cama de matrimonio double bed

cama individual single bed

cámara f camera; inner tube

cámara fotográfica camera

camarera f [kamaraira] waitress; chambermaid

camarero m waiter

camarote m [kamarotay] cabin

cambiar [kamb-yar] to change

cambiarse (de ropa) [kamb-yarsay] to get changed

cambio m change; exchange; exchange rate

cambio de divisas currency exchange

cambio de moneda currency exchange

cambio de sentido junction, take filter lane to exit and cross flow of traffic

caminar to walk

camino m path

camino cerrado (al tráfico) road closed to (traffic)

camino privado private road

camión m lorry, truck

camioneta f van

camisa f shirt

camiseta f T-shirt; vest

camisón m nightdress

campana f bell

camping m camping; campsite; caravan site, (US) trailer park

campo m countryside; pitch; court; field

campo de deportes sports field

campo de futból football ground

campo de golf golf course

Campsa State-owned oil company

canadiense [kanad-yensay] Canadian

Canal de la Mancha m English Channel

Canarias fpl [kanar-yass] Canaries

cancelado [kanthelado] cancelled

cancelar [kanthelar] to cancel

cancha f court; pitch

canción f [kanth-yon] song

canguro m/f [kangooro] baby-sitter

canoso greying; grey

cansado tired

cantar to sing

cantina f buffet

canto m singing

caña f [kan-ya] small glass of beer

caña de pescar fishing rod

capaz: ser capaz (de) [sair kapath] to be able (to)

capazo m [kapatho] carry-cot

capilla f [kapee-ya] chapel

capitán m captain

capó(t) m bonnet, (US) hood

cara f face

caramelos mpl [karamayloss] sweets, candies

caravana f caravan

carburador m carburettor

cárcel f [karthel] prison

cardenal m bruise

carne f [karnay] flesh

carné de conducir m [karnay day kondootheer] driving licence

carnet de identidad m identity card

carnicería f [karneethairee-a] butcher's

caro expensive

carpintería f [karpeentairee-a] joiner's, carpenter's

carrera f [karraira] race

carrete m [karraytay] film (for camera)

carretera f [karretaira] road

carretera comarcal district highway

carretera cortada road blocked, road closed

carretera de circunvalación by-pass

carretera de doble calzada two-lane road

carretera nacional national highway

carretera principal main highway

carril m lane

carrito m trolley, cart

carrito portaequipajes [porta-aykeepaHess] baggage trolley
carta f letter; menu
cartel m poster
cartelera de espectáculos f [kartelaira] entertainments guide
cartera f [kartaira] briefcase; wallet
carterista m pickpocket
cartero m postman, mailman
cartón m cardboard; carton
casa f house
  en casa at home
  en casa de Juan at Juan's
casa de huéspedes [wespedess] guesthouse
casa de socorro emergency first-aid centre
casado married
casarse [kasarsay] to get married
cascada f waterfall
casi almost
casino m leisure club; casino
caso m case
  en caso de que in case
caso urgente [oorHentay] emergency
casete f, cassette f [kaset] cassette
casete m, cassette m cassette player
caspa f dandruff
castaño (m) [kastan-yo] sweet chestnut; brown
castañuelas fpl [kastan-waylass] castanets
castellano [kastay-yano]

Castilian; another word for the Spanish language
Castilla [kastee-ya] Castile
castillo m castle
casualidad: por casualidad [kaswaleeda] by chance
Cataluña [kataloon-ya] Catalonia
catarro: tengo catarro I've got a cold
católico (m) Catholic
catorce [katorthay] fourteen
caucho m [kowcho] rubber
causa f [kowsa] cause
  a causa de because of
cayó [ka-yo] he fell
caza f [katha] hunting
cazadora f [kathadora] bomber jacket, blouson
cazar [kathar] to hunt
cazo m [katho] saucepan
ceda el paso give way, yield
ceder el paso [thedair] to give way
ceja f [thayHa] eyebrow
celoso [theloso] jealous
cementerio m [thementair-yo] cemetery
cena f [thayna] dinner
cenar to have dinner
cenicero m [thayneethairo] ashtray
central telefónica f [thentral] telephone exchange
centro comercial m [thentro komairthee-al] shopping centre
centro urbano/ciudad m [th-yooda] city/town centre
ceñido [then-yeedo] tight-

fitting

cepillo m [thepee-yo] brush

cepillo de dientes [d-yentess] toothbrush

cepillo del pelo hairbrush

cera f [thaira] wax

cerámica f [thairameeka] ceramics

cerca de [thairka] near

cercanías m [thairkanee-ass] local short-distance train

cerilla f [thairee-ya] match

cero [thairo] zero

cerrado [thairrado] closed

cerrado por defunción closed due to bereavement

cerrado por descanso del personal closed for staff holidays

cerrado por obras/reforma/vacaciones closed for alteration/renovation/holidays

cerradura f [thairradoora] lock

cerramos los ... we close on ...

cerrar [thairrar] to close

cerrar con llave [yabay] to lock

cerrojo m [thairroHo] bolt

certificado m [thairteefeekado] certificate; registered letter

cervecería f [thairbethair-ee-a] bar specializing in beer

cerveza f [thairbaytha] beer

césped m [thesped] lawn

cesta f [thesta] basket

cesto de la compra m shopping basket

CH (casa de huespedes) f

[wespedess] boarding house, low-price hostel

chaleco m waistcoat

chalecos salvavidas life-jackets

chalet m [chalay] villa

champú m shampoo

chandal m tracksuit

chaparrón m shower; downpour

chaqueta f [chakayta] cardigan; jacket

chaquetón m [chaketon] jacket; three-quarter length jacket

charcutería f delicatessen

charlar to chat

cheque m [chaykay] cheque, (US) check

cheque de viaje m [day b-yaHay] travellers' cheque

chica f girl

chicle m [cheeklay] chewing gum

chico m boy

chillar [chee-yar] to shout

chino Chinese

chiringuito m [cheereengeeto] open-air bar

chiste m [cheestay] joke

chocar con to run into

chocolate con leche m [chokolatay kon lechay] milk chocolate

chocolate de hacer [athair] plain chocolate

chubasco m sudden short shower

chubasquero m [choobaskairo] cagoule

chupa-chups® m lollipop

Cía. (compañía) company

cicatriz f [theekatreeth] scar

ciclismo m [theekleesmo] cycling

ciclista m/f [theekleesta] cyclist

ciego [th-yaygo] blind

cielo m [th-yaylo] sky

cien [th-yen] hundred

ciencia f [th-yenth-ya] science

ciento ... [th-yento] a hundred and ...

cierren las puertas close the doors

cierro [th-yairro] I close

cigarrillo m [theegarree-yo] cigarette

cinco [theenko] five

cincuenta [theen-kwenta] fifty

cine m [theenay] cinema

cinta f [theenta] tape; ribbon

cintura f [theentoora] waist

cinturón m [theentooron] belt

cinturón de seguridad seat belt

circo m [theerko] circus

circulación f [theerkoolath-yon] traffic; circulation

circulación en ambas direcciones two-way traffic

circule despacio drive slowly

circule por la derecha keep to your right

circunvalación f [theerkoonbalath-yon] ring road

cistitis f [theesteeteess] cystitis

cita f [theeta] appointment

ciudad f [thee-oo-da] town, city

claro clear

¡claro! of course!

clase f [klasay] class

clavo m nail

claxon m [klakson] horn

clima m climate

climatizado [-thado] air-conditioned

clínica f hospital; clinic

cobrador m conductor

cobre m [kobray] copper

cocer [kothair] to cook; to boil

coche m [kochay] car

en coche by car

coche-cama m sleeper, sleeping car

cochecito m [kochetheeto] pram

coche comedor dining car

coche de línea [leenay-a] long-distance bus

coche de niño [neen-yo] pram; pushchair, baby buggy

coche-restaurante m [-restowrantay] restaurant car

cocina f [kotheena] kitchen; cooker

cocinar [kotheenar] to cook

cocinera f [kotheenaira], cocinero m cook

código de la circulación m [theerkoolath-yon] highway code

código postal postcode, zip code

codo m elbow

coger [koнair] to catch; to take

cojo (m) [koнo] I catch; I take; person with a limp

cola f tail; queue

hacer cola to queue

colchas fpl bedspreads

colchón m mattress

colchoneta inflable f [eenflablay] air mattress

colección f [kolekth-yon] collection

colegio m [kolayH-yo] school

colgante m [kolgantay] pendant

colina f hill

collar m [ko-yar] necklace

colocar to place, to put

color m colour

columna vertebral f spine

combinación f [kombeenath-yon] petticoat

combustible m [komboosteeblay] fuel

comedor m dining room

comenzar [komenthar] to begin

comer [komair] to eat

comerciante m [komairth-yantay] shopkeeper; dealer

comida f lunch; food; meal

comidas para llevar take-away meals

comienzo [kom-yentho] I begin

comisaría f police station

comisaría de policía [polee-thee-a] police station

como as; like

¿cómo? pardon?; how?

¿cómo dice? [deethay] pardon?

¿cómo está? how are you?

¿cómo le va? [lay] how are things?

como quieras [k-yairass] it's

up to you

compañera f [kompan-yaira] girlfriend

compañero m mate; boyfriend

compañía f [kompan-yee-a] company

compañía aérea [a-airay-a] airline

comparar to compare

compartir to share

completamente [-mentay] completely

completo full, no vacancies

complicado complicated

compra: hacer la compra [athair] to do the shopping

compramos a ... buying rate

comprar to buy

comprender [komprendair] to understand

no comprendo I don't understand

compras: ir de compras to go shopping

compresa m [kompraysa] sanitary towel, sanitary napkin

comprimido efervescente m soluble tablet

comprimidos tablets

computadora f computer

comunicando engaged; busy

con with

concha f shell

concierne [konth-yairnay] it concerns

concierto m [konth-yairto] concert

condición: a condición de que [kondeeth-yon] on condition that

condón m condom

conducir [kondootheer] to drive

conductor m, conductora f driver

conduzca con cuidado drive with care

conduzco [kondoothko] I drive

conejo m [konay-Ho] rabbit

confección f [konfekth-yon] clothing industry

confección de caballero [kabayairo] menswear

confección de señoras ladies' fashions

confecciones fpl ready-to-wear clothes

conferencia internacional f [konfairenth-ya eentairnath-yonal] international call

conferencia interurbana long-distance call

confesar to admit, to confess

confirmar to confirm

confitería f [konfeetairee-a] sweetshop, candy store

conforme [konformay] as

estar conforme to agree

conformidad f agreement

congelado [konHaylado] frozen

congelador m [konHaylador] freezer

congelados mpl [konHayladoss] frozen foods

conjunto m [konHoonto] group; band

conmigo with me

conmoción cerebral f [konmoth-yon thairebral] concussion

conocer [konothair] to know

conozco [konothko] I know

conque [konkay] so, so then

conserje m [konsairHay] janitor, porter

conservas fpl jams, preserves

consérvese en sitio fresco store in a cool place

consigna f [konseeg-na] left luggage (office), baggage check

consigna automática left luggage lockers

consigo with himself; with herself; with yourself; with themselves; with yourselves

consulado m consulate

consulta médica surgery, doctor's office

consúmase antes de ... best before ...

contable m/f [kontablay] accountant

contacto: ponerse en contacto con to contact

contado: pagar al contado to pay cash

contagioso [kontaH-yoso] contagious

contaminado polluted

contar to count; to tell

contener [kontenair] to contain

contenido m contents

contento happy

contestar to reply, to answer

contigo with you

continuación: a continuación

[konteen-wath-yon] then, next

continuar [konteen-war] to continue

contorno de cadera m hip measurement

contorno de cintura [theentoora] waist measurement

contorno de pecho bust/chest measurement

contra against

contradecir [kontradetheer] to contradict

contraindicaciones fpl contra-indications

contraventanas fpl shutters

control de pasaportes m passport control

convalecencia f [konbalethenth-ya] convalescence

¡coño! [kon-yo] fuck!

copa f glass

coquetear [koketay-ar] to flirt

corazón m [korathon] heart

corbata f tie, necktie

cordero m [kordairo] lamb

cordones mpl [kordoness] (shoe)laces

correa del ventilador f [korray-a] fan belt

correo m [korray-o] mail

correo aéreo [a-airay-o] airmail

correo urgente [oorнentay] express

correos m post office

Correos y Telégrafos Post Office

correr [korrair] to run

corrida de toros f bullfight

corriente peligrosa dangerous current

corrimiento de tierras danger: landslides

cortadura f cut

cortar to cut

cortarse [kortarsay] to cut oneself

cortauñas m [korta-oon-yass] nail clippers

corte de pelo m [kortay] haircut

corte y confección [konfekth-yon] dressmaking

cortina f curtain

corto short

cosa f thing

coser [kosair] to sew

costa f coast

costar to cost

costilla f [kostee-ya] rib

costumbre f [kostoombray] custom

cráneo m [kranay-o] skull

crédito m credit; unit(s)

creer [kray-air] to believe

crema f [krayma] cream

crema base [basay] foundation cream

crema de belleza [bay-yaytha] cold cream

crema hidratante [eedratantay] moisturizer

crema limpiadora [leemp-yadora] cleansing cream

cremallera f [krema-yaira] zip, zipper

creyó [kray-yo] he believed

crisis nerviosa f [nairb-yosa]

nervous breakdown

cristal m [kreestal] crystal; glass

cristalería f glassware

crítica f criticism

criticar to criticize

cruce m [kroothay] junction, intersection; crossing; crossroads

cruce de ganado danger: cattle crossing

cruce de ciclistas danger: cyclists crossing

crucero m [kroothairo] cruise

Cruz Roja f [krooth roHa] Red Cross

cruzar [kroothar] to cross

CTNE f Spanish national telephone company

cuaderno m [kwadairno] notebook

cuadrado [kwadrado] square

cuadro m [kwadro] painting
de cuadros checked

cual [kwal] which; who

¿cuándo? [kwando] when?

¿cuánto? [kwanto] how much?
en cuanto... as soon as...
¡cuánto lo siento! [s-yento] I'm so sorry!

¿cuántos? how many?

cuarenta [kwarenta] forty

cuartel de la guardia civil m civil guard barracks

cuartilla f [kwartee-ya] writing paper

cuarto (m) [kwarto] quarter; fourth; room
cuarto de hora [ora] quarter of an hour

cuarto de baño [ban-yo] bathroom

cuarto de estar sitting room

cuarto piso fourth floor, (US) fifth floor

cuatro [kwatro] four

cuatrocientos [kwatro-th-yentoss] four hundred

cubierta f [koob-yairta] deck

cubierto (m) covered; overcast; meal

cubiertos mpl cutlery

cubo m bucket; cube

cubo de la basura dustbin, trashcan

cucaracha f cockroach

cuchara f spoon

cucharilla f [koocharee-ya] teaspoon

cuchilla de afeitar f [koochee-ya day afay-eetar] razor blade

cuchillería f [koochee-yairee-a] cutlery

cuchillo m [koochee-yo] knife

cuelgue, espere y retire la tarjeta hang up, wait and remove card

cuello m [kway-yo] neck; collar

cuenco m [kwenko] bowl

cuenta f [kwenta] bill; account

cuentas corrientes current accounts

cuento m [kwento] tale

cuerda f [kwairda] rope; string

cuero m [kwairo] leather

cuerpo m [kwairpo] body

cuesta (f) [kwesta] it costs; slope

cueva f [kweba] cave

cuidado (**m**) [kweedado] take care; look out; care

cuidado con ... caution ...

cuidado con el perro beware of the dog

cuidado con el escalón mind the step

cuidar to look after; to nurse

culebra f snake

culpa f fault, blame; guilt

es culpa mía it's my fault

culturismo m body building

cumplas: ¡que cumplas muchos más! many happy returns!

cumpleaños m [koomplay-an-yoss] birthday

cuna f cot, (US) crib

cuneta f [koonayta] gutter

cuñada f [koon-yada] sister-in-law

cuñado m brother-in-law

cura m priest

curado cured; smoked

curar to cure; to dress

curarse [koorarsay] to heal up

curva f bend; curve

curva peligrosa dangerous bend

cuyo [koo-yo] whose; of which

D

D. (Don) Mr

damas fpl ladies' toilet, ladies' restroom

danés Danish

danza f [dantha] dancing; dance

daños mpl [dan-yoss] damage

dar to give

dar el visto bueno a [bwayno] to approve

dcha. (derecha) right

de of; from

de 2 metros de alto two metres high

debajo de [debaHo] under

deber (**m**) [debair] to have to; to owe; duty

deberes mpl [debairess] homework

débil weak

decepción f [dethepth-yon] disappointment

decepcionado [dethepth-yonado] disappointed

decidir [detheedeer] to decide

décimo [detheemo] tenth

decir [detheer] to say; to tell

declaración f [deklarath-yon] declaration; statement

declarar to declare, to state

dedo m [daydo] finger

dedo del pie [p-yay] toe

defectuoso [defekt-woso] faulty

degustación f [degoostath-yon] café specializing in coffee

dejar [dayHar] to leave; to let

dejar de beber to stop drinking

delante de [delantay] in front of

delantera f [delantaira] front (part)

delantero front

la parte delantera [partay] the

front (part)

delgado thin

delicioso [deleeth-yoso] delicious

demás: los demás the others

demasiado [demass-yado] too

demasiados too many

demora f delay

dentadura postiza f [posteetha] dentures

dentista m/f dentist

dentro (de) inside

dentro de dos semanas in two weeks' time

depende [dependay] it depends

dependiente m/f [depend-yentay] shop assistant

deporte m [deportay] sport

deportes de invierno mpl [eemb-yairno] winter sports

deportivo [deporteebo] sports

deportivos mpl trainers

depósito m tank; deposit

deprimido depressed

derecha f right

a la derecha (de) on the right (of)

derecho: todo derecho straight ahead

derribar to wreck, to demolish

desacuerdo m [desak-wairdo] disagreement

desafortunadamente [-amentay] unfortunately

desagradable [-dablay] unpleasant

desagradar to displease

desaparecer [desaparaythair] to

disappear

desastre m [desastray] disaster

desayunar [desa-yoonar] to have breakfast

desayuno m [desa-yoono] breakfast

descansar to rest

descarado cheeky

descarrilar to be derailed

descolgar el aparato lift receiver

descubierto [deskoob-yairto] discovered

descubrir to discover

descuelgue el auricular lift the receiver

descuentos [deskwentoss] discounts

descuidado [deskweedado] careless

desde (que) [desday] since

desde luego [lwaygo] of course

desear [desay-ar] to want; to wish

¿qué desea? [kay desay-a] what can I do for you?

desembarcadero m [desembarkadairo] quay

desfile de modelos m [desfeelay] fashion show

desgracia: por desgracia [desgrath-ya] unfortunately

deshacer las maletas [dess-athair] to unpack

desinfectante m [-tantay] disinfectant

desmaquillarse [desmakee-yarsay] to remove one's

makeup

desmayarse [desmayarsay] to faint

desnudo naked

desobediente [desobayd-yentay] disobedient

desodorante m [-rantay] deodorant

desordenado untidy

desorientarse [desor-yentarsay] to lose one's way

despachador automático m ticket machine

despacho de billetes m [bee-yaytess] ticket office

despacio [despath-yo] slowly

despedirse [despedeersay] to say goodbye

despegar to take off

despegue m [despay-gay] take-off

despejado [despayнado] clear

despertador m [despairtador] alarm clock

despertar to wake

despertarse [-tarsay] to wake up

despierto [desp-yairto] awake

desprendimiento de terreno danger: landslides

despreocupado [despray-okoopado] thoughtless

después [despwess] afterwards

después de after

destinatario m addressee

destino m destination

destornillador m [destornee-yador] screwdriver

destruir [destr-weer] to destroy

desvestirse [desbesteersay] to undress

desviación f [desb-yath-yon] diversion

desvío m [desbee-o] detour, diversion

desvío provisional temporary diversion

detener [detenair] to arrest; to stop

detergente en polvo m [detairнentay] washing powder

detergente lavavajillas [lababaнee-yass] washing-up liquid

detestar to detest

detrás (de) behind

devolver [debolbair] to give back; to vomit

di I gave; tell me

día m [dee-a] day

día festivo public holiday

diamante m [d-yamantay] diamond

diapositiva f [d-yaposeeteeba] slide

diario (m) [d-yar-yo] diary; daily newspaper

diarrea f [d-yarray-a] diarrhoea

días azules [athooless] cheap travel days

días festivos public holidays

días laborables weekdays

dibujar [deebooнar] to draw

dibujos animados mpl [deebooнoss] cartoons

diccionario m [deekth-yonar-yo] dictionary

dice [deethay] he/she says;

you say

dicho said

¿qué ha dicho? what did you say?; what did he/she say?

diciembre m [deeth-yembray] December

diecinueve [d-yetheenwaybay] nineteen

dieciocho [d-yethee-ocho] eighteen

dieciséis [d-yetheesay-eess] sixteen

diecisiete [d-yethees-yaytay] seventeen

diente m [d-yentay] tooth

dieron [d-yairon] they gave; you gave

dieta f [d-yayta] diet

diez [d-yeth] ten

difícil [deefeetheel] difficult

diga tell me

dígame [deegamay] hello, yes

digo I say

dije [deeHay] I said

dijeron [deeHairon] they said; you said

dijiste [deeHeestay] you said

dijo [deeHo] he/she said; you say

diminuto tiny

Dinamarca f Denmark

dinero m [deenairo] money

dinero suelto [swelto] small change

Dios m [dee-oss] God

¡Dios mío! [mee-o] my God!

dirección f [deerekth-yon] direction; address; steering; management

dirección única one-way traffic

dirección prohibida no entry

director m, **directora** f manager; director; headteacher

dirigir [deereeHeer] to direct; to lead

disco m record

disco compacto compact disc

disco obligatorio parking disk must be displayed

disconformidad f disagreement

discoteca f disco, discotheque

disculparse [deeskoolparsay] to apologize

disculpe [deeskoolpay] excuse me

disculpen las molestias we apologize for any inconvenience

discurso m speech

discusión f [deeskoos-yon] discussion; argument

discutir to argue

diseñador de modas m [deesen-yador] fashion designer

distancia f [deestanth-ya] distance

distinto different

distraído [deestra-eedo] absent-minded

distribuidor m [deestreebweedor] distributor

distrito postal m postcode, zip code

disuélvase en agua dissolve in water

divertido entertaining; funny

divertirse [deebairteersay] to have a good time

divisas fpl foreign currency

divorciado [deeborth-yado] divorced

divorciarse [deeborth-yarsay] to divorce

divorcio m [deeborth-yo] divorce

doble [doblay] double

doce [dothay] twelve

docena (de) f [dothayna] dozen

dólar m dollar

doler [dolair] to hurt

dolor m pain

dolor de cabeza [kabaytha] headache

dolor de garganta sore throat

dolor de muelas toothache

dolor de oídos [o-eedoss] earache

doloroso painful

domicilio m [domeetheel-yo] place of residence; commercial headquarters

domingo m Sunday

domingos y festivos Sundays and public holidays

¡dominguero! [domeengairo] learn to drive!

don Mr

donaciones donations

donde [donday] where

doña [don-ya] Miss; Mrs

dorado gold, golden

dormido asleep

dormir to sleep

dormitorio m [dormeetor-yo] bedroom; dormitory

dos two

doscientos [doss-thyentoss] two hundred

doy I give

droga f drug

droguería f [drogairee-a] drugstore; household cleaning materials

ducha f shower

ducharse [doocharsay] to have a shower

dudar to doubt; to hesitate

duele [dwaylay] it hurts

dulce [doolthay] sweet; gentle

dunas fpl sand dunes

durante [doorantay] during

duro (m) hard; tough guy; five peseta coin

E

e and

ebanistería f [ebaneestairee-a] cabinetmaker's

echar to throw

echo de menos a mi ... [dee maynoss] I miss my ...

echar al buzón [boothon] to post, to mail

echar el cerrojo [thairoHo] to bolt

echar al correo [korray-o] to post, to mail

echarse la siesta [echarsay] to have a nap

edad f age

edificio m [edeefeeth-yo] building

edredón m quilt, eiderdown;

duvet
educado polite
EE.UU. (Estados Unidos) USA
efectivo: en efectivo in cash
eje m [ayнay] axle
eje del cigüeñal [theegwen-yal]
crankshaft
ejemplo m [eнemplo] example
  por ejemplo for example
el the
él he; him
elástico elastic
electricidad f [elektreetheeda]
electricity
electricista m [elektreetheesta]
electrician
eléctrico electric
electrodomésticos mpl
electrical appliances
elegir [elayнeer] to choose
ella [ay-ya] she; her
ellas they; them
ellos they; them
embajada f [embaнada]
embassy
embarazada [embarathada]
pregnant
embarque m [embarkay]
embarcation
embotellado en ... bottled
in ...
embotellamiento m [embotay-
yam-yento] traffic jam
embrague m [embragay] clutch
embudo m funnel
emergencia f [emairнenth-ya]
emergency
emergencias casualty;
emergencies

emisión f [emeess-yon]
programme; emission;
distribution date; issue
emocionante [emoth-yonantay]
exciting
empalme m [empalmay]
junction
empaquetado m [empaketado]
packing
empaste m [empastay] filling
empeorar [empay-orar] to get
worse
empinado steep
empleada f [emplay-ada],
empleado m shop assistant,
employee
empujar [empooнar] to push
en in; at; on; by
enagua de medio cuerpo f
[enagwa day mayd-yo kwairpo]
underskirt
enamorados: día de los
enamorados m St Valentine's
Day
encantado delighted
¡encantado! pleased to meet
you!
encantador lovely
encantar to please
encendedor m [enthendedor]
lighter
encender [enthendair] to light;
to switch on
encender luces de cruce
switch headlights on
encendido m [enthendeedo]
ignition
enchufe m [enchoofay] plug;

socket

encienda las luces switch on your lights

encierro [enth-**yai**rro] bull-running in Pamplona, the bulls loose in the streets

encima [en**thee**ma] above

encima de on (top of)

encontrar to find

encontrarse (con/a) [-**trar**say] to meet

encuentro (m) [en**kwen**tro] meeting, encounter; I find

enero m [e**nai**ro] January

enfadado angry

enfadarse [-**dar**say] to get angry

enfermedad f [enfairme**da**] disease

enfermedad venérea [bena**iray**-a] VD

enfermera f [enfairm**ai**ra] nurse

enfermero m male nurse

enfermo [en**fair**mo] ill

enfrente de [en**fren**tay] opposite

enhorabuena:

¡enhorabuena! [enorab**wai**na] congratulations!

dar la enhorabuena a to congratulate

enlace m [en**la**thay] connection; wedding

enlatados mpl canned food

enorme [e**nor**may] enormous

enseñar [ensen-**yar**] to teach

entender [enten**dair**] to understand

entero [en**tai**ro] whole

entiendo [ent-**yen**do] I understand

entierro m [ent-**yai**rro] funeral

entonces [en**ton**thess] then; therefore

entrada f entrance, way in; ticket

entrada por delante entry at the front

entrada libre admission free

entrada gratis admission free

entrar to go in

entre [**en**tray] among; between

entre sin llamar enter without knocking

entreacto m [entray-**ak**to] intermission

entretanto meanwhile

enviar [emb-**yar**] to send

envolver [embol**bair**] to wrap up; to involve

equipaje m [ekeepa**hay**] luggage, baggage

equipaje de mano hand baggage

equipajes mpl left-luggage office, (US) baggage check

equipo m [e**kee**po] team

equitación f [ekeetath-**yon**] horse riding

equivocado [ekeebo**ka**do] wrong

equivocarse [ekeebo**kar**say] to make a mistake

equivocarse de número to dial the wrong number

era [**ai**ra] I/he/she/it was; you were

erais [**ai**ra-eess] you were

éramos we were

eran they were; you were

eras you were

eres you are

erupción f [airoopth-yon] rash; eruption

es he is; you are

ésa [aysa] that one

esa that

ésas those ones

esas those

escala f intermediate stop; scale; ladder

escalera automática f escalator

escaleras fpl stairs

escalón lateral ramp; uneven road surface; no hard shoulder

escandaloso shocking

Escandinavia f Scandinavia

escarcha f frost

escayola f [eska-yola] plaster cast

escocés [eskothayss] Scottish

Escocia f [eskoth-ya] Scotland

escoger [eskoHair] to choose

esconder [eskondair] to hide

escribir to write

escrito written

escuchar to listen; to listen to

escuela f [eskwayla] school

escuela de párvulos kindergarten

escurrir a mano to wring by hand

ése [aysay] that one

ese that

esencial [esenth-yal] essential

esfuerzo m [esfwairtho] effort

esmalte de uñas m [esmaltay day oon-yass] nail polish

esmeralda f emerald

eso [ayso] that

eso es that's it, that's right

ésos those ones

esos those

espalda f back

espantoso dreadful; frightening

España f [espan-ya] Spain

español (m) [espan-yol] Spanish; Spaniard

española f Spaniard, Spanish woman/girl

especialista m/f specialist

especialmente [espeth-yalmentay] especially

espejo m [espayHo] mirror

esperar [espairar] to wait; to hope

espere [espairay] please wait

¡espéreme! [espairemay] wait for me!

espere tono más agudo wait for higher pitched tone

espeso [espayso] thick

esponja f [esponHa] sponge

esposa f wife

esposo m husband

espuma de afeitar f [afay-eetar] shaving foam

esquí m [eskee] ski; skiing

esquí acuático [akwateeko] waterski; waterskiing

esquiar [eskee-ar] to ski

esquina f [eskeena] corner

esta this

ésta this one

estación f [estath-yon] station; season

estación de autobuses [owtoboosess] bus station

estación de servicio [sairbeeth-yo] service station

estación de trenes train station

estación principal central station

estacionamiento vigilado supervised parking

estacionamiento limitado restricted parking

estacionarse [estath-yonarsay] to park

estadio de fútbol m [estad-yo] football stadium

Estados Unidos mpl United States

estampado (m) pattern; printed

estanco m tobacconist's

estanque m [estankay] pond

estaño m [estan-yo] tin; pewter

estar to be

estárter m [estartair] choke

estas these

éstas these ones

estatua f [estatwa] statue

este m [estay] east

este this

éste this one

esterilizado [estaireeleethado] sterilized

esto this

estómago m stomach

estornudar to sneeze

estos these

éstos these ones

estoy I am

estrecho narrow; tight

Estrecho de Gibraltar m [Heebraltar] Strait of Gibraltar

estrella f [estray-ya] star

estrellarse contra [estray-yarsay] to run into

estreno m [estrayno] new film release

estreñido [estren-yeedo] constipated

estreñimiento m [estren-yeem-yento] constipation

estropear [estropay-ar] to damage

estudiante m/f [estood-yantay] student

estudiar [estood-yar] to study

estupendo wonderful, great

estúpido stupid

etiqueta f [eteekayta] label

... de etiqueta formal ...

europeo [ay-ooropay-o] European

evidente [ebeedentay] obvious

exactamente [-mentay] exactly

¡exacto! exactly!

excelente [esthelentay] excellent

excepto ... except ...

excepto domingos y festivos except Sundays and holidays

excepto sábados except Saturdays

exceso de equipaje m [esthayso day ekeepaнay] excess baggage

exceso de velocidad [belotheeda] speeding

excursión f [eskoors-yon] trip

expedir [espedeer] to dispatch

explicación f [espleekath-yon] explanation

explicar explain

explorar to explore

exportación f [esportath-yon] export

exposición f [esposeeth-yon] exhibition

exprés m slow night train stopping at all stations

expreso m fast train; special delivery

exterior (m) [estairee-or] exterior, outer; foreign; overseas

extintor (de incendios) m [eenthend-yoss] fire extinguisher

extra 4-star, (US) premium

extranjera f [estranHaira] foreigner

extranjero (m) [estranHairo] foreign; abroad; overseas; foreigner

en el extranjero abroad

extraño [estran-yo] strange

F
▬

fábrica f factory

fabricado por ... made by ...

fácil [fatheel] easy

factura f bill; invoice

facturación f [faktoorath-yon] check-in

facturar el equipaje [ekeepaHay] to check in

falda f skirt; hillside

falda pantalón culottes

falso false

falta f lack; mistake; defect; fault

no hace falta que ... [athay] it's not necessary to ...

falta de visibilidad poor visibility

familia f [fameel-ya] family

famoso famous

farmacia f [farmath-ya] chemist's, pharmacy

farmacia de guardia [gward-ya] emergency chemist's/ pharmacy, duty chemist

faro m light; headlight; lighthouse

faro antiniebla [anteen-yebla] fog lamp

favor: a favor de [fabor] in favour of

por favor please; please do; excuse me

febrero m [febrairo] February

fecha f date

fecha de caducidad [kadootheeda] expiry date

fecha de caducación [kadookath-yon] expiry date

fecha de nacimiento [natheem-yento] date of birth

fecha límite de venta sell-by date

¡felices Pascuas y próspero Año Nuevo! [feleethess paskwass ee prospairo an-yo nwaybo] merry Christmas and a happy New Year!

felicidad f [feleetheeda] happiness

¡felicidades! [feleetheedadess] happy birthday!; congratulations!

felicitar [feleetheetar] to congratulate

feliz [feleeth] happy

¡feliz cumpleaños! [koomplay-an-yoss] happy birthday!

feo [fay-o] ugly

feria de ... ... fair

ferias fpl [fair-yass] fair

ferretería f [fairraytairee-a] hardware store

ferrobús m local short-distance train

ferrocarril m railway, railroad

festividad f celebration

festivos bank holidays, public holidays

fibras naturales [natooraless] natural fibres

fiebre f [f-yebray] fever

fiebre del heno [ayno] hay fever

fiesta f public holiday; party

fiesta de ... feast of ...

fiesta nacional [nath-yonal] bullfighting

fila f row

filtro m filter

fin m [feen] end; purpose

a fin de que [day kay] so that

fin de semana weekend

fin de serie [sair-yay] discontinued articles

final m [feenal] end

final de autopista end of

motorway/highway

fingir [feenHeer] to pretend

fino fine; delicate

firma f signature; company

firmar to sign

firme deslizante slippery surface

firme en mal estado bad surface

flaco skinny

flequillo m [flekee-yo] fringe

flor f flower

floristería f florist

flotador m rubber ring

flotadores mpl [flotadoress] lifebelts

folleto m [fo-yayto] leaflet

fonda f (simple) restaurant; boarding house

fondo m bottom; background

en el fondo (de) at the bottom (of)

fontanero m [fontanairo] plumber

footing m jogging

forma f form

en forma fit

foto f photograph

hacer fotos to take photographs

fotografía f photograph; photography

fotografiar [fotograf-yar] to photograph

fotógrafo m photographer

fotómetro m light meter

francamente [-mentay] frankly

francés [franthayss] French

Francia f [franth-ya] France

franqueo m [frank**ay**-o] postage

fregadero m sink

fregar: fregar los platos to do the washing up

freír [fray-**eer**] to fry

frenar [fren**ar**] to brake

freno m [fr**ay**no] brake

freno de mano handbrake

frente f [fr**ent**ay] forehead

fresco fresh

frigorífico m fridge

frío [fr**ee**-o] cold

  hace frío [**a**thay] it's cold

frontera f [front**ai**ra] border

frutería f fruit shop/store; greengrocer

fue [fway] he/she/it went; he/she/it was; you went; you were

fuego m [fw**ay**go] fire

  ¿tiene fuego? have you got a light?

fuegos artificiales [arteefeeth-**yal**ess] fireworks

fuente f [fw**ent**ay] fountain; source; font

fuera [fw**ai**ra] outside; he/she/it was; he/she/it went; you were; you went

fuera de servicio out of order

fuera de apart from

fuera de horas punta off-peak hours

fuerais [fw**ai**ra-eess] you were; you went

fuéramos [fw**ai**ramoss] we were; we went

fueran [fw**ai**ran] they were; they went; you were; you

went

fueras [fw**ai**rass] you were; you went

fueron [fw**ai**ron] they were; they went; you were; you went

fuerte [fw**ai**rtay] strong; loud

fuerza f [fw**ai**rtha] force; strength

fui [fwee] I was; I went

fuimos [fw**ee**moss] we were; we went

fuiste [fw**ee**stay] you were; you went

fuisteis [fw**ee**stay-eess] you were; you went

fumadores smoking

fumar to smoke

funcionar [foonkth-yon**ar**] to work

funcionario m [foonkth-yon**ar**-yo] civil servant

funeraria f undertaker's

furgón m van

furgoneta f van

furioso [foor-**yos**o] furious

furúnculo m abscess; boil

fusible m [foos**ee**blay] fuse

fútbol m football

futuro (m) [foot**oo**ro] future

G

gabardina f raincoat

gafas fpl glasses, eyeglasses

gafas de sol sunglasses

gafas de bucear [boothay-**ar**] goggles

galería f [galair**ee**-a] gallery

galería de arte [day artay] art gallery

galerías fpl store

Gales m [galess] Wales

galés Welsh

gallego [ga-yay-go] Galician

ganar to win; to earn

ganga f bargain

ganso m goose

garaje m [garaHay] garage

garantía f guarantee

garganta f throat

gas-oil m diesel

gasóleo m [gasolay-o] diesel

gasolina f petrol, fuel

gasolina normal two-star petrol, (US) regular (gas)

gasolina super four-star petrol, (US) premium (gas)

gasolinera f [gasoleenaira] petrol/gas station, filling station

gastar to spend

gato m cat; jack

gemelos mpl [Haymayloss] twins; cufflinks

generalmente [Henairalmentay] generally; usually

¡genial! [Hayn-yal] great!, fantastic!

genio: tener mal genio [Hayn-yo] to be bad-tempered

gente f [Hentay] people

gerente m [Hairentay] manager

¡gilipollas! [Heeleepo-yass] stupid idiot!

gimnasia f [Heemnas-ya] gymnastics

gimnasio m gymnasium

ginecólogo m [Heenekologo] gynaecologist

girar [Heerar] to turn

giro [Heero] money order; turn

gitano m [Heetano] gypsy

glorieta f [glor-yayta] roundabout

gobierno m [gob-yairno] government

gol m goal

Golfo de Vizcaya m [beethka-ya] Bay of Biscay

golpe m [golpay] blow

de golpe all of a sudden

golpear [golpay-ar] to hit

goma f rubber; glue

goma elástica rubber band

gordo fat

gorra f cap

gorro m bonnet, cap

gorro de baño [ban-yo] bathing cap

gorro de ducha shower cap

gota f drop

gotera f [gotaira] leak

gracias [grath-yass] thank you

gracias, igualmente [eegwalmentay] thank you, the same to you

gracioso [grath-yoso] funny

grados mpl degrees

gramática f grammar

gramo m gramme

Gran Bretaña f [bretan-ya] Great Britain

grande [granday] big, large

grandes rebajas [rebaHass] sales

grandes almacenes mpl
[almath**ay**ness] large
department store
granizo m [gran**ee**tho] hail
granja f [gran**H**a] farm
granjero m [gran**H**airo] farmer
grano m spot
grasa f fat
grasiento [grass-**y**ento] greasy
graso greasy
gratificación f [grateefeekath-
yon] reward; tip
gratis free
grave [gra**b**ay] serious
gravilla f [gra**bee**-ya] loose
chippings
Grecia f [gr**e**th-ya] Greece
grifo m tap, (US) faucet
gripe f [gr**ee**pay] flu
gris grey
gritar to shout
grosero [gro**ss**airo] rude
grúa f [gr**oo**-a] tow truck,
breakdown lorry; crane
grueso [grw**ay**so] thick
grupo m group
grupo sanguíneo [sang**ee**nay-o]
blood group
guante m [gw**a**ntay] glove
guapo [gw**a**po] handsome
guardacostas m/f
[gwardak**o**stass] coastguard
guardar [gward**a**r] to keep; to
put away
guardarropa m [gwardarr**o**pa]
cloakroom, (US) checkroom
guardería (infantil) f [gwardair**ee**-
a (infant**ee**l)] crèche; nursery
school

guárdese en sitio fresco keep
in a cool place
guardia civil m/f [gw**a**rd-ya
theeb**eel**] police; policeman/
policewoman
guateque m [gwat**ay**-kay] party
guerra f [g**ai**rra] war
guerra civil civil war
guía m/f [g**ee**-a] guide
guía telefónica f phone book,
telephone directory
guía turística tourist guide
guisar [gees**a**r] to cook
guitarra f [geet**a**rra] guitar
gustar to please
me gusta ... I like ...
gusto: mucho gusto pleased
to meet you!
con mucho gusto certainly,
with great pleasure
el gusto es mío how do you
do, it is a pleasure

H

h is not pronounced in Spanish

ha he/she/it has; you have
habéis [ab**ay**-eess] you have
habilidoso skilful
habitación f [abeetath-**y**on]
room
habitación doble [d**o**blay]
double room
habitación individual
[eendeebeed**wal**] single room
habitación con dos camas
twin room
habitar to live

h is not pronounced in Spanish

hablador talkative
hablar to speak
hable aquí speak here
habrá there will be; he/she/it will have; you will have
habrán they will have; you will have
habrás you will have
habré [abray] I will have
habréis [abray-eess] you will have
habremos we will have
habría [abree-a] I would have; he/she/it would have; you would have
habríais [abree-a-eess] you would have
habríamos [abree-amoss] we would have
habrían [abree-an] they would have; you would have
habrías [abree-ass] you would have
hace [athay]: hace ... días ... days ago
hace calor it is hot
hacer [athair] to make; to do
hacerse [athairsay] to become
hacia [ath-ya] towards
hago I do; I make
hambre: tengo hambre [ambray] I'm hungry
hamburguesería f [amboorgaysairee-a] restaurant selling hamburgers, hot

dogs
han [an] they have; you have
haré [aray] I will do
harto: estar harto (de) [arto] to be fed up (with)
has [ass] you have
hasta [asta] even; until
hasta que [kay] until
¡hasta la vista! see you!
¡hasta luego! [lwaygo] cheerio!; see you later!
¡hasta mañana! [man-yana] see you tomorrow!
¡hasta pronto! see you soon!
hay [ī] there is; there are
hay ... we sell ...
haya [ī-a] I have; he/she/it has; you have
haz [ath] do; make
he [ay] I have
hecho m [ay-cho] fact
hecho made; done
hecho a la medida made-to-measure
helada f frost
heladería f [eladairee-a] ice-cream parlour
helado f [elado] ice-cream
helar to freeze
hembra female
hemos we have
herida f [aireeda] wound
herido injured
hermana f [airmano] sister
hermano m brother
hermoso [airmoso] beautiful
herramientas fpl [airram-yentass] tools
hervir [airbeer] to boil

hice [eethay] I made; I did

hidratante: crema hidratante f [eedratantay] moisturizer

hidropedales mpl [eedropedaless] pedalos

hielo m [yaylo] ice

hierba f [yairba] grass

hierro m [yairro] iron

hija f [eeHa] daughter

hijo m son

hilo m thread

hipermercado [eepairmairkado] hypermarket

hipo m hiccups

hipódromo m horse-racing track

historia f [eestor-ya] history; story

hizo [eetho] he/she made; he/she did; you made; you did

hogar m home; household goods

hoja f [oHa] leaf; sheet of paper

hoja de afeitar [day afay-eetar] razor blade

¡hola! hello!, hi!

hombre m [ombray] man

¡hombre! hey there!; you bet; oh come on!

hombre de negocios [negoth-yoss] businessman

hombro m shoulder

hondo deep

honrado honest

hora f [ora] hour

¿qué hora es? what time is it?

hora local local time

horario m [orar-yo] timetable, (US) schedule

horario de autobuses [owtoboosess] bus timetable/schedule

horario de invierno [eemb-yairno] winter timetable/schedule

horario de recogidas [rekoHeedass] collection times

horario de trenes train timetable/schedule

horario de verano summer timetable/schedule

horas de consulta surgery hours, (US) office hours (of doctor)

horas de oficina [ofeetheena] opening hours

horas de visita visiting hours

horas punta rush hour

hormiga f ant

horno m oven

horquilla f [orkee-ya] hairpin

hospedarse [ospedarsay] to stay

hostal m [ostal] restaurant specializing in regional dishes; boarding house

hostal-residencia m [reseedenth-ya] long-stay boarding house

hostería f [ostairee-a] restaurant specializing in regional dishes

hotel-residencia m residential hotel

hoy [oy] today

h is not pronounced in Spanish

HR (hostal-residencia) **m**
boarding house where no
meals are served, often
lower-priced, residential
hotel

hube [oobay] I had

hubieron [oob-yairon] they had;
you had

hubimos [oobeemoss] we had

hubiste [oobeestay] you had

hubisteis [oobeestay-eess] you
had

hubo [oobo] he/she/it had;
you had; there was/were

huelga f [welga] strike

hueso m [wayso] bone

huésped m/f [wesped] guest

huevo m [waybo] egg

humedad m humidity,
dampness

húmedo damp

humo m smoke

humor m humour

hundirse [oondeersay] to sink

hurto m theft

Hr

I

idéntico (a/que) identical (to)

idioma m [eed-yoma] language

idiota m/f [eed-yota] idiot

iglesia f [eeglays-ya] church

igual [eegwal] equal; like
me da igual it's all the same
to me

imbécil (m) [eembaytheel]
nutter; stupid

impaciente [eempath-yentay]
impatient

imperdible m [eempairdeeblay]
safety pin

impermeable (m)
[eempairmay-ablay] waterproof;
raincoat

importación f [eemportath-yon]
imported goods

importante [eemportantay]
important

importar: no importa it doesn't
matter
¿le importa si ...? do you
mind if ...?

importe m [eemportay]
amount

importe del billete [bee-yaytay]
fare

importe total total due

imposible [eemposeeblay]
impossible

impreso m [eemprayso] form

impuesto m [eempwesto] tax

incendiar [eenthend-yar] to set
fire to

incendio m [eenthend-yo] fire
(blaze)

incluido [eenkl-weedo] included

incluso even

increíble [eenkray-eeblay]
incredible

indemnizar [eendemneethar] to
compensate

independiente [eendepend-
yentay] independent

indicaciones fpl instructions
for use

indicador m indicator

indicador de nivel gauge

indicar to indicate

indicativos provinciales area codes

indicativos de paises country codes

indignado indignant

indispuesto [eendeespwesto] unwell

infantil children's

infarto m heart attack

infectarse [eenfektarsay] to become infected

inflamado swollen

inflamarse [eenflamarsay] to swell

influenciar [eenflwenth-yar] to influence

información f [eenformath-yon] information

información de vuelos [bwayloss] flight information

información turística tourist information

información y turismo tourist information office

informar to inform

informarse (de/sobre) [-marsay (day/sobray)] to get information (on/about)

infracción f [eenfrakth-yon] offence

Inglaterra f [eenglatairra] England

inglés (m) [een-glayss] English; Englishman

inglesa f Englishwoman

ingresos mpl deposits; income

iniciales fpl [eeneeth-yaless] initials

inmediatamente [eenmed-yatamentay] immediately

inocente [eenothentay] innocent

insertar monedas insert coins

inserte moneda insert coin

insistir to insist

insolación f [eensolath-yon] sunstroke

instituto de belleza m [bay-yaytha] beauty salon

instrucciones de lavado mpl washing instructions

inteligente [eenteleeHentay] intelligent

intentar to try

interés m [eentairayss] interest

interesante [eentairesantay] interesting

interior (m) [eentairee-or] interior, inner; domestic, home

intermedio (m) [eentairmayd-yo] intermediate; intermission, interval

intermitente m [eentairmeetentay] indicator

interruptor m switch

interurbana long-distance

intoxicación alimenticia f [eentokseekath-yon aleementeeth-ya] food poisoning

introduzca moneda insert coin

introduzca el dinero exacto

insert exact amount
introduzca la tarjeta y marque
  insert card and dial
inútil useless, pointless
invierno m [eemb-**yair**no]
  winter
invitada f, invitado m guest
invitar to invite
inyección f [eenyekth-**yon**]
  injection
ir to go
ir de paseo [pas**ay**-o] to go for
  a walk
Irlanda f [eer**lan**da] Ireland
Irlanda del Norte [**nor**tay]
  Northern Ireland
irlandés (m) [eerland**ayss**] Irish;
  Irishman
irlandesa f Irishwoman
irse [**eer**say] to go away
isla f island
Islas Canarias fpl [kanar-**yass**]
  Canary Islands
itinerario m [eeteenair**ar**-yo]
  itinerary
IVA (impuesto sobre el valor
  añadido) [**eeba**] VAT

In

izq. (izquierda) left
izquierda f [eethk-**yair**da] left
  a la izquierda (de) on the left
  (of)

J

jabón m [Hab**on**] soap
jabón de afeitar [afay-**ee**tar]
  shaving soap
jamonería f [Hamonair**ee**-a]
  hams (shop)

jarabe m [Hara**bay**] syrup
jardín m [Hard**een**] garden
jardines públicos [Hard**ee**ness]
  park, public gardens
jarra f [**Ha**rra] jug
jarrón m [Ha**rron**] vase
jefe m [**Hay**fay] boss
jefe de tren guard
jersey m [Hairs**ay**-ee] jumper
jersey de cuello alto [**kway**-yo]
  polo neck jumper
¡Jesús! [Hays**ooss**] bless you!
¡joder! [Hod**air**] hell!
joven (m/f) [**Ho**ben] young;
  young man; young woman
joyas fpl [**Ho**yass] jewellery
joyería f [Hoyair**ee**-a] jewellery;
  jeweller's
judío [Hood**ee**-o] Jewish
juego (m) [**Hway**go] game; I
  play
jueves m [**Hway**bess] Thursday
jugar [Ho**ogar**] to play
juguete m [Hoo**gay**tay] toy
juguetería f [Hoogaytair**ee**-a] toy
  shop
juicio m [H**weeth**-yo]
  judgement; opinion;
  reason
julio m [**Hool**-yo] July
junio m [**Hoon**-yo] June
junto (a) [**Hoon**to] next (to)
juntos together
justo [**Hoo**sto] just

K

kiosko de periódicos m
  [k-**yo**sko day pairee-**o**deekoss]

newsagent's, newsstand
kiosko de prensa newsagent's, newsstand

L

la the; her; it
labio m [lab-yo] lip
laborables [laborabless] weekdays, working days
laca f hair spray
lado m side
 al lado de beside, next to
ladrillo m [ladree-yo] brick
ladrón m thief
lagartija f [lagarteeHa] lizard
lago m lake
lámpara f lamp
lana f wool
lana pura pure wool
lanas al peso wool sold by weight
lápiz m [lapeeth] pencil
lápiz de ojos [oHoss] eyeliner
largo (m) length; long
 a lo largo de along
largura f length
las the; them; you
 las que ... the ones that ...
lástima: es una lástima it's a pity
lastimarse la espalda [lasteemarsay] to hurt one's back
lata f can; nuisance
latón m brass
lavabo m [lababo] washbasin
lavabos toilets, rest room
lavado m [labado] washing

lavadora f [labadora] washing machine
lavandería f [labandairee-a] laundry
lavandería automática [owtomateeka] launderette, laundromat
lavaplatos m [labaplatoss] dishwasher
lavar [labar] to wash
lavar a mano wash by hand
lavar en seco dry clean
lavar la ropa to do the washing
lavarse [labarsay] to wash
lavar separadamente wash separately
laxante m [laksantay] laxative
le [lay] him; her; you
lección f [lekth-yon] lesson
leche f [lechay] milk
leche limpiadora f [leemp-yadora] skin cleanser
lechería f [lechairee-a] dairy shop; dairy produce
leer [lay-air] to read
lejía f [leHee-a] bleach
lejos [layHoss] far away
 lejos de far from
lencería f [lenthairee-a] drapery
lentillas fpl [lentee-yass] contact lenses
lentillas blandas soft lenses
lentillas duras hard lenses
lentillas porosas gas permeable lenses
lento slow
leotardos mpl [lay-otardoss] tights, pantyhose

les them; you

letra f letter; banker's draft

levantar [lebantar] to raise, to lift

levantarse [lebantarsay] to get up

ley f [ay-ee] law

libra f pound

libre [eebray] free; vacant

libre de impuestos duty-free

librería f [leebrairee-a] bookshop, bookstore

libreta de ahorros f [leebrayta day a-orross] savings account book

libreta de direcciones [deerekth-yoness] address book

libro m book

libro de frases phrase book

libros de bolsillo [bolsee-yo] paperbacks

líder m [leedair] leader

ligero [leeHairo] light

lima de uñas f [oon-yass] nailfile

límite f [leemeetay] limit

límite de altura maximum height

límite de peso [payso] weight limit

límite de velocidad [day belotheedad] speed limit

limpiaparabrisas m [leemp-yaparabreesass] windscreen wiper

limpiar [leemp-yar] to clean

limpieza f [leemp-yaytha] cleanliness; cleaning

limpieza de coches car wash

limpieza en seco dry-cleaning

limpio [leemp-yo] clean

línea f [eenay-a] line

linterna f [leentairna] torch

lío m [lee-o] mess

liquidación f [leekeedath-yon] sale

liquidación total clearance sale

liso flat; plain; straight

lista f list

lista de correos [korray-oss] poste restante, (US) general delivery

lista de espera [espaira] standby

listo clever; ready

litera f [leetaira] couchette

litro m litre

llamada f [yamada] call

llamada a cobro revertido [rebairteedo] reverse charge call

llamar [yamar] to call; to name

llamar por teléfono [telayfono] to call, to phone

llamarse [yamarsay] to be called

llame a la puerta please knock

llame al timbre please ring

llame antes de entrar knock before entering

llamo: me llamo ... [may yamo] my name is ...

llave f [yabay] key; spanner

llave inglesa [eenglaysa] spanner

llegada f [yaygada] arrival

llegadas internacionales international arrivals

llegadas nacionales domestic arrivals

llegar [yegar] to arrive; to get to

llegué [yegay] I arrived

llenar [yenar] to fill

llenar el depósito to fill up

lleno [yayno] full

llevar [yebar] to carry; to take; to bring; to give a lift to

llevar a juicio [Hweeth-yo] to prosecute

llevarse [yebarsay] to take away

llorar [yorar] to cry

llover [yobair] to rain

lloviendo: está lloviendo [yob-yendo] it's raining

llovizna f [yobeethna] drizzle

llueve [y-way-bay] it is raining

lluvia f [yoob-ya] rain

lo it; the

localidad f place

localidades tickets

loción antimosquitos f [loth-yon anteemoskeetoss] insect repellent

loción bronceadora [bronthay-adora] suntan lotion

loción para después del afeitado [despwess del afay-eetado] after-shave

loco (m) mad; madman

locomotora f engine

locutorio telefónico m telephone booth

Londres [londress] London

longitud f [lonHeetoo] length

los the

los que ... the ones that ...

loza f [lotha] crockery

luces de posición fpl [loothess day poseeth-yon] sidelights

luces traseras [trasairass] rear lights

luego [lwaygo] then

luego que after

lugar m place

en lugar de instead of

lugar de veraneo [bairanay-o] summer resort

lugares de interés places of interest

lujo m [looHo] luxury

lujoso luxurious

luna f moon

lunes m [looness] Monday

luz f [looth] light

luz de carretera main beam

luz de cruce [kroothay] dipped headlights

M

machista m male chauvinist, sexist

madera f [madaira] wood

madre f [madray] mother

madrileño [madreelayn-yo] from Madrid, Madrid

madrugada f small hours

maduro ripe

maestra f [ma-estra], **maestro m** primary school teacher

mal (m) badly; unwell, ill, sick; evil

¡maldita sea! [say-a] damn!

maleducado rude

malentendido m misunderstanding

maleta f suitcase
  hacer las maletas to pack

maletero m [maletairo] boot, (US) trunk

mal genio m [Hayn-yo] bad temper

mal humor m bad mood; bad temper; anger

Mallorca [ma-yorka] Majorca

malo bad

mamá f mum

manantial m [manant-yal] spring

mancha f stain

mandar to send; to order

mandíbula f jaw

manera: de esta manera [manaira] in this way

de manera que so (that)

mano f hand

manoplas fpl mittens

manta f blanket

mantel m tablecloth

mantelerías fpl [mantelairee-ass] table linen

mantenga limpia España keep Spain tidy

mantenga limpia la ciudad keep our city tidy

manténgase en sitio fresco store in a cool place

manténgase alejado de los niños keep out of the reach of children

manual de conversación m [manwal day konbairsath-yon] phrasebook

mañana (f) [man-yana] morning; tomorrow

por la mañana in the morning

¡hasta mañana! see you tomorrow!

mañana por la mañana tomorrow morning

mañana por la tarde [tarday] tomorrow afternoon; tomorrow evening

mapa m map

mapa de carreteras road map

mapa de recorrido network map

maquillaje m [makee-yaHay] make-up

maquillarse [makee-yarsay] to put one's makeup on

máquina de afeitar eléctrica f [makeena day afay-eetar] electric shaver

máquina de escribir typewriter

máquina de fotos camera

máquina tragaperras [makeena] slot machine

maquinaria f [makeenar-ya] machinery

maquinilla de afeitar f [makeenee-ya] razor

mar m sea
  la mar de ... lots of ...; very ...

maravilloso [marabee-yoso] marvellous

marca registrada f [reHeestrada] registered trade mark

marcar to dial

marcar el número dial the number

marcha f gear

marcha atrás reverse gear

marcharse [marcharsay] to go away

marea f [maray-a] tide

mareado [maray-ado] sick; merry, drunk

mares: a mares loads

marica m poofter

marido m husband

mariposa f butterfly; fairy, pansy

marisquería f [mareeskairee-a] shellfish restaurant

marque ... dial ...

marrón brown

marroquinería f [marrokeen-airee-a] fancy leather goods

Marruecos m [marrway-koss] Morocco

martes m [martess] Tuesday

martes de carnaval Shrove Tuesday

martillo m [martee-yo] hammer

marzo m [martho] March

más more

más de more than

más pequeño smaller

el más caro the most expensive

ya no más no more

más o menos [maynoss] more or less

matar to kill

matrícula f number plate; registration; registration fees

máximo personas maximum number of people

mayo m [ma-yo] May

mayor [mayor] adult; bigger; older; biggest; oldest

la mayor parte (de) [partay] most (of)

mayor de edad of age, adult

mayoría: la mayoría [mayoree-a] most

me me; myself

me duele aquí [dwaylay] I have a pain here

mecánico m mechanic

mechas fpl highlights

media docena (de) f [dothayna] half a dozen

media hora f half an hour

media pensión f [pens-yon] half board, (US) European plan

mediano [mayd-yano] medium; average

medianoche f [mayd-yanochay] midnight

medias fpl [mayd-yass] stockings

ir/pagar a medias to go Dutch

medias panty tights, pantyhose

medicina f [medeetheena] medicine

médico m [maydeeko] doctor

médico general [Hay-nairal] GP

medida: a medida que as

medida del cuello f [kway-yo] collar size

medio m [mayd-yo] middle

por medio de by (means of)

medio: de tamaño medio

medium-sized

medio billete m [bee-yaytay] half(-price ticket)

medio litro half a litre

mediodía m [mayd-yodee-a] midday

medir to measure

medusa f jellyfish

mejor [mayHor] best; better

mejorar [mayHorar] to improve

mejoría f [mayHoree-a] recovery

mencionar [menth-yonar] to mention

menor [menor] smaller; younger; smallest; youngest

menor de edad minor

menos [maynoss] less; fewest; least

a menos que unless

menudo tiny, minute

a menudo often

menú turístico m set menu

mercadillo m [mairkadee-yo] street market

mercado m market

mercado cubierto [koob-yairto] indoor market

mercado de divisas exchange rates

mercería f [mairthairee-a] haberdashery

merendar to have an afternoon snack

merendero m [mairendairo] open-air café

merienda f [mair-yenda] tea, afternoon snack

mes m month

mesa f table

mesón m inn

meta [mayta] goal

metro m metre; underground, (US) subway

mezquita f [methkeeta] mosque

mí me

mi my

mía [mee-a] mine

microbús m minibus

miedo m [m-yaydo] fear

tengo miedo (de/a) I'm afraid (of)

mientras [m-yentrass] while

mientras que whereas

mientras tanto meanwhile

miércoles m [m-yairkoless] Wednesday

miércoles de ceniza [theneetha] Ash Wednesday

¡mierda! [m-yairda] shit!

mil [meel] thousand

militar m serviceman

millón m [mee-yon] million

minifalda f mini-skirt

ministerio de ... ministry of ...

minúsculo tiny

minusválido (m) disabled; disabled person

minuto m minute

mío [mee-o] mine

miope [m-yopay] short-sighted

mirador m scenic view, vantage point

mirar to look (at)

mis my

misa f mass

mismo same

mitad f half

mitad de precio [**pray**th-yo] half price

mobilette f [mobeel**e**ttay] moped

mochila f rucksack

moda f fashion
de moda fashionable

moda jóvenes [Hob**ay**ness] young fashions

moda juvenil [Hoobayn**eel**] young fashions

modas caballeros [kaba-y**ai**ross] men's fashions

modas niños/niñas [neen-yoss] children's fashions

modas pre-mamá maternity fashions

modas señora ladies' fashions

modelo m model; design; style

moderno [mod**ai**rno] modern

modista f dressmaker; fashion designer

modisto m fashion designer

modo: de modo que so (that)

modo de empleo instructions for use

mojado [mo**Ha**do] wet

moldeado con secador de mano [molday-**a**do] blow-dry

molestar to disturb; to bother

molesto annoying

monedas fpl coins

monedero m [moned**ai**ro] purse

montacargas m service lift, service elevator

montaña f [mont**an**-ya] mountain

montañismo m [montan-y**ee**smo] climbing

montar to get in; to ride; to assemble

montar a caballo [ka**ba**-yo] to go horse-riding

montar en bici [bee**thee**] to cycle

moquetas fpl [mok**ay**tass] carpets

morado purple

mordedura f bite

moreno [mor**ay**no] dark-haired

morir to die

moros mpl Moors

morriña: tengo morriña [morr**ee**n-ya] I'm homesick

mosca f fly

mostrador m counter

mostrador (de equipajes) [day ekeepa**Hess**] check-in

mostrar to show

moto f motorbike

motora f motorboat

mover [mob**ai**r] to move

mozo m [**mo**tho] porter

muchacha f girl

muchacho m boy

muchas gracias [grath-yass] thank you very much

muchísimas gracias thank you very much indeed

muchísimo enormously, a great deal

mucho much; a lot; a lot of

mucho más a lot more

mucho menos [may**noss**] a lot less

muchos/muchas a lot; a lot

169

of; many

muebles mpl [mwaybless] furniture

muela f [mwayla] back tooth

muela del juicio [Hweeth-yo] wisdom tooth

muelle m [mway-yay] spring; quay

muerte f [mwairtay] death

muerto [mwairto] dead

mujer f [mooHair] woman; wife

muletas fpl crutches

multa f fine; parking ticket

multa por uso indebido penalty for misuse

mundo m world

muñeca f [moon-yeka] wrist; doll

muro m wall

músculo m muscle

museo m [moosay-o] museum

museo de arte [artay] art gallery

música f music

muslo m thigh

musulmán Muslim

muy [mwee] very

muy bien [b-yen] very well

N

N (carretera nacional) national highway

nacido [natheedo] born

nacimiento m [natheem-yento] birth

nacional [nath-yonal] domestic

nacionalidad f [nath-yonaleeda] nationality

nada nothing

de nada you're welcome, don't mention it

nada que declarar nothing to declare

nadar to swim

nadie [nad-yay] nobody

naranja f [naranHa] orange

nariz f [nareeth] nose

natación f [natath-yon] swimming

naturaleza f [natooralaytha] nature

naturalmente [-mentay] naturally; of course

náusea: siento náuseas [s-yento nowsay-ass] I feel sick

navaja f [nabaHa] penknife

Navidad f Christmas

¡feliz Navidad! [feleeth] merry Christmas!

neblina f mist

necesario [nethesar-yo] necessary

necesitar: necesito ... [netheseeto] I need ...

negar to deny

negativo (m) negative

negocio m [negoth-yo] business

negro (m) black; furious

nena f [nayna] baby girl; little girl

nene m [naynay] baby boy; little boy

nervioso [nairb-yoso] nervous

neumático m [nay-oomateeko] tyre

neumáticos - se reparan, se arreglan tyres repaired

neurótico [nay-oor**o**teeko]
neurotic

nevar to snow

ni neither, nor

ni ... ni ... neither ... nor ...

niebla f [n-y**e**bla] fog

nieta f [n-y**ay**ta] granddaughter

nieto m grandson

nieva [n-y**ay**ba] it is snowing

nieve f [n-y**ay**bay] snow

ningún [neeng**oo**n] nobody;
none; not one; no ...

en ningún sitio [s**ee**t-yo]
nowhere

ninguno nobody; none; not
one; no ...

niña f [n**ee**n-ya] child

niñera f [neen-y**ai**ra] nanny

niño m [n**ee**n-yo] child

nivel del aceite m [ath**ay**-eetay]
oil level

no no; not

no admite plancha do not
iron

no aparcar no parking

no aparcar, llamamos grúa
illegally parked vehicles will
be towed away

no contiene alcohol does not
contain alcohol

no entrada por detrás no
entry at the rear

no exceda la dosis indicada
do not exceed the stated
dose

no fumadores no smoking

no funciona out of order

no hay de qué [no ī day kay]
you are welcome

no hay localidades sold out

no molestar do not disturb

no para en ... does not stop
in ...

no ... pero sí not ... but

no pisar el césped keep off
the grass

no recomendada para
menores de 18 años not
recommended for those
under 18 years of age

no se admiten caravanas no
caravans allowed

no se admiten devoluciones
no refunds given

no se admiten perros no dogs
allowed

no tocar please do not touch

no utilizar lejía do not bleach

noche f [n**o**chay] night

esta noche tonight

por la noche at night

nochebuena f [nochay-bw**ay**na]
Christmas Eve

nochevieja f [nochay-b-y**ay**нa]
New Year's Eve

nombre m [n**o**mbray] name

nombre de soltera [solt**ai**ra]
maiden name

nombre de pila first name

nordeste m [nord**e**stay] northeast

normal (m) [n**o**rmal] normal;
lower grade petrol, (US)
regular

normalmente [-m**e**ntay] usually

noroeste m [noro-**e**stay] northwest

norte m [nortay] north
  al norte de la ciudad north of
  the town
Noruega f [norwayga] Norway
nos us; ourselves
nosotras, nosotros we; us
noticias fpl [noteeth-yass]
  news
novecientos [nobay-th-yentoss]
  nine hundred
novela f novel
noveno [nobayno] ninth
noventa ninety
novia f [nob-ya] girlfriend;
  fiancée; bride
noviembre m [nob-yembray]
  November
novillada f [nobee-yada]
  bullfight featuring young
  bulls
novio m [nob-yo] boyfriend;
  fiancé; groom
nube f [noobay] cloud
nublado cloudy
nuboso cloudy
nuera f [nwaira] daughter-
  in-law

nuestra [nwestra], nuestras,
  nuestro, nuestros our
Nueva York [nwayba] New
  York
nueve [nwaybay] nine
nuevo new
número m [noomairo] number
número de teléfono phone
  number
número (de calzado) [day
  kalthado] (shoe) size
nunca never

172

O

o or
o ... o ... either ... or ...
objeción f [ob-Heth-yon]
  objection
objetar [obHaytar] to object
objetivo m [obHayteebo] lens;
  objective
objetos de escritorio [obHaytoss
  day eskreetor-yo] office supplies
objetos perdidos lost
  property, lost and found
obra f work; play
obras fpl roadworks
obstruido [obstr-weedo]
  blocked
obturador m shutter
ocasión f [okass-yon] occasion;
  opportunity; bargain
  de ocasión second hand
occidental [oktheedental]
  Western
ochenta eighty
ocho eight
ocho días mpl [dee-ass] week
ochocientos [ochoth-yentoss]
  eight hundred
octavo eighth
octubre m [oktoobray] October
oculista [okooleesta] optician
ocupado engaged; occupied;
  busy
ocupantes del coche mpl
  [okoopantess del kochay]
  passengers
odiar [od-yar] to hate
oeste m [o-estay] west

al oeste de la ciudad west of
the town
ofender [ofendair] to offend
oferta (especial) f [ofairta
(espeth-yal)] special offer
oficina f [ofeetheena] office
oficina de reclamaciones
[reklamath-yoness] complaints
department
oficina de registros
[reHeestross] registrar's office
oficina de turismo tourist
information office
oficina de objetos perdidos
[obHaytoss] lost property
office, lost and found
oficina de información y
turismo [eenformath-yon]
tourist information office
oficina de correos [korray-oss]
post office
oficina de correos y telégrafos
post office and telegrams
oficinista m/f [ofeetheeneesta]
office worker
oficio m [ofeeth-yo] job
ofrecer [ofrethair] to offer
oído (m) [o-eedo] ear; hearing;
heard
¡oiga! [oyga] listen here!;
excuse me!
oigo I hear
oír [o-eer] to hear
ojo m [oHo] eye
ojo al tren beware of the train
ola f wave; fashion
ola de calor heatwave
oler [olair] to smell
olor m smell

olvidar to forget
omnibús m local short-
distance train
once [onthay] eleven
operadora f operator
operarse [opairarsay] to have
an operation; to come about
oportunidad f chance,
opportunity
oportunidades bargains
óptica f optician's
óptico m optician
optimista optimistic
orden m order
ordenador m computer
oreja f [oray-Ha] ear
organizar [organeethar] to
organize
orgulloso [orgoo-yoso] proud
orilla f [oree-ya] shore
oro m gold
orquesta f [orkesta] orchestra
os you; to you
oscuro dark
otoño m [oton-yo] autumn,
(US) fall
otorrinolaringólogo ear, nose
and throat specialist
otra vez [bayth] again
otro another (one); other
oveja f [obay-Ha] sheep
oye [o-yay] he/she hears; you
hear; listen

P

p (paseo) street; parking
paciente [path-yentay] patient
pacotilla: de pacotilla [pakotee-

ya] rubbishy; second-rate

padecer de [padeth**air**] to suffer from

padecer del corazón [korath**on**] to have a heart condition

padre m [p**a**dray] father

padres mpl parents

pagadero payable

pagar to pay

página f [p**a**нeena] page

páginas amarillas [amar**ee**-yass] yellow pages

pagos mpl deposits

pague el importe exacto (please tender) exact money

país m [pa-**ee**ss] country

País Vasco Basque Country

País de Gales: el País de Gales [g**a**less] Wales

paisaje m [pa-eesa**н**ay] scenery

pájaro m [p**a**нaro] bird

pala f spade

palabra f word

palacio m [pal**a**th-yo] palace

palacio real [ray-**a**l] royal palace

palacio de congresos conference hall

Palacio de Justicia [нoost**ee**th-ya] Law Courts

Palacio de la Opera opera house

palanca de velocidades f [beloth**ee**d**a**dess] gear lever

palco m box (at theatre)

palomitas de maíz fpl [ma-**ee**th] popcorn

palos de golf mpl golf clubs

pan m bread

panadería f [panadair**ee**-a] baker's

pantalla f [panta-ya] screen

pantalón corto m shorts

pantalones mpl [pantal**o**ness] trousers, (US) pants

pantalones cortos mpl shorts

pantalones vaqueros [bak**ai**ross] jeans

panties mpl tights

pantorrilla f [pantorr**ee**-ya] calf

pañal m [pan-y**a**l] nappy, (US) diaper

pañería f [pan-yair**ee**-a] drapery

pañuelo m [panw**ay**lo] handkerchief; scarf

pañuelo (de cabeza) [day kab**ay**tha] (head)scarf

papá m dad

papel m [pap**el**] paper; rôle

papel celo® [th**ay**lo] sellotape®, Scotch tape®

papel de envolver [embolb**air**] wrapping paper

papel de escribir writing paper

papel de plata silver foil

papel higiénico [eeн-y**ay**neeko] toilet paper

papelera f litter; litter bin

papelería f [papelair**ee**-a] stationery, stationer's

papeles pintados mpl wallpaper

paquete m [pak**ay**tay] packet

par m pair

para for; in order to

para automáticas for automatic washing machines

para que [kay] in order that

para uso del personal staff only

para uso externo not to be taken internally

parabrisas m windscreen

paracaidismo m [paraka-eedeesmo] parachuting

parachoques m [parachokess] bumper, (US) fender

parada f stop

parada de autobuses bus stop

parada de taxis taxi rank

parador m hotel restaurant; luxury hotel

parador nacional [nath-yonal] state-owned hotel, often a historic building which has been restored

paraguas m [paragwass] umbrella

parar to stop

parecer [parethair] to seem; to resemble

parecido [paretheedo] similar

pared f [parayd] wall

pareja f [paray-ʜa] pair; couple

parezco [parethko] I seem

pariente m/f [par-yentay] relative

parking m car park, (US) parking lot

paro: en paro unemployed

parque m [parkay] park

parque de atracciones [atrakth-yoness] amusement park

parque de bomberos [bombaiross] fire station

parque de recreo [rekray-o] amusement park

parque infantil children's park; playpen

parrilla f [parree-ya] grill

parte f [partay] part

en todas partes everywhere

en otra parte elsewhere

en alguna parte somewhere

¿de parte de quién? [day k-yen] who's calling?

parte antigua [anteegwa] old town

parte meteorológico m [maytay-oroloʜeeko] weather forecast

particular private

partida f game

partido m match

pasado last

la semana pasada last week

pasado mañana the day after tomorrow

pasado de moda out of fashion

poco pasado rare

pasador m hairslide

pasaje m [pasaʜay] plane ticket

pasajero m [pasaʜairo] passenger

pasajeros de tránsito transit passengers

pasaporte m [pasaportay] passport

pasaportes passport control

pasar to pass; to overtake; to happen

pasar la aduana [ad-wana] to go through customs

pasarlo bien [b-yen] to enjoy oneself

pasarlo bomba to have a great time

pasatiempo m [pasat-yempo] hobby

Pascua [pask-wa] Easter

pasear [pasay-ar] to go for a walk

pasen enter; cross, walk

paseo m [pasay-o] walk; drive; ride

paseo de ... ... avenue

pasillo m [pasee-yo] corridor

paso m passage; pass; step

 estar de paso to be passing through

paso a nivel level crossing, (US) grade crossing

paso de cebra [thaybra] zebra crossing

paso de contador unit

paso de peatones [pay-atoness] pedestrian crossing

paso subterráneo pedestrian underpass

pasta de dientes f [d-yentess] toothpaste

pastelería f [pastelairee-a] cake shop

pastilla f [pastee-ya] tablet

pastillas para la garganta throat pastilles

patatas fritas chips, French fries; crisps, potato chips

patinaje m [pateenaHay] skating

patinar to skid; to skate

patio de butacas m stalls

peaje m [pay-aHay] toll

peatón m [pay-aton] pedestrian

peatón, camine por la

izquierda pedestrians keep to the left

peatón, circula por tu izquierda pedestrians keep to the left

peatonal pedestrian

peatones pedestrians

peatones, caminen por la izquierda pedestrians keep to the left

pecho m chest; breast

pedazo m [pedatho] piece

pediatra m/f [pedee-atra] pediatrician

pedir to order; to ask for

pedir disculpas to apologize

pedir hora [ora] to make an appointment

peinar [pay-eenar] to comb

peinarse [pay-eenarsay] to comb one's hair

peine m [pay-eenay] comb

pelea f [pelay-a] fight

peletería f [peletairee-a] furs, furrier

película f film, movie

película en color colour film

película en versión original [bairs-yon oreeHeenal] film in the original language

peligro m danger

peligro de incendio danger: fire hazard

peligro deslizamientos slippery road surface

peligroso dangerous

es peligroso bañarse danger: no swimming

es peligroso asomarse al

exterior do not lean out
pelirrojo [peleerroHO] redheaded
pelo m [paylo] hair
me está tomando el pelo
you're pulling my leg
pelón bald
pelota f ball
peluca f wig
peluquería f [pelookairee-a]
hairdresser's
peluquería de caballeros [kaba-
yaiross] gent's hairdresser's
peluquería de señoras ladies'
salon
peluquera f [pelookaira],
peluquero m hairdresser
pena f [payna] grief, sorrow
¡qué pena! [kay] what a pity!
pendiente de pago
outstanding
pendientes mpl [pend-yentess]
earrings
pene m [paynay] penis
penicilina f [peneetheeleena]
penicillin
pensar to think
pensión f [pens-yon]
guesthouse, boarding house;
pension
pensión completa [komplayta]
full board, (US) American
plan
pensionista m [pens-yoneesta]
old-age pensioner
peor [pay-or] worse; worst
pequeño (m) [pekayn-yo] small;
child
percha f [paircha] coathanger
perder [pairdair] to lose; to

miss
perderse [pairdairsay] to get
lost
pérdida f loss
perdón sorry, excuse me;
pardon, pardon me
perezoso [pairethoso] lazy
perfecto [pairfekto] perfect
perfumería f [pairfoomairee-a]
perfumes (shop)
periódico m [pairee-odeeko]
newspaper
periodista m [pair-yodeesta]
journalist
período m [pairee-odo] period
perla f [pairla] pearl
permanente f [pairmanentay]
perm
permiso m [pairmeeso] licence
permitido allowed
permitir to allow
pero [pairo] but
perra: no tengo una perra I'm
broke
perro m [pairro] dog
persona f [pairsona] person
persuadir [pairswadeer] to
persuade
pesadilla f [pesadee-ya]
nightmare
pesado heavy
pésame: dar el pésame
[paysamay] to offer one's
condolences
pesar weight
a pesar de que despite the
fact that
a pesar de in spite of
pesca f fishing

ir de pesca to go fishing
pescadería f [peskadairee-a]
  fishmonger's
pescar to fish; to catch out
peso m [payso] weight
peso neto net weight
peso máximo maximum
  weight
pestañas fpl [pestan-yass]
  eyelashes
petición de mano f [peteeth-
  yon] engagement
pez m [peth] fish
picadura f bite
picante [peekantay] hot
picar to sting; to itch
picor m itch
pidió [peed-yo] he/she asked
  for; you asked for
pie m [p-yay] foot
a pie on foot
piedra f [p-yedra] stone
piedra preciosa [preth-yosa]
  precious stone
piel f [p-yayl] skin
pienso [p-yenso] I think
pierna f [p-yairna] leg
pieza de repuesto f [p-yaytha
  day repwesto] spare part
piezas de recambio [rekamb-
  yo] spares
pijama m [peeHama] pyjamas
pila f battery; pile
píldora f pill
piloto m pilot
pilotos mpl rear lights
pincel m [peenthayl] paint
  brush
pinchazo m [peenchatho]

puncture
pintar to paint
pintura f painting; paint
pinza de la ropa f clothes peg
pinzas fpl [peenthass] tweezers
piña f [peen-ya] pineapple
pipa f pipe
piragua f [peeragwa] canoe
piragüismo m [peeragweesmo]
  canoeing
Pirineos mpl [peereenay-oss]
  Pyrenees
piscina f [peestheena]
  swimming pool
piscina cubierta [koob-yairta]
  indoor swimming pool
piso m floor; flat, apartment
piso amueblado [amweblado]
  furnished apartment
piso bajo [baHo] ground floor,
  (US) first floor
piso sin amueblar [amweblar]
  unfurnished apartment
pista f track; clue
pista de baile [ba-eelay] dance
  floor
pista de patinaje [pateenaHay]
  skating rink
pista de tenis tennis court
pistas de esquí [eskee] ski
  runs
pistola f gun
plancha f iron
planchar to iron
plano (m) flat; map
planta f plant; floor
planta baja [baHa] ground
  floor, (US) first floor
planta primera [preemaira] first

floor, (US) second floor
planta sótano lower floor;
basement
planta superior [soopair-**yor**]
upper floor
plástico (**m**) plastic
plata f silver
plateado [platay-**ado**] silver
platillo m [platee-**yo**] saucer
plato m plate; dish, course
playa f [pla-**ya**] beach
playeras fpl [pla-**yairass**]
trainers
plaza f [**platha**] square; seat
en plaza current prices
plaza de abastos marketplace
plaza de toros bullring
plazas libres [**leebress**] seats
available
pluma f pen; feather
población f [poblath-**yon**]
village; town; population
pobre [**pobray**] poor
poco little
poco profundo shallow
pocos few
unos pocos a few
poder (**m**) [pod**air**] to be able
to; power
podrido rotten
policía f [poleethee-**a**] police
policía m/f policeman;
policewoman
policía municipal f
[mooneetheep**al**] municipal
police
polideportivo m sports centre
polígono industrial m
industrial estate

política f politics
político political
póliza de seguros f insurance
policy
polo m ice lolly
polvos mpl powder
pomada f ointment
pon put
poner [pon**air**] to put
ponerse en marcha [pon**airsay**]
to set off
ponerse en pie [p-**yay**] to
stand up
poney m pony
pongo I put
poquito: un poquito [pok**eeto**]
a little bit
por by; through; for
por allí [a-**yee**] over there
por fin at last
por lo que [**kay**] for which
reason
por lo menos [**maynoss**] at
least
por qué [**kay**] why
por semana per week
por si in case
por ciento [th-**yento**] per cent
por favor please
por favor, use un carrito please
take a trolley
por favor, use una cesta please
take a basket
porcelana f [porthe**lana**]
porcelain
porque [**porkay**] because
portaequipajes m [porta-
ekeepa**Hess**] luggage rack
portátil [porta**teel**] portable

portero m [portairo] porter;
doorman; goalkeeper

portugués [portoogayss]
Portuguese

posada f inn

posible [poseeblay] possible

postal f postcard

precaución f [prekowth-yon]
caution

precio m [preth-yo] price

precioso [preth-yoso] beautiful;
precious

precio unidad unit price

precios fijos [feeHoss] fixed
prices

preferencia f [prefairenth-ya]
right of way; preference

preferir [prefaireer] to prefer

prefijo m [prefeeHo] dialling
code, area code

pregunta f question

preguntar to ask

prendas fpl clothing

prensa f press; newspapers

preocupado [pray-okoopado]
worried

preocupes: ¡no te preocupes!
[no tay pray-okoopess] don't
worry

preparar to prepare

prepararse [prepararsay] to get
ready

presentar to introduce

preservativo m [presairbateebo]
condom

presión f [press-yon] pressure

presión de los neumáticos
[nay-oomateekoss] tyre
pressure

prestado: pedir prestado to
borrow

prestar to lend

prima f cousin

primavera f [preemabaira]
spring

primer [preemair] first

primer piso m first floor, (US)
second floor

primer plato m first course

primera (clase) f [klasay] first
class

primero first

primeros auxilios [owk-seel-
yoss] first-aid post

primo m cousin

princesa f [preenthaysa]
princess

principal [preentheepal] main

príncipe m [preentheepay]
prince

principiante m/f [preentheep-
yantay] beginner

principio m [preentheep-yo]
beginning

principio de autopista start of
motorway/highway

prioridad de paso priority

prioridad a la derecha give
way/yield to vehicles
coming from your right

prisa: darse prisa [darsay] to
hurry

¡dese prisa! [daysay] hurry
up!

privado private

probablemente [probablementay]
probably

probador m fitting room

probar to try
probarse to try on
problema m problem
procesiones de Semana Santa fpl [prothess-**yo**ness] Holy Week processions
producido en ... produce of ...
producto preparado con ingredientes naturales product prepared using natural ingredients
productos alimenticios [aleement**eeth**-yoss] foodstuffs
productos de belleza [bay-**yay**tha] beauty products
profesor m, profesora f teacher; lecturer
profundidad f depth
profundo deep
programa infantil m children's programme
prohibida la entrada a menores de ... no admission for those under ... years of age
prohibida su reproducción copyright reserved
prohibida su venta not for sale
prohibida la entrada no entry, no admission
prohibido [pro-eeb**ee**do] prohibited, forbidden; no
prohibido acampar no camping
prohibido adelantar no overtaking, no passing
prohibido aparcar no parking
prohibido aparcar excepto

carga y descarga no parking except for loading and unloading
prohibido asomarse do not lean out
prohibido asomarse a la ventana do not lean out of the window
prohibido asomarse a la ventanilla do not lean out of the window
prohibido bañarse no swimming
prohibido cambiar de sentido no U-turns
prohibido cantar no singing
prohibido el paso no entry; no trespassing
prohibido encender fuego no campfires
prohibido escupir no spitting
prohibido estacionar no parking
prohibido fijar carteles stick no bills
prohibido fumar no smoking
prohibido girar a la izquierda no left turn
prohibido hablar con el conductor do not speak to the driver
prohibido hacer auto-stop no hitch-hiking
prohibido hacer sonar el claxon/la bocina do not sound your horn
prohibido pescar no fishing
prohibido pisar el césped keep off the grass

prohibido pisar la hierba keep off the grass

prohibido tirar basura no litter

prohibido tirar escombros no dumping

prohibido tocar la bocina/el claxon do not sound your horn

prohibido tomar fotografías no photographs

prometer [prometair] to promise

prometida f fiancée

prometido (m) engaged; fiancé

pronóstico del tiempo m [t-yempo] weather forecast

pronto soon

¡hasta pronto! [asta] see you soon!

llegar pronto [yegar] to be early

pronunciar [pronoonth-yar] to pronounce

propiedad privada private property

propietario m [prop-yetar-yo] owner

propina f tip

propósito: a propósito deliberately

proteger [protay-Hair] to protect

provecho: ¡buen provecho! [bwen probay-cho] enjoy your meal!

provincia f [probeenth-ya] district

provocar to cause

próximo next

la semana próxima next

week

prudente [proodentay] careful

prueba de alcoholemia f [pr-wayba day alko-olaym-ya] breath test

pts (pesetas) pesetas

pub bar in which no meals are served, often higher priced and disco music played

público (m) public; audience

pueblo m [pweblo] village; people

puede [pwayday] he/she can; you can

puede ser [sair] maybe

puedo [pwaydo] I can

puente m [pwentay] bridge

puente aéreo [a-airay-o] shuttle plane

puente de fuerte pendiente humpbacked bridge

puente de peaje [pay-aHay] toll bridge

puente romano Roman bridge

puerta f [pwairta] door; gate

por la otra puerta use other door

puerta de embarque [embarkay] gate

puerta nº. gate no.

puerto m harbour; pass; port

puerto deportivo marina

puerto de montaña [montan-ya] (mountain) pass

pues [pwayss] since; so

puesta de sol f [pwesta] sunset

puesto de periódicos [paireeodeekoss] newspaper kiosk

puesto de socorro m first-aid post

puesto que [kay] since

pulga f flea

pulmones mpl lungs

pulmonía f [poolmonee-a] pneumonia

pulse botón para cruzar press button to cross

pulsera f [poolsaira] bracelet

pulso m pulse

puntual: llegar puntual [poont-wal] to arrive on time

punto de vista m point of view

punto: hacer punto [athair] to knit

¡puñeta! [poon-yayta] hell!

¡vete a hacer puñetas! [baytay a athair] bugger off!

pura lana virgen [beerHen] pure new wool

puro m cigar

puse [poosay] I put

Q

que [kay] who; that; which; than

que ... o que whether ... or

¿qué? what?

¿qué hay? [ī] how's things?

¿qué tal?, mucho gusto how do you do?, nice to meet you

¡qué va! no way!

quedarse [kedarsay] to stay

quedarse con to keep

quedarse sin gasolina to run out of petrol/gas

quejarse [kayнarsay] to complain

quemadura f [kemadoora] burn

quemadura de sol sunburn

quemar [kemar] to burn

quemarse [kemarsay] to burn oneself

querer [kerair] to love; to want

querido [kaireedo] dear

¿quién? [k-yen] who?

quiero [k-yairo] I want; I love

no quiero I don't want to

quince [keenthay] fifteen

quince días [dee-ass] fortnight

quinientos [keen-yentoss] five hundred

quinto [keento] fifth

quiosco m [k-yosko] kiosk

quisiera [keess-yaira] I would like; he/she would like; you would like

quiso [keeso] he/she wanted; you wanted

quitaesmalte m [keeta-esmaltay] nail polish remover

quitar [keetar] to remove

quizá(s) [keetha(ss)] maybe

R

rabioso [rab-yoso] furious

R.A.C.E (Real Automóvil Club de España) Spanish Royal Automobile Club

ración f [rath-yon] portion

radiador m [rad-yador] radiator

radio m [rad-yo] spoke
radio f radio
radiografía f [rad-yografee-a]
  X-ray
rápidamente [-mentay] quickly
rápido fast
rápido m train stopping at
  many stations
raqueta de tenis f [rakayta]
  tennis racket
raro rare; strange
rata f rat
ratón m mouse
rayas: a rayas [ra-yass] striped
razón f [rathon] reason; rate
  razón aquí apply within
  tiene razón you're right
razonable [rathonablay]
  reasonable
rea sale
realmente [ray-almentay] really
rebajado [rebaHado] reduced
rebajas fpl [rebaHass]
  reductions, sale
rebajas de verano [bairano]
  summer sale
rebanada f slice
recado m message
recepción f [rethepth-yon]
  reception
recepcionista m/f [rethepth-
  yoneesta] receptionist
receta f [rethayta] recipe;
  prescription
  con receta médica only
  available on prescription
recetar [rethaytar] to prescribe
recibir [retheebeer] to receive
recibo m [retheebo] receipt

recién [reth-yen] recently
recién pintado wet paint
reclamación de equipajes f
  [reklamath-yon day ekeepaHess]
  baggage claim
reclamaciones fpl [reklamath-
  yoness] complaints
recoger [rekoHair] to collect;
  to pick up
recogida de equipajes f
  [rekoHeeda] baggage claim
recoja su ticket take your
  ticket
recomendar to recommend
reconocer [rekonothair] to
  recognize; to examine
recordar to remember
recorrido m journey
recto straight
recuerdo (m) [rekwairdo]
  souvenir; I remember
red f network; net
redondo round
reduzca la velocidad reduce
  speed now
reembolsar [ray-embolsar] to
  refund
reembolsos refunds
reestreno [ray-estrayno] re-
  release (of a classic movie)
regalo m present
regatear [regatay-ar] to haggle
régimen m [ray-Heemen] diet
registrar [reHeestrar] to search
regla f rule; period
registro de equipajes m
  [reHeestro day ekeepaHess]
  check in
registros sanitarios

government health certificate

regresar to return

reina f [ray-eena] queen

Reino Unido m United Kingdom

reír [ray-eer] to laugh

rejoneador m [reHonay-ador] bullfighter on horseback

relajarse [relaHarsay] to relax

rellenar [ray-yaynar] to fill in

reloj m [ray-loH] watch; clock

reloj de pulsera [poolsaira] (wrist)watch

relojería f [ray-loHairee-a] watches and clocks

remar to row

remite m [remeetay] sender's name and address

remitente m/f [remeetentay] sender

remo m [raymo] oar

remolque m [remolkay] trailer

remonte m [remontay] ski tow

Renacimiento m [renatheem-yento] Renaissance

RENFE (Red Nacional de Ferrocarriles Españoles) Spanish Railways/Railroad

reparación f [reparath-yon] repair(s)

reparación de calzado shoe repairs

reparaciones faults service

reparar to repair

repente: de repente [repentay] suddenly

repetir to repeat

replicar to reply

reponerse [reponairsay] to recover

reposar to rest

representante m/f [repraysentantay] representative, agent

repuestos mpl [repwestoss] spare parts

repugnante [repoognantay] disgusting

resaca f hangover

resbaladizo [resbaladeetho] slippery

resbalar to slip

rescatar to rescue

reserva f [resairba] reservation

reserva de asientos seat reservation

reservado reserved

reservado el derecho de admisión the management reserve the right to refuse admission

reservado socios members only

reservar to reserve; to book

reservas fpl reservations

resfriado m [resfree-ado] cold

respirar to breathe

responder [respondair] to answer

responsable [responsablay] responsible

respuesta f [respwesta] answer

resto m rest

retales mpl [retaless] remnants

retrasado late

retrasado mental mentally handicapped

retraso m delay

retrete m [retraytay] toilets, (US) rest rooms

reumatismo m [ray-oomateesmo] rheumatism

reunión f [ray-oon-yon] meeting

revelado m film processing

revelar to develop; to reveal

revisar to check

revisor m ticket collector

revista m magazine

rey m [ray] king

Reyes: día de los Reyes m [dee-a day loss ray-ess] 6th of January, Epiphany

rico rich

ridículo ridiculous

rímel m mascara

rincón m corner

riñón m [reen-yon] kidney

río m [ree-o] river

rizado [reethado] curly

robar to steal

robo m theft

roca f rock

rodilla f [rodee-ya] knee

rojo [roHo] red

románico romanesque

rómpase en caso de emergencia break in case of emergency

romper to break

ropa f clothes

ropa confeccionada ready-to-wear clothes

ropa de caballeros [kaba-yaiross] men's clothes

ropa de cama bed linen

ropa de señoras ladies' clothes

ropa infantil children's clothes

ropa interior f [eentair-yor] underwear

ropa sucia [sooth-ya] laundry

rosa (f) pink; rose

roto broken

rotulador m felt-tip pen

rubéola f [roobay-ola] German measles

rubí m [roobee] ruby

rubio [roob-yo] blond

rueda f [rwayda] wheel

rueda de repuesto f [repwesto] spare wheel

ruedo m bullring

ruego [rwaygo] I request

ruido m [rweedo] noise

ruidoso [rweedoso] noisy

ruinas fpl [weenass] ruins

rulo m roller, curler

rulot(a) f caravan, (US) trailer

ruta f route

S

S.A. (Sociedad Anónima) PLC, Inc

sábado m Saturday

sábana f sheet

saber [sabair] to know

saber a to taste of

sabor m taste

sabroso tasty

sacacorchos m [sakakorchoss] corkscrew

sacar to take out; to get out

sacar un billete [bee-yaytay] to buy a ticket

saco de dormir **m** sleeping bag
sal (**f**) salt; leave
sala **f** room; hall
sala climatizada air conditioned
sala de baile [ba-**ee**lay] dance hall
sala de cine [thee**nay**] cinema, movie theater
sala de conciertos [konth-**yair**toss] concert hall
sala de embarque [embar**kay**] departure lounge
sala de espera [espa**ira**] waiting room
sala de exposiciones [esposeeth-**yo**ness] exhibition hall
sala de tránsito transit lounge
sala X X-rated cinema
salado salty
saldar to sell at a reduced price
saldo **m** clearance; balance
saldos sales
sales de baño **fpl** [**sal**ess day **ban**-yo] bath salts
salgo I leave
salida **f** exit; departure
salida ciudad take this direction to leave the city
salida de ambulancias ambulance exit
salida de autopista end of motorway/highway; motorway exit
salida de camiones heavy goods vehicle exit, works exit

salida de emergencia [aymair**h**enth-ya] emergency exit
salida de fábrica factory exit
salida de incendios fire exit
salida de socorro **f** emergency exit
salidas **fpl** departures
salidas de noche night life
salidas internacionales international departures
salidas nacionales domestic departures
salir to go out; to leave
salón **m** lounge
salón de belleza [bay-**yay**tha] beauty salon
salón de demostraciones exhibition hall
salón de peluquería [pelookai**ree**-a] hairdressing salon
saltar to jump
salud **f** [sa**loo**] health
¡salud! cheers!
saludar to greet
saludos best wishes
salvo que [kay] except that
sandalias **fpl** [sandal-**yass**] sandals
San Fermín [fair**meen**] July 7th, when the 'encierro' happens
sangrar to bleed
sangre **f** [**san**gray] blood
sano healthy
Santiago [sant-**yago**] July 25th, a national holiday
sarampión **m** [saramp-**yon**] measles

sartén f frying pan

sastre m [sastray] tailor

se [say] himself; herself; itself; yourself; themselves; yourselves; oneself

sé [say] I know
 no sé I don't know

se aceptan tarjetas de crédito we accept credit cards

se alquila for hire, to rent

se alquila piso flat to let, apartment for rent

se alquilan habitaciones rooms to rent

se alquilan hidropedales pedalos for hire

se alquilan sombrillas parasols for hire

se alquilan tumbonas deckchairs for hire

se habla inglés English spoken

se hacen fotocopias photocopying service

se necesita ... ... needed

se precisa ... ... needed

se prohibe ... ... forbidden

se prohibe fumar no smoking

se prohibe hablar con el conductor do not speak to the driver

se prohibe la entrada no entry, no admittance

se prohibe tirar basura no litter

se ruega ... please ...

se ruega desalojen su habitación antes de las doce please vacate your room by

12 noon

se ruega no ... please do not ...

se ruega no aparcar no parking please

se ruega no molestar please do not disturb

se ruega pagar en caja please pay at the desk

se vende for sale

secador de pelo m [paylo] hair dryer

secadores mpl dryers

secar to dry

secarse el pelo [sekarsay] to dry one's hair, to have a blow-dry

sección f [sekth-yon] department

seco dry

secretaria f, **secretario** m secretary

secreto secret

sed: tengo sed [seth] I'm thirsty

seda f silk

seda natural pure silk

seguida: en seguida [segeeda] immediately, right away

seguir [segeer] to follow

según according to

segunda clase f [klasay] second class

segundo (m) second
 de segunda mano second-hand

segundo piso m second floor, (US) third floor

segundo plato m main course

188

seguridad f [segooreeda] safety; security

seguro (m) safe; sure; insurance

seguro de viaje m [b-yaHay] travel insurance

seis [say-eess] six

seiscientos [say-eess-th-yentoss] six hundred

sello m [say-yo] stamp

semáforos mpl traffic lights

semana f week

Semana Santa Holy Week

semanarios mpl weeklies

sencillo [senthee-yo] simple

sensible [senseeblay] sensitive

sentar: sentar bien (a) [b-yen] to suit

sentarse [sentarsay] to sit down

sentido m direction; sense; meaning

sentir to feel

señal de tráfico f [sen-yal day trafeeko] roadsign

señas fpl [sen-yass] address

señor [sen-yor] gentleman, man; sir

  el señor Brown Mr Brown

señora f [sen-yora] lady, woman; madam

  la señora Brown Mrs Brown

señoras fpl ladies' toilet, ladies' room; ladies' department

señores mpl [sen-yoress] gents' toilet, men's room

señorita f [sen-yoreeta] young lady, young woman; miss

  la señorita Brown Miss Brown

separado separate; separated

  por separado separately

septiembre m [sept-yembray] September

séptimo seventh

sequía f [sekee-a] drought

ser [sair] to be

  a no ser que unless

serio [sair-yo] serious

servicio m [sairbeeth-yo] service; toilet

servicio a través de operadora operator-connected calls

servicio automático direct dialling

servicio de habitaciones room service

servicio de fotocopias photocopying service

servicio (no) incluido service charge (not) included

servicios mpl [sairbeeth-yoss] toilets, (US) rest rooms

servicios de rescate mountain rescue

servicios de socorro emergency services

servilleta f [sairbee-yayta] serviette

servir [sairbeer] to serve

sesenta [saysenta] sixty

sesión continua continuous showing

sesión de noche late showing

sesión de tarde early showing

setecientos [saytay-th-yentoss] seven hundred

setenta [setenta] seventy
sexto [sesto] sixth
si [see] if
sí [see] yes; oneself; herself;
  itself; yourself; themselves;
  yourselves; each other
si no otherwise
SIDA m AIDS
sido been
siempre [s-yempray] always
siempre que [kay] whenever;
  so long as
siento [s-yento] I sit down; I
  feel; I regret
  lo siento I'm sorry
siete [s-yaytay] seven
siga adelante straight ahead
siglo m century
siglo de oro XVI-XVII
  century
significar to mean
siguiente [seeg-yentay] next
  el día siguiente [dee-a] the
  day after
silencio m [seelenth-yo] silence
silla f [see-ya] chair
silla de ruedas [rwaydass]
  wheelchair
sillita de ruedas [see-yeeta]
  pushchair, buggy
sillón m [see-yon] armchair
similar (a) similar (to)
simpático nice
sin [seen] without
sin duda undoubtedly
sin embargo however
sin plomo unleaded
sinagoga f synagogue
sincero [seenthairo] sincere

sino but
sino que [kay] but
siquiera [seek-yaira] even if
sírvase [seerbasay] please
sírvase coger una cesta please
  take a basket
sírvase frío serve cold
sírvase usted mismo help
  yourself
sitio m [seet-yo] place
  en ningún sitio [neen-goon]
  nowhere
smoking m dinner jacket
sobrar to be left over; to be
  too many
sobre (m) [sobray] envelope;
  on; above
sobrecarga [sobraykarga] excess
  weight; extra charge
sobrina f niece
sobrino m nephew
sobrio [sobr-yo] sober
sociedad f [soth-yayda] society;
  company
socio m [soth-yo] associate;
  member
socorrer [sokorair] to help
socorrista mf lifeguard
¡socorro! help!
sois [soyss] you are
sol m sun
  al sol in the sun
solamente [solamentay] only
soleado [solay-ado] sunny
solo alone
sólo only
  no sólo ... sino también [tamb-
  yen] not only ... but also
sólo carga y descarga loading

and offloading only

sólo laborables weekdays only

sólo monedas de nueva emisión only new coins

sólo motos motorcycles only

solo para residentes (del hotel) hotel patrons only

soltero (m) [soltairo] single; bachelor

solterón m bachelor

solterona f spinster

solución ... gotas solution ... drops

sombra f shade; shadow

sombra de ojos [oHoss] eye shadow

sombrero m [sombrairo] hat

sombrilla f [sombree-ya] parasol

somnífero m [somneefairo] sleeping pill

somos we are

son they are; you are

sonreír [sonray-eer] to smile

sordo deaf

sorprendente [sorprendentay] surprising

sorpresa f surprise

sortija f [sorteeHa] ring

sótano m basement

soy [soy] I am

sport: de sport casual

Sr (Señor) Mr

Sra (Señora) Mrs

Sres (Señores) Messrs

Srta (Señorita) Miss

starter m choke

stop m stop sign

su [soo] his; her; its; their;

your

suave [swabay] soft

subir to go up; to get on; to get in; to put up

subtitulada sub-titled

subtítulos mpl subtitles

suburbios mpl [sooboorb-yoss] suburbs

suceder [soothedair] to happen

sucio [sooth-yo] dirty

sucursal f branch

sudar to sweat

Suecia f [swayth-ya] Sweden

sueco [swayko] Swedish

suegra f [swaygra] mother-in-law

suegro m father-in-law

suela f [swayla] sole

suelo (m) [swelo] floor; I am used to

suelto m [swelto] change

sueño m [swayn-yo] dream; I dream

tener sueño to be sleepy

suerte f [swairtay] luck

por suerte luckily, fortunately

¡buena suerte! [bwayna] good luck!

suéter m [swaytair] sweater

suficiente: es suficiente [soofeeth-yentay] that's enough

sugerencias de presentación serving suggestions

Suiza f [sweetha] Switzerland

sujetador m [sooHay-tador] bra

sumar to add

supe [soopay] I knew

súper soopair] four-star petrol, (US) premium (gas);

supermarket

supermercado m
[soopairmairkado] supermarket

supuesto: por supuesto
[soopwesto] of course

sur m south

al sur de south of

sureste m [soorestay] south-east

suroeste m [sooro-estay] south-west

surtido m assortment

sus [sooss] his; her; its; their; your

susto m shock

susurrar to whisper

sutil subtle

suyo [soo-yo] his; hers; its; theirs; yours

T

T.V.E. (Television Española)
Spanish Television

Tabacalera SA Spanish tobacco monopoly

tabaco m tobacco

tabla de surf f surfboard

tabla de windsurf sailboard

tablero de instrumentos m dashboard

tablón de anuncios m notice board, (US) bulletin board

tablón de información [tablon day eenformath-yon] indicator board

tacón m heel

tacones altos [takoness] high heels

tacones planos flat heels

TAF m slow diesel train

Tajo m [taHo] Tagus

tal such

con tal (de) que provided that

tal vez [bayth] maybe

talco m talcum powder

TALGO m fast diesel train, luxury train (supplement required)

talla f [ta-ya] size

tallas sueltas odd sizes

tallas grandes large sizes

taller (de reparaciones) m [ta-yair (day reparath-yoness)] garage

talón m heel

talón de equipajes [ekeepaHess] baggage slip

talonario de cheques m [talonar-yo day chekess] cheque book

tamaño m [taman-yo] size

también [tamb-yen] also

yo también me too

tampoco neither, nor

yo tampoco me neither

tan: tan bonito so beautiful

tan pronto como as soon as

tancat closed (in Catalan)

tanto (**m**) so much; point

tanto ... como ... both ... and ...

tantos so many

tapa f lid

tapas fpl savoury snacks, tapas

tapón m plug

taquilla f [takee-ya] ticket

office

tarde (f) [tarday] afternoon;
  evening; late

  a las tres de la tarde at 3
  p.m.

  esta tarde this afternoon,
  this evening

  por la tarde in the evening

  llegar tarde [yegar] to be late

tarifa f charge, charges

tarifa especial estudiante
  [espeth-yal estood-yantay]
  student reduced rate

tarifa normal standard rate

tarifa reducida [redootheeda]
  reduced rate

tarifas de servicio fares

tarjeta f [tarHayta] card

tarjeta bancaria cheque card

tarjeta de crédito credit card

tarjeta de embarque [embarkay]
  boarding pass

tarjeta de transporte público
  [transportay] travel card

tarjeta postal postcard

tarjeta telefónica phonecard

tauromaquia f [towromak-ya]
  bullfighting

taxista m/f taxi driver

taza f [tatha] cup

te [tay] you; yourself

teatro m [tay-atro] theatre

techo m ceiling

teclado m keyboard

tejado m [teHado] roof

tejanos mpl [teHanoss] jeans

tejidos mpl [teHeedoss]
  materials, fabrics

tela f [tayla] material; dosh

tele f [taylay] TV

telecabina f cable car

teleférico m cable car

telefonear [telefonay-ar] to
  telephone

teléfono m telephone

teléfono interurbano long-
  distance phone

teléfonos para casos urgentes
  emergency telephone
  numbers

telesilla m [telesee-ya] chairlift

telesquí m [teleskee] ski lift

televisor m television (set)

temer [temair] to fear

temor m fear

tempestad f storm

temporada f season

temprano early

ten hold

tenedor m fork

tener [tenair] to have

  tener derecho to have the
  right

  tener prisa to be in a hurry

  tener prioridad [pree-oreeda]
  to have right of way

  tener que [kay] to have to

  tengo que I have to, I must

  ¡tenga cuidado! [kweedado] be
  careful!

tenis m tennis

tensión f [tens-yon] blood
  pressure

teñirse el pelo [ten-yeersay el
  paylo] to dye one's hair, to
  have one's hair dyed

TER m fast luxury diesel
  trains, a supplement is

required

tercer piso m [tairthair] third floor, (US) fourth floor

tercero [tairthairo] third

tercio m [tairth-yo] third

terciopelo m [tairth-yopaylo] velvet

terco stubborn

terminal f [tairmeenal] terminus; terminal

terminal nacional domestic terminal

terminar to finish

termo m vacuum flask

termómetro m thermometer

test del embarazo [embaratho] pregnancy test

testigo m witness

tetera f [tetaira] teapot

tfno (teléfono) telephone

ti [tee] you

tía f [tee-a] aunt; bird, woman

tibio [teeb-yo] lukewarm

tiburón m shark

tiempo m [t-yempo] time; weather

a tiempo on time

tiempo de recreo [rekray-o] leisure

tiempo libre [leebray] free time

tienda f [t-yenda] shop, store; tent

esta tienda se translada a ... business is transferred to ...

tienda de artículos de piel [p-yayl] leather goods shop

tienda de artículos de regalo gift shop

tienda de comestibles [komesteebless] grocer's

tienda de deportes [deportess] sports shop

tienda de discos record shop

tienda de electrodomésticos electrical goods shop

tienda de lanas woollen goods shop

tienda de muebles [mwaybless] furniture shop

tienda de regalos gift shop

tienda de ultramarinos grocer's

tienda de vinos y licores off-licence, (US) liquor store

tienda libre de impuestos [leebray day eempwestoss] duty-free shop

tiendas: ir de tiendas to go shopping

tiene que [t-yaynay kay] he must

¿tiene ...? have you got ...?

tierra f [t-yairra] earth

tijeras fpl [teeHairass] scissors

timbre m [teembray] bell

timbre de alarma alarm bell

tímido shy

tintorería f [teentorairee-a] dry-cleaner's

tío m [tee-o] uncle; bloke, guy

tipo de cambio m [kamb-yo] exchange rate

tirar to pull; to throw; to throw away

tirita f Elastoplast®, Bandaid®

toalla f [to-a-ya] towel

toalla de baño [ban-yo] bath

towel

tobillo m [tobee-yo] ankle

tocadiscos m record player

tocar to touch; to play

todavía [todabee-a] still; yet

 todavía no not yet

todo all, every; everything

 todos los días every day

todo derecho straight on

todo seguido [segeedo]
 straight ahead

todos everyone

tomamos la tensión we take
 your blood pressure

tomar to take

tomar el sol to sunbathe

tomavistas m cine-camera

tome usted take

tómese antes de las comidas
 to be taken before meals

tómese después de las
 comidas to be taken after
 meals

tómese ... veces al día to be
 taken ... times per day

tonelada f tonne

tono m dialling tone; shade

tonto silly

torcer [torthair] to twist; to
 sprain

torcerse un tobillo [oon tobee-
 yo] to twist one's ankle

torero m [torairo] bullfighter

tormenta f storm

tormentoso stormy

tornillo m [tornee-yo] screw

toro m bull

toros mpl bullfighting

torpe [torpay] clumsy

torre f [torray] tower

tos f cough

toser [tosair] to cough

tosferina f [tosfaireena]
 whooping cough

total: en total altogether

totalmente [-mentay]
 absolutely

tóxico [tokseeko] poisonous

trabajador [trabaHador]
 industrious

trabajar [trabajar] to work

trabajo m [trabaHo] work

traducir [tradootheer] to
 translate

traer [tra-air] to bring

tragar to swallow

traigo [tra-eego] I bring

traje [traHay] I brought

traje m suit; dress

traje de baño [ban-yo]
 swimming costume

traje de noche [nochay]
 evening dress

traje de señora lady's suit

traje típico traditional
 regional costume

tranquilizante [trankeeleethantay]
 tranquillizer

tranquilizarse [trankeeleetharsay]
 to calm down

tranquilo [trankeelo] quiet

transbordo m transfer; change
 hacer transbordo en ...
 change at ...

transferencia f [transfairenth-ya]
 transfer

tras after

trasero (m) [trasairo] bottom;

back; rear
tratar to treat
través: a través de across, through
travieso [trab-**yay**so] mischievous
trece [**tray**thay] thirteen
treinta [**tray**-eenta] thirty
tren m [tren] train
tren de carga goods train
trenes de cercanías [**tren**ess day thair**kan**ee-ass] local trains, suburban trains
tren de lavado automático car wash
tren de pasajeros [pasa**H**air**oss**] passenger train
tren directo through train
tren tranvía [tran**bee**-a] stopping train
tres [tress] three
tres cuartos de hora mpl three quarters of an hour
trescientos [tress-th-**yen**toss] three hundred
tripulación f [treepoolath-yon] crew
triste [**tree**stay] sad
tristeza f [tree**stay**tha] sadness
tronco m body; buddy
tropezar [trope**thar**] to trip
trozo (de) m [**tro**tho (day)] piece (of)
trueno m [tr**way**no] thunder
tu [too] your
tú [too] you
tú mismo yourself
tubería f [toobair**ee**-a] pipe
tubo de escape m [es**ka**pay]

exhaust
tubo de respirar snorkel
tuerza [**twair**tha] turn
tumbona f deck chair
túnel m tunnel
Túnez m [**tooneth**] Tunisia
turista m/f tourist
turno m turn; round
es mi turno it's my turn/round
turrón m [toor**ron**] nougat
tus [tooss] your
tuyo [**too**yo] yours

U

u [oo] or
Ud (usted) [**oo**stay] you (sing)
Uds (ustedes) [**oo**stay**dess**] you (plural)
úlcera (de estómago) f [**ool**thaira] (stomach) ulcer
últimamente [oolteemamentay] recently, lately
último last; latest
últimos días [**dee**-ass] last days
ultramarinos m grocer's
un [oon] a
una [**oo**na] a
unas some
uno one; someone
unos some; a few
uña f [**oon**-ya] fingernail
urbana local
urbanización f [oorbaneethath-**yon**] housing estate
urgencias [oor**H**en-yass] casualty department, emergencies

usado used; secondhand

usar to use

uso use

el uso del tabaco es perjudicial para su salud smoking can damage your health

uso externo not to be taken internally

uso obligatorio cinturón de seguridad seatbelts must be worn

Usted [oostay] you

Ustedes [oostaydess] you

útil useful

utilice sólo moneda fraccionaria small change only

V

va he/she/it goes; you go

vaca f cow

vacaciones fpl [bakath-yoness] holiday, vacation

vacío [bathee-o] empty

vacuna f vaccination

vacunarse [bakoonarsay] to be vaccinated

vado permanente no parking at any time

vagón m carriage

vagón restaurante [restowrantay] restaurant car

vagón de literas [leetairass] sleeping car

vainilla f [ba-eenee-ya] vanilla

vais [ba-eess] you go

vajilla f [baHee-ya] crockery

vale [balay] OK

valer [balair] to be worth

valiente [bal-yentay] brave

valla f [ba-ya] fence

valle m [ba-yay] valley

valores mpl [baloress] securities

válvula f valve

vamos we go

van they go; you go

vapor m steamer

vaqueros mpl [bakaiross] jeans; cowboys

varicela f [bareethay-la] chickenpox

varios [bar-yoss] several

varón m male

varonil manly

vas you go

vasco Basque

Vascongadas fpl the Basque country

vaso m glass

vaya [ba-ya] go; I/he/she go; you go

¡vaya por Dios! [dee-oss] oh Christ!

¡váyase! [ba-yasay] go away!

¡váyase a paseo! [pasay-o] get lost!

Vd (usted) [oostay] you (sing)

Vds (ustedes) you (plural)

ve [bay] go; he/she sees; you see

veces: a veces [baythess] sometimes

vecino m [betheeno] neighbour

vehículos pesados heavy vehicles

veinte [bay-eentay] twenty

v is pronounced more like a b than an English v

vejiga f [beHeega] bladder
vela f [bayla] candle; sail
velero m [belairo] sailing boat
velocidad f [belotheeda] speed
velocidad controlada por radar radar speed checks
velocidad limitada speed limits apply
velocidades fpl [belotheedadess] gears
velocímetro m [beloth**ee**metro] speedometer
ven [ben] come; they see; you see
vena f [bayna] vein
venda f bandage
vendar to dress (wound)
vendemos a ... selling rate
vender [bend**air**] to sell
veneno m [ben**ay**no] poison
vengo I come
venir to come
venta f sale
 de venta aquí on sale here
venta de localidades tickets (on sale)
venta de sellos stamps sold here
ventana f window
ventanilla f [bentan**ee**-ya] window; ticket office
ventas a crédito credit terms available
ventas a plazos hire purchase, (US) installment plan
ventas al contado cash sales

ventilador m fan
ver [bair] to see; to watch
veraneante m [bairanay-**an**tay] holidaymaker, vacationer
veranear [bairanay-**ar**] to holiday
verano m [bairano] summer
verbena f [bair**bay**na] open-air dance
verdad f [bair**da**] truth
 ¿de verdad? is that so?
 ¿verdad? don't you?; do you?; isn't he?; is he? etc
verdadero [bairda**dair**o] true
verde (m) [**bair**day] green
versión f [bairs-**yon**] version
 en versión original in the original language
vestido m dress
vestir to dress
 de vestir formal
vestirse [best**ee**rsay] to get dressed
vestuarios mpl [bestwar-**yoss**] fitting rooms
vez f [bayth] time
 una vez once
 en vez de instead of
vi [bee] I saw
vía aérea: por vía aérea by air mail
vía oral orally
vía rectal per rectum
viajar [b-ya**Har**] to travel
viaje m [b-ya**Hay**] journey
 ¡buen viaje! [bwen] have a good trip!
viaje de negocios [negoth-**yoss**] business trip

viaje de novios [nob-yoss] honeymoon

viaje organizado [organeethado] package tour

viajero m [b-yaHairo] passenger

vida f life

vidrio m [beedr-yo] glass

viejo [b-yayHo] old

viene: la semana que viene [b-yaynay] next week

viento m [b-yento] wind

vientre m [b-yentray] stomach

viernes [b-yairness] Friday

Viernes Santo m Good Friday

vine [beenay] I came

vinos y licores wines and spirits

viñedo [been-yaydo] vineyard

violación f [b-yolath-yon] rape

violar [b-yolar] to rape

violento [b-yolento] violent; embarrassing, awkward
  sentirse violento to feel awkward

visado m visa

visita f visit

visita con guía [gee-a] guided tour

visitante m/f [beeseetantay] visitor

visitar to visit

visor m viewfinder

víspera f [beespaira] the day before

vista f view
  ¡hasta la vista! see you!

vista turística scenic view

visto seen

viuda f [b-yooda] widow

viudo m widower

vivir to live

vivo alive; I live

VO (versión original) original language

volante m [bolantay] steering wheel

volar to fly

voltaje [boltaHay] voltage

volver [bolbair] to come back

volver a hacer algo to do something again

volver a casa to go home

vomitar to vomit

vosotras, vosotros you

v.o. subtitulada version in the original language with subtitles

voy I go

voz f [both] voice

vuelo m [bwaylo] flight

vuelo nacional [nath-yonal] domestic flight

vuelo regular scheduled flight

vuelta f [bwelta] change
  la vuelta al colegio [kolay-Hyo] back to school

vuelvo [bwelbo] I return

vuestra [bwestra], vuestras, vuestro, vuestros your; yours

W

wáter [batair] toilet, rest room

Y

y [ee] and
ya already
 ya está there you are
 ya ... ya sometimes ...
 sometimes
ya que [kay] since
yerno m [yairno] son-in-law
yo I; me
yo mismo myself

Z

zapatería f [thapatairee-a] shoe
 shop/store
zapatero m [thapatairo]
 cobbler; shoe repairer
zapatillas fpl [thapatee-yass]
 slippers
zapatos mpl [thapatoss] shoes
zona f [thona] area
zona de avalanchas frequent
 avalanches
zona monumental historic
 monuments
zona (reservada) para
 peatones pedestrian precinct
zona azul [athool] restricted
 parking area, permit holders
 only
zona de servicios [sairbeeth-
 yoss] service area
zurdo [thoordo] left-handed

Menu Reader:
Food

Essential Terms

bread el pan
butter la mantequilla [mantekee-ya]
cup la taza [tatha]
dessert el postre [postray]
fish (food) el pescado
fork el tenedor
glass (wine glass) la copa
knife el cuchillo [koochee-yo]
main course el plato principal
meat la carne [karnay]
menu el menú [menoo]
pepper (spice) la pimienta [peem-yenta]
plate el plato
salad la ensalada
salt la sal
set menu el menu del día [menoo]
soup la sopa
spoon la cuchara
starter (food) la entrada
table la mesa [maysa]

another ..., please otro/otra ..., por favor [fabor]
excuse me! (to call waiter/waitress) ¡por favor! [fabor]
could I have the bill, please? la cuenta, por favor [kwenta]

aceite [athay-eetay] oil

aceite de oliva [day oleeba] olive oil

aceitunas [athay-eetoonass] olives

aceitunas aliñadas [aleen-yadass] olives with salad dressing

aceitunas negras black olives

aceitunas rellenas [ray-yaynass] stuffed olives

aceitunas verdes [bairdess] green olives

acelgas [athelgass] chard, spinach beet

achicoria [acheekor-ya] chicory

aguacate [agwakatay] avocado

aguja de ternera [agooHa day tairnaira] veal for stewing

ahumados [a-oomadoss] smoked fish

ahumados variados [baree-adoss] smoked fish

ajillo [aHee-yo] garlic

ajo [aHo] garlic

alaju [ala-Hoo] nougat-type sweet made from walnuts or pine nuts, toasted breadcrumbs and honey

albahaca [alba-aka] basil

albaricoque [albareekokay] apricot

albóndigas meatballs

albóndigas de lomo [day] pork meatballs

alcachofas artichokes

alcachofas en vinagreta [beenagrayta] artichokes in vinaigrette dressing

alcachofas a la andaluza [andalootha] artichokes with ham and bacon

alcachofas a la romana artichokes in batter

alcaparras capers

aliñada [aleen-yada] with salad dressing

ali oli garlic mayonnaise

almejas [almay-Hass] clams

almejas a la buena mujer [bwayna mooHair] clams stewed with chillies, white wine, lemon and herbs

almejas a la marinera [mareenaira] clams stewed in white wine and parsley

almejas a la valenciana [balenth-yana] clams in a white wine sauce

almejas al natural [natooral] live clams

almejas en salsa verde [bairday] clams in parsley and white wine sauce

almejas naturales [natooraless] live clams

almendra almond

alubias [aloob-yass] beans

alubias blancas white kidney beans

alubias rojas [roHass] red kidney beans

ancas de rana frogs' legs

ancas de rana albuferena [aboofairayna] frogs' legs in a sauce made from chicken soup, mushrooms and paprika anchoas [ancho-ass] anchovies

anchoas a la barquera [barkaira] marinated anchovies with capers

anguila [angeela] eel

anguila ahumada [a-oomada] smoked eel

angulas baby eels

angulas al all-i-pebre [all-ee-pebray] baby eels with garlic and black pepper

añojo [an-yoHo] veal

apio [ap-yo] celery

arenques frescos [arenkess] fresh herrings

arroz [arroth] rice

arroz a la cubana boiled rice with fried eggs and either bananas or tomato sauce

arroz a la emperatriz [empairatreeth] rice with milk, apricots, truffles, raisins, Cointreau and gelatine

arroz a la turca [toorka] boiled rice with curry sauce, onions and tomatoes

arroz a la valenciana [balenth-yana] paella

arroz blanco boiled white rice

arroz con leche [lechay] rice pudding

asado roast

asados roast meats

asadurilla [asadooree-ya] lambs' liver stew

atún [atoon] tuna

atún al horno [orno] baked tuna

avellana [abay-yana] hazelnut

aves [abess] poultry

azafrán [athafran] saffron

azúcar [athookar] sugar

bacalao a la catalana [bakala-o] cod with ham, almond, garlic and parsley

bacalao al ajo arriero [aHo arr-yairo] cod with garlic, peppers and chillies

bacalao a la vizcaína [beethka-eena] cod served with ham, peppers and chillies

bacalao al pil pil [peel] cod cooked in olive oil

baveresa de coco [babairaysa day] cold coconut sweet

becadas snipe

becadas a la vizcaína [beethka-eena] snipe served with bacon, onion and sherry sauce

becadas asadas baked snipe

berenjena [bairenHayna] aubergine, eggplant

berenjenas a la mallorquina [ma-yorkeena] aubergines/ eggplants with garlic mayonnaise

berza [bairtha] cabbage

besugo bream

besugo al horno [al orno] baked sea bream

besugo asado baked sea bream

besugo mechado sea bream stuffed with ham and bacon

bien hecho [b-yen echo] well done

bistec a la riojana [r-yoHana] steak with fried red peppers

bistec de ternera [tairnaira] veal steak

bizcocho [beethkocho] sponge finger

bocadillo [bokadee-yo] sandwich, snack

bogavante [bogabantay] lobster

bollo [bo-yo] roll

bomba helada [elada] baked alaska

bonito tuna

bonito al horno [orno] baked tuna

boquerones en vinagre [bokaironess en beenagray] anchovies in vinaigrette

boquerones fritos fried fresh anchovies

brandada de bacalao [bakala-o] creamy cod purée

brazo de gitano [bratho day Heetano] swiss roll

brevas [brebass] figs

broqueta de riñones [broketa day reen-yoness] kidney kebabs

buey [boo-ay] beef

buñuelos [boon-ywayloss] light fried pastry

buñuelos de bacalao [bakala-o] fried pastry containing flaked, dried, salted cod

buñuelos de cuaresma rellenos [day kwaresma ray-yaynoss] light fried pastries with chocolate and cream

butifarra Catalan sausage – contains bacon

butifarra con rovellons [robay-yons] Catalan sausage with mushrooms

butifarra con setas Catalan sausage with mushrooms

buvangos rellenos [boobangoss ray-yaynoss] stuffed courgettes/zucchini

cabello de ángel [kabay-yo day] sweet pumpkin filling (used in cakes)

cabracho mullet

cabrito asado roast kid

cacahuetes [kakawaytess] peanuts

cachelada [kachelada] pork stew with eggs, tomato, onion and boiled potatoes

cachelos [kachayloss] boiled potatoes served with spicy sausage and bacon

calabacines [kalabatheeness] courgettes, zucchini; marrow

calabaza [kalabatha] pumpkin

calamares a la romana [kalamaress] squid rings fried in batter

calamares en su tinta [teenta] squid cooked in their ink

calamares fritos fried squid

caldeirada [kalday-eerada] fish soup

caldera de dátiles de mar [kaldaira day dateeless] seafood stew

caldereta de cordero a la pastora [kaldairayta day kordairo] lamb and vegetable stew caldereta gallega [ga-**yay**ga] vegetable stew

caldo clear soup

caldo de gallina [ga-**yee**na] chicken soup

caldo de perdiz [pair**deeth**] partridge soup

caldo de pescado clear fish soup

caldo gallego [ga-**yay**go] clear soup with green vegetables, beans and pork

caldo guanche [**gwan**chay] soup made from potatoes, onions, tomatoes and courgettes/zucchini

callos a la madrileña [ka-**yoss** a la madre**een**-ya] tripe cooked with chillies

camarones [kama**ron**ess] baby prawns

canela [ka**nay**la] cinnamon

canelones [kane**lon**ess] canneloni

cangrejo [kang**ray**-HO] crab

cangrejos de río river crabs

caracoles [kara**kol**ess] snails

caracoles a la madrileña [madre**een**-ya] snails cooked with chillies

carbonada de buey [boo-**ay**] beef cooked in beer

cardo type of thistle, eaten as a vegetable

carne [**kar**nay] meat

carne de cerdo [**thair**do] pork

carne de membrillo [membree-yo] quince jelly (dessert)

carne de vaca [**bak**a] beef

carne picada minced meat

carnero [kar**nair**o] mutton

carnes [**kar**ness] meat; meat dishes

carro de queso [**kay**so] cheese board

carta menu

castaña [kas**tan**-ya] chestnut

caza [**kath**a] game

cazuela [kath**way**la] casserole

cazuela de chichas meat casserole

cazuela de hígado [**ee**gado] liver casserole

cebolla [thebo-ya] onion

cebolletas [thebo-**yet**ass] spring onions

cecina [the**thee**na] dry cured meat

centollo [then**to**-yo] spider crab

centollo relleno [ray-**yay**no] spider crab cooked in its shell

cerdo [**thair**do] pork, pig

cereza [thai**ray**tha] cherry

cesta de frutas [**thes**ta day **froo**tass] a selection of fresh fruit

champiñón a la crema [champeen-**yon** – **kray**ma] mushrooms in cream sauce

champiñón al ajillo [aHee-yo] mushrooms fried with garlic

champiñón a la plancha grilled mushrooms

champiñones [champeen-**yon**ess] mushrooms

chanfaina [chanfa-**ee**na] rice and black pudding stew

chanfaina castellana [kastay-yana] rice and sheeps' liver stew

changurro spider crab cooked in its shell

chanquetes [chankaytess] fish (like whitebait)

chateaubrian [chatobree-an] thick steak

chicharros horse mackerel

chipirones [cheepeeroness] baby squid

chipirones en su tinta [teenta] baby squid cooked in their ink

chipirones rellenos [ray-yaynoss] stuffed baby squid

chirimoyas [cheereemo-yass] custard apples

chocos squid

chocos con habas [abass] squid with broad beans

chorizo [choreetho] spicy red sausage

chuleta [choolayta] chop

chuleta de buey [day boo-ay] beef chop

chuleta de cerdo [thairdo] pork chop

chuleta de cerdo empanada breaded pork chop

chuleta de cordero [kordairo] lamb chop

chuleta de ternera [tairnaira] veal chop

chuleta de ternera empanada breaded veal chop

chuletas de gamo venison chops

chuletas de lomo ahumado [a-oomado] smoked pork chops

chuletas de venado [benado] venison chops

chuletitas de cordero [day kordairo] small lamb chops

chuletón large chop

chuletón de ternera a la diable roja [d-yablay roHa] large, grilled, breaded veal chop

churros fried pastry strips

cigala [theegala] crayfish

cigalas a la parrilla [parree-ya] grilled crayfish

cigalas cocidas [kotheedass] boiled crayfish

ciruela [theerwayla] plum, greengage

ciruelas pasas prunes

civet de liebre [theebet day l-yaybray] marinated hare

coca amb pinxes [koka am peensess] sardine pie

cochinillo asado [kocheenee-yo] roast sucking pig

cocido [kotheedo] stew made from meat, chickpeas and vegetables

cocido castellano/madrileño [kastay-yano/madreelen-yo] stew made from meat, chickpeas, vegetables etc

cocochas (de merluza) [mairlootha] hakes' gills

cóctel de bogavante [bogabantay] lobster cocktail

cóctel de gambas prawn cocktail

cóctel de langostinos king

prawn cocktail

cóctel de mariscos seafood cocktail

codillo de cerdo con chucrut [kodee-yo day thairdo kon chookroot] pigs' trotters with sauerkraut

codoñate [kodon-yatay] cake made with chestnuts, honey and quince

codoñate de nueces [nwaythess] cake made with walnuts

codornices [kodorneethess] quail

codornices con uvas [oobass] quail stewed with grapes

codornices estofadas braised quail

col cabbage

coles de Bruselas [koless day broosaylass] Brussels sprouts

coliflor cauliflower

coliflor con bechamel cauliflower cheese

comino cumin

conejo [konay-Ho] rabbit

conejo encebollado [enthebo-yado] rabbit served with onions

conejo estofado braised rabbit

congrio [kongr-yo] conger eel

consomé al jerez [konsomay al Haireth] consommé with sherry

consomé con yema [yayma] consommé with egg yolk

consomé de ave [abay] chicken consommé

consomé de pollo [po-yo] chicken consommé

contra de ternera con guisantes [tairnaira kon geesantess] veal stew with peas

contrafilete de ternera [kontrafeelaytay day] veal fillet

copa de helado [elado] assorted ice cream served in a stemmed glass

cordero [kordairo] lamb

cordero chilindrón lamb stew with onion, tomato, peppers and eggs

corvina [korbeena] Mediterranean fish, similar to sea bass

costillas de cerdo [kostee-yas day thairdo] pork ribs

costillas de cerdo con chucrut [chookroot] pork ribs with sauerkraut

crema catalana [krayma] crème caramel

cremada dessert made from egg, sugar and milk

crema de cangrejos [krayma day kangray-Hoss] cream of crab soup

crema de espárragos cream of asparagus soup

crema de espinacas cream of spinach soup

crema de legumbres/verduras [legoombrays/bairdoorass] cream of vegetable soup

crep(e) pancake

crep(e)s imperiales [eempairyaless] crêpe suzette

criadillas [kree-adee-yass] bulls' testicles; truffles (edible fungus); root vegetable

criadillas de ternera [tairnaira] calves' testicles

criadillas de tierra [t-yairra] truffles (edible fungus)

criadillas en salsa verde [bairday] root vegetable in parsley sauce

crocante [krokantay] ice cream with chopped nuts

croquetas [krokaytass] croquettes

crudo raw

cuajada [kwaHada] junket, curds

dátiles [dateeless] dates

dátiles de mar shellfish

delicias de queso [deleeth-yass day kayso] cheese croquettes

dulce de membrillo [doolthay day membree-yo] quince jelly

embutidos cured pork sausages

embutidos de la tierra [t-yairra] local sausages

empanada gallega [ga-yayga] pie with chicken, chorizo sausage, peppers, ham, onions and tuna

empanada santiaguesa [sant-yagaysa] fish pie

empanado in breadcrumbs

empanadillas [empanadee-yass] small pies

empanadillas de chorizo [choreetho] small pies filled with spicy sausage

endivias [endeeb-yass] endive

ensaimada mallorquina [ensa-eemada ma-yorkeena] large, spiral-shaped bun

ensalada salad

ensalada de frutas fruit salad

ensalada ilustrada mixed salad

ensalada mixta [meesta] mixed salad

ensalada simple [seemplay] green salad

ensaladilla [ensaladee-ya] Spanish salad

ensaladilla rusa [roosa] Russian salad

entrantes [entrantess] entrées, starters

entrecot a la parrilla [entrekot – parree-ya] grilled entrecôte steak

entrecot a la pimienta [peem-yenta] entrecôte in black pepper sauce

entremés [entremayss] hors d'oeuvre, starter

entremeses [entremaysess] hors d'oeuvres

entremeses de la casa hors d'oeuvres – house speciality

entremeses variados [bar-yadoss] assorted hors d'oeuvres

escabeche de ... [eskabechay] marinated ...

escalibada flaked cod and vegetable salad (Catalan dish)

escalope a la milanesa
[eskalopay] breaded veal
escalope with cheese

escalope a la parrilla [parree-
ya] grilled veal

escalope a la plancha grilled
veal

escalope Cordon Bleu veal
escalope with ham and
cheese

escalope de cerdo [thairdo]
pork escalope

escalope de lomo de cerdo
escalope of fillet of pork

escalope de ternera [tairnaira]
veal escalope

escalopines al vino de Marsala
[eskalopeeness – beeno] veal
escalopes cooked in wine

escalopines de ternera
[tairnaira] veal escalopes

escarola endive

espadín a la toledana kebab

espaguetis italiana
[espagayteess eetal-yana]
spaghetti

espárragos asparagus

espárragos calientes [kal-
yentess] grilled asparagus with
béchamel sauce

espárragos dos salsas
asparagus with mayonnaise
and vinagrette dressing

espárragos en vinagreta
[beenagrayta] asparagus in
vinaigrette dressing

espárragos trigueros
[treegayross] green asparagus

especia [espayth-ya] spice

especialidad speciality

espina fishbone

espinacas spinach

espinazo de cerdo con
patatas [espeenatho day thairdo]
pork ribs with potatoes

espuma de jamón [day Hamon]
boiled ham mousse

estofado stew; stewed

estofado de liebre [l-yaybray]
hare stew

estofado de liebre con
níscalos hare stew with wild
mushrooms

estofados stews

estragón tarragon

fabada (asturiana) [astoor-yana]
bean stew with red sausage,
black pudding and pork

fabricación: de fabricación
casera homemade

faisán [fa-eesan] pheasant

faisán trufado [troofado]
pheasant with truffles

farinato fried sausage

fiambres [f-yambress] cold
meats, cold cuts

fideos [feeday-oss] thin pasta;
noodles; vermicelli

filete [feelaytay] steak; fillet

filete a la parrilla [parree-ya]
grilled beef steak

filete a la plancha grilled beef
steak

filete de cerdo [thairdo] pork
steak

filete de ternera [tairnaira] veal
steak

flan crème caramel

flan con nata crème caramel with whipped cream

flan de café [day kafay] coffee-flavoured crème caramel

flan de caramelo [karamaylo] crème caramel

flan (quemado) al ron [kemado] crème caramel with rum

frambuesa [frambwaysa] raspberry

fresa [fraysa] strawberry

fresas con nata strawberries and cream

fritanga al modo de Alicante [day aleekantay] dish of fried peppers, tuna and garlic

frito fried

fritos de la casa fried hors d'oeuvres – house speciality

fritos variados [bar-yadoss] fried hors d'oeuvres

fruta fruit

frutas en almíbar fruit in syrup

fruta variada [bar-yada] assorted fresh fruit

gachas manchegas type of sweet or savoury porridge

galleta [ga-yayta] biscuit

gallina a la cairatraca [ga-yeena a la ka-eeratraka] stewed chicken

gallina en pepitoria [pepeetor-ya] stewed chicken with peppers, onions and tomato

gamba prawn

gambas a la americana prawns with brandy and garlic

gambas al ajillo [aHee-yo] prawns with garlic

gambas a la plancha grilled prawns

gambas cocidas [kotheedass] boiled prawns

gambas en gabardina prawns in batter

gambas rebozadas [rebothadass] prawns in batter

garbanzos [garbanthoss] chickpeas

garbanzos a la catalana chickpeas with sausage, boiled eggs and pine nuts

gazpacho andaluz [gathpacho andalooth] cold soup made from tomatoes, onions, garlic, peppers and cucumber

gazpacho manchego rabbit stew with tomato and garlic, sometimes also with partridge meat

gelatina [Helateena] jelly

gratén de ... ... au gratin

grelo turnip

guisado de cordero [geesado day kordairo] stewed lamb

guisado de costillas de ternera [kostee-yass day tairnaira] rib of veal stew

guisado de ternera stewed veal

guisantes [geesantess] peas

habas [abass] broad beans

habas fritas fried young broad

beans

habichuelas [abeechwaylass] haricot beans; white kidney beans

hamburguesa [amboorgaysa] hamburger

harina [areena] flour

helado [elado] ice cream

helado de caramelo [karamaylo] caramel ice cream

helado de mantecado dairy ice cream

helado de nata dairy ice cream

helado de vainilla [ba-eenee-ya] vanilla ice cream

hierbas [yairbass] herbs

hígado [eegado] liver

hígado de ternera estofado [tairnaira] braised calves' liver

hígado encebollado [entheboyado] liver in an onion sauce

hígado estofado braised liver

higos [eegoss] figs

higos secos dried figs

hornazo [ornatho] Easter cake

horno: al horno baked

huevo [waybo] egg

huevo duro [dooro] hard-boiled egg

huevo hilado [eelado] shredded boiled eggs used as a garnish

huevo pasado por agua [agwa] boiled egg

huevos a la española [espan-yola] fried eggs

huevos a la flamenca baked eggs with sausage, tomato, peas, asparagus and peppers

huevos cocidos [kotheedoss] hard-boiled eggs

huevos con picadillo [peekadee-yo] eggs with minced sausage meat

huevos duros con mayonesa [ma-yonaysa] egg mayonnaise

huevos escalfados poached eggs

huevos fritos fried eggs

huevos fritos con chorizo [choreetho] fried eggs with Spanish sausage

huevos pasados por agua [agwa] boiled eggs

huevos rellenos [ray-yaynoss] stuffed eggs

huevos revueltos [rebweltoss] scrambled eggs

incluye pan, postre y vino includes bread, dessert and wine

IVA no incluido VAT not included

jamón [Hamon] ham

jamón con huevo hilado [waybo eelado] ham with shredded egg garnish

jamón de Jabugo [day Haboogo] jamón ibérico from Jabugo, Huelva

jamón ibérico [eebaireeko] Spanish ham

jamón serrano [sairrano] cured ham, similar to Parma ham

jamón York boiled ham

jarrete de ternera [Harraytay day

tairn**air**a] veal hock
jeta [**H**eta] pigs' cheeks
jeta rebozada [rebo**tha**da] pigs'
cheek in batter
judías [H**oodee-ass**] beans
judías verdes [**bair**dess] green
beans
judías verdes a la española
[espan-**yo**la] French bean stew
judías verdes al natural
[nat**oo**ral] plain green beans
judías verdes con jamón
[H**am**on] French beans with
ham
judiones [Hood-**yo**ness] broad
beans

lacón con grelos bacon with
turnip tops
langosta lobster
langosta a la americana
lobster with brandy and
garlic
langosta a la catalana lobster
with mushrooms and ham in
a white sauce
langosta con mahonesa
[ma-**on**aysa] lobster with
mayonnaise
langosta fría con mayonesa
cold lobster with mayonnaise
langosta gratinada lobster au
gratin
langostinos a la plancha
grilled king prawns
langostinos dos salsas king
prawns cooked in two sauces
laurel [**low**rel] bay leaves
lebrato hare

leche frita [**le**chay **free**ta] slices
of thick custard fried in
breadcrumbs
leche merengada cold
milk with meringues and
cinnamon
lechuga [lech**oo**ga] lettuce
lengua [**len**gwa] tongue
lengua de buey [boo-**ay**] ox
tongue
lenguado a la parrilla [**len**gwado
a la parr**ee**-ya] grilled sole
lenguado a la plancha grilled
sole
lenguado a la romana sole in
batter
lenguado al chacolí con
hongos [**on**goss] sole with
mushrooms and white wine
lenguado frito fried sole
lenguado grillado [gree-**ya**do]
grilled sole
lenguado menie/meuniere
[men-**yair**] sole meunière –
sole coated in flour, fried and
served with butter, lemon
juice and parsley
lenguado rebozado [rebo**tha**do]
sole in batter
lentejas [len**tay**-Hass] lentils
lentejas aliñadas [aleen-**ya**dass]
lentils in vinaigrette dressing
lentejas onubenses
[onoob**en**sess] lentils with
spicy sausage, onion and
garlic
liba rebozada [rebo**tha**da] sea
bass fried in batter
liebre estofada [l-**yay**bray]

stewed hare
lima [**lee**ma] lime
limón lemon
lombarda red cabbage
lomo curado [koo**ra**do] cured pork sausage
lomo de liebre [l-**yay**bray] loin of hare
lonchas de jamón [Ha**mon**] slices of cured ham
longaniza [longa**nee**tha] cooked Spanish sausage
lubina a la cantábrica sea bass with garlic, lemon juice and white wine
lubina a la marinera [maree**nai**ra] sea bass in a parsley sauce

macarrones [maka**rro**ness] macaroni
macarrones gratinados macaroni cheese
macedonia de fruta [mathe**don**-ya] fruit salad
maduro [ma**doo**ro] ripe
magdalena [magda**lay**na] muffin
magras con tomate [to**ma**tay] slices of cured ham with tomato
mahonesa [ma-o**nay**sa] mayonnaise
maíz [ma-**eeth**] sweetcorn
mandarinas tangerines
manises [ma**nee**sess] peanuts
manitas de cordero [kor**dai**ro] leg of lamb
manos de cerdo [**thai**rdo] pigs'

trotters
mantecadas small sponge cakes
mantecado vanilla ice cream
mantequilla [mante**kee**-ya] butter
manzana [man**tha**na] apple
manzanas a la malvasía [malbass**ee**-a] apples in syrup
manzanas asadas baked apples
mariscada cold mixed shellfish
mariscos seafood
mariscos del día fresh shellfish
mariscos del tiempo [t-**yem**po] seasonal shellfish
marmitako tuna and vegetable stew
mayonesa [ma-yo**nay**sa] mayonnaise
mazapán [matha**pan**] marzipan
medallones de anguila [meda-**yo**ness day ang**ee**la] eel steaks
medallones de merluza [mair**loo**tha] hake steaks
mejillones [may-Hee-**yo**ness] mussels
mejillones a la marinera [maree**nai**ra] mussels in wine sauce with garlic and parsley
mejillones con salsa mussels with tomato and herb sauce
melocotón peach
melocotones en almíbar [meloko**to**ness] peaches in syrup
melón melon
melón al calisay [kalee**si**]

melon with a spirit or
liqueur poured over it

melón con jamón [Hamon]
melon with cured ham

membrillo [membree-yo] quince

menestra de legumbres
[legoombress] vegetable stew
made from pulses

menestra de verduras
[bairdoorass] vegetable stew

menú [menoo] set menu

menú de la casa fixed price
menu

menú del día today's set menu

merluza a la castellana
[mairlootha – kastay-yana] hake
with clams, prawns, linseeds,
eggs and chilli

merluza a la cazuela
[kathwayla] hake casserole

merluza al ajo arriero [aHo arr-
yairo] hake with garlic and
chillies

merluza a la riojana [r-yoHana]
hake with chillies

merluza a la romana hake
steaks in batter

merluza a la vasca [baska]
hake in a garlic sauce

merluza caldo corto hake with
vegetable sauce

merluza en salsa verde
[bairday] hake in parsley and
white wine sauce

merluza fría [free-a] cold hake

merluza frita fried hake

merluza koskera [koskaira]
hake in a garlic sauce

merluza (lomos de) con

angulas y almejas [ee almay-
Hass] hake fillet with baby
eels and clams

mermelada [mairmelada] jam;
marmalade

mero [mairo] grouper (fish)

mero a la levantina [lebanteena]
grouper with lemon juice
and rosemary

mero en salsa verde [bairday]
grouper with garlic, parsley
and white wine sauce

miel [m-yel] honey

mojete [moHay-tay] 'dipping'
sauce for bread, usually made
from vegetables

mojojones [moHoHoness]
mussels

mollejas con setas [mo-yay-
Hass] lambs' gizzards with
mushrooms

mollejas de ternera [tairnaira]
calves' sweetbreads

mora blackberry

morcilla [morthee-ya] black
pudding, blood sausage

morcilla de ternera [tairnaira]
black pudding made from
calves' blood

morros de cerdo [thairdo] pigs'
cheeks

morros de vaca [day baka]
cows' cheeks

morros de vaca pastora cows'
cheeks with vegetables

mortadela salami-type sausage

morteruelo [mortair-waylo]
breaded minced liver

mostaza [mostatha] mustard

mousse de limón lemon
  mousse
mújol guisado [mooHol geesado]
  red mullet

nabo turnip
naranja [naranHa] orange
nata cream
nata batida whipped cream
natillas [natee-yass] cold
  custard with cinnamon
natillas de chocolate
  [chokolatay] cold custard with
  chocolate
níscalos wild mushrooms
nísperos [neespaiross] medlars
  – fruit similar to crab apple
nueces [nwaythess] walnuts
nuez [nwayth] nut
ñoquis [n-yokeess] potato
  gnocchi

oca en adobo marinaded
  goose
orejas de cerdo [oray-Has day
  thairdo] pigs' ears
orejas y pie de cerdo [ee p-yay]
  pigs' ears and trotters
ostra oyster
otros mariscos según precios
  en plaza other shellfish,
  depending on current prices

pa amb tomaquet bread
  spread with olive oil and
  tomato sauce
paella [pa-ay-ya] fried rice
  with seafood and chicken
paella castellana [kastay-yana]

meat paella
paella de marisco shellfish
  paella
paella de pollo [po-yo] chicken
  paella
paella especial [espeth-yal]
  paella house speciality
paella mixta [meesta] shellfish
  and chicken paella
paella valenciana [balenth-yana]
  paella with assorted shellfish
  and chicken
paleta de cordero lechal
  [kordairo] shoulder of lamb
paloma pigeon
pan bread
panaché de verduras [panachay
  day bairdoorass] vegetable stew
pan blanco white bread
panceta [panthayta] bacon
pan de higos [eegoss] dried fig
  cake with cinnamon
pan integral wholemeal bread
parrilla: a la parrilla grilled
parrillada de caza [parree-yada
  day katha] mixed grilled game
parrillada de mariscos mixed
  grilled shellfish
pasas raisins
pasta biscuit; pastry; pasta
pastel cake; pie
pastel de hígado de cerdo
  [eegado day thairdo] pigs' liver
  pie
pastel de higos [eegoss] fig
  cake
pastel de ternera [tairnaira]
  veal pie
pastel de verduras con salsa

de champiñones silvestres
[bairdoorass –champeen-yoness
seelbestress] vegetable pie
with wild mushroom sauce

pasteles [pastayless] cakes

patas de cordero [kordairo]
stewed leg of lamb

patata potato

patatas a la pescadora
potatoes with fish

patatas asadas roast potatoes

patatas bravas [brabass]
potatoes in cayenne sauce

patatas con nabos potatoes
with turnips

patatas estofadas boiled
potatoes

patatas fritas chips, French
fries; crisps, potato chips

patitos rellenos [ray-yaynoss]
stuffed duckling

pato duck

pato a la naranja [naran-Ha]
duck à l'orange

pavipollo [pabeepo-yo] large
chicken

pavo [pabo] turkey

pavo a la Asturiana [astoor-
yana] turkey with red wine
and paprika

pavo relleno a la catalana
turkey stuffed with sausage,
pork and plums

pavo trufado turkey stuffed
with truffles

pecho de ternera [tairnaira]
breast of veal

pechuga de pollo [po-yo]
breast of chicken

peixo-palo a la marinera [pesho
– mareenaira] stock-fish with
potatoes and tomato

pepinillos [pepeenee-yoss]
gherkins

pepinillos en vinagreta
[beenagrayta] gherkins in
vinaigrette dressing

pepino cucumber

pera pear

percebes [pairthaybess]
barnacles (shellfish)

perdices [pairdeethess]
partridges

perdices a la campesina
partridges with vegetables

perdices a la manchega
partridges cooked in red
wine, garlic, herbs and
pepper

perdiz encebollada [pairdeeth
enthebo-yada] partridge with
onion sauce

perejil [pairay-Heel] parsley

pescaditos fritos fried sprats

pescado fish

pestiños [pesteen-yoss] sugared
pastries flavoured with
aniseed

pestiños con miel [m-yel] fried
sugared pastries flavoured
with aniseed and honey

pez [payth] fish

pez espada ahumado
[a-oomado] smoked swordfish

picadillo [peekadee-yo] salad
of diced vegetables; stew of
pork, bacon, garlic and eggs

picadillo de ternera [tairnaira]

217

minced veal

pichones estofados
[peech**o**ness] stewed pigeon

pimentón paprika

pimienta (negra) [peem-y**e**nta]
black pepper

pimienta blanca white pepper

pimienta de cayena [ka-y**ay**na]
cayenne pepper

pimiento pepper

pimientos a la riojana
[r-yo**H**ana] baked red peppers
fried in oil and garlic

pimientos fritos fried peppers

pimientos morrones
[m**o**rr**o**ness] strong peppers

pimientos rellenos [ray-y**ay**noss]
stuffed peppers

pimientos verdes [b**ai**rdess]
green peppers

pinchitos snacks/appetizers
served in bars; kebabs

pinchos snacks served in bars

pinchos morunos kebabs

pintada guinea fowl

piña [p**ee**n-ya] pineapple

piña al gratén pineapple au
gratin

piña fresca fresh pineapple

piñones [peen-y**o**ness] pine nuts

piparrada vasca [b**a**sca]
pepper and tomato stew with
ham and eggs

piriñaca [peereen-y**a**ka] tuna
and vegetable salad

pisto fried peppers, onions,
tomatoes and courgettes/
zucchini

pisto manchego marrow,

onion and tomato stew

plancha: a la plancha grilled

plátano banana

plátanos flameados [flamay-
adoss] flambéed bananas

platos combinados meat and
vegetables, hamburgers and
eggs etc, mixture of various
foods served as one dish; set
menu

pochas con almejas [almay-
Hass] white beans with clams

poco hecho [**e**cho] rare

pollo [p**o**-yo] chicken

pollo al ajillo [a**H**ee-yo] fried
chicken with garlic

pollo a la parrilla [parr**ee**-ya]
grilled chicken

pollo a la riojana [r-yo**H**ana]
chicken with peppers and
chillies

pollo asado roast chicken

pollo braseado [brasay-**a**do]
braised chicken

pollo en cacerola [kathair**o**la]
chicken casserole

pollo en chanfaina [chanfa-
eena] chicken with fried
peppers, onions, tomatoes
and courgettes/zucchini

pollo en pepitoria [pepeet**o**r-ya]
chicken in wine with saffron,
garlic and almonds

pollo reina clamart [r**ay**-eena]
roast chicken with vegetables

**pollos tomateros con
zanahorias** [tomat**ai**ros kon
thana-**o**r-yass] baby chickens
with carrots

polvorones [polbor**o**ness]
sugar-based dessert (eaten at
Christmas)

pomelo grapefruit

postre [p**o**stray] dessert

postre sorpresa al DYC
[sorpr**ay**sa al deek] whisky-
flavoured dessert

potaje castellano [pota**H**ay
kastay-**y**ano] thick broth

potaje de garbanzos
[garb**a**nthoss] chickpea stew

potaje de habichuelas
[habeechw**ay**lass] white bean
stew

potaje de lentejas [lent**ay**-Hass]
lentil stew

primer plato starters

pucherete al estilo montañés
[poochair**e**tay al est**ee**lo montan-
yess] black pudding and spicy
sausage stew

puchero canario [poochairo
kan**a**r-yo] casserole of meat,
chickpeas and corn

puerro [pw**ai**rro] leek

pulpitos con cebolla [thebo-ya]
baby octopuses with onions

pulpo octopus

puré de patata [poor**ay** day
potato purée, mashed
potatoes

purrusalda cod soup with
leeks and potatoes

PVP price

queso [k**ay**so] cheese

queso con membrillo [mem-
br**ee**-yo] cheese with quince

jelly

queso de bola Edam

queso de Burgos soft white
cheese

queso de cabrales [kabr**a**less]
Spanish Roquefort-type
cheese

queso de cerdo [th**ai**rdo]
similar to the pork in a pork
pie, usually in slices

queso de Idiazábal [eed-
yath**a**bal] strong sheeps' cheese
from the Basque country

queso del país [pa-**ee**ss] local
cheese

queso de oveja [ob**ay**-Ha]
sheep's cheese

queso de Roncal strong
sheep's cheese from Navarra

queso gallego [ga-y**ay**go]
creamy cheese from Galicia

queso manchego hard, strong
cheese from La Mancha

quisquillas [keeskee-yass]
shrimps

rábanos radishes

rabas squid rings fried in
batter

rabo de buey [boo-**ay**] oxtail

ración [rath-yon] portion

ración pequeña para niños
[pek**ay**n-ya – n**ee**n-yoss]
children's portion

ragout de ternera [rag**oo**t day
tairn**ai**ra] veal ragoût

rape a la americana [r**a**pay]
monkfish with brandy and
herbs

rape a la cazuela [kathwayla] monkfish casserole

rape a la plancha grilled monkfish

ravioles [rab-yoless] ravioli

raya [ra-ya] skate

raya con manteca negra skate in butter and vinegar sauce

redondo al horno [orno] roast fillet of beef

redondo de ternera [tairnaira] fillet of veal

redondo en su jugo [Hoogo] fillet of beef cooked in its own sauce

relleno [ray-yayno] stuffed; stuffing

remolacha beetroot

repollo [repo-yo] cabbage

repostería de la casa cakes and desserts made on the premises

requesón [rekay-son] cream cheese, curd cheese

revuelto de ajos [rebwelto day aHoss] scrambled eggs with garlic

revuelto de ajos tiernos [t-yairnoss] scrambled eggs with spring garlic

revuelto de espárragos trigueros [treegaiross] scrambled eggs with asparagus

revuelto de sesos scrambled eggs with brains

revuelto de setas scrambled eggs with mushrooms

revuelto mixto [meesto] scrambled eggs with mixed vegetables

riñones a la plancha [reen-yoness] grilled kidneys

riñones al jerez [Haireth] kidneys in a sherry sauce

rodaballo [rodaba-yo] turbot

rodaballo al cava [kaba] turbot with champagne

romero [romairo] rosemary

romesco de pescado mixed fish

roscas sweet pastries

rosquillas [roskee-yass] small sweet pastries

rovellons [robay-yons] mushrooms (Catalan)

sal salt

salchicha sausage

salchichas blancas fried sausages with onions

salchichas de Frankfurt frankfurters

salchichón cured white sausage with pepper

salmón [sal-mon] salmon

salmón ahumado [a-oomado] smoked salmon

salmonetes [sal-monaytess] red mullet

salmonetes en papillote [papee-yotay] red mullet cooked in foil

salmón frío [sal-mon free-o] cold salmon

salmorejo [salmoray-Ho] thick sauce made from bread, tomatoes, olive oil, vinegar, green pepper and garlic, served cold with hard-boiled eggs and ham

salpicón de mariscos shellfish with vinaigrette dressing

salsa sauce

salsa ali oli/all-i-oli [alee-**o**lee] garlic mayonnaise

salsa bechamel béchamel sauce, white sauce

salsa de tomate [to**ma**tay] tomato sauce

salsa holandesa [oland**ay**sa] hollandaise sauce – hot sauce made with eggs and butter

salsa mayonesa [ma-yon**ay**sa] mayonnaise

salsa romesco sauce made from peppers, tomatoes and garlic

salsa tártara tartare sauce

salsa vinagreta [beenagra**y**ta] vinaigrette dressing

salteado [saltay-**a**do] sautéed

sandía [sand**ee**-a] water melon

sandwich mixto [m**ee**sto] cheese and ham sandwich

sangre de cerdo [**sa**ngray day th**ai**rdo] pigs' blood

sardina sardine

sardinas a la asturiana [astoor-**ya**na] sardines in cider sauce

sardinas a la brasa barbecued sardines

sardinas a la parrilla [parr**ee**-ya] grilled sardines

sardinas fritas fried sardines

segundo plato main course

sesos brains

sesos a la romana brains in batter

sesos rebozados [reboth**a**doss] brains in batter

setas a la bordalesa [bordal**ay**sa] mushrooms cooked in red wine and onions

setas a la plancha grilled mushrooms

setas rellenas [ray-y**ay**nass] stuffed mushrooms

sobrasada soft red sausage with cayenne pepper

soldados de Pavia [pab**ee**-a] fillets of cod, marinaded and fried

solomillo al vino [solom**ee**-yo al b**ee**no] fillet steak with red wine

solomillo con guisantes [gees**a**ntess] fillet steak with peas

solomillo con patatas fritas fillet steak with chips/French fries

solomillo de cerdo [th**ai**rdo] fillet of pork

solomillo de ternera [tair**na**ira] fillet of veal

solomillo de vaca [**ba**ka] fillet of beef

solomillo frío [**free**-o] cold roast beef

solomillo Roquefort [rokayf**or**] fillet steak with Roquefort cheese

sopa soup

sopa al cuarto de hora [kw**a**rto

day **o**ra] soup made from
ham, veal, chicken, almonds,
vegetables and eggs
sopa castellana [kastay-y**a**na]
vegetable soup
sopa de ajo [day a**HO**] bread
and garlic soup
sopa de almendras almond-
based pudding
sopa de calducho clear soup
sopa de cola de buey [boo-**ay**]
oxtail soup
sopa de fideos [feed**ay**-oss]
noodle soup
sopa de frutos de mar
shellfish soup
sopa de gallina [ga-y**ee**na]
chicken soup
sopa del día soup of the day
sopa de legumbres
[leg**oo**mbress] vegetable soup
sopa de lentejas [lent**ay**-Hass]
lentil soup
sopa de marisco fish and
shellfish soup
sopa de pescado fish soup
sopa de rabo oxtail soup
sopa de rabo de buey [boo-**ay**]
oxtail soup
sopa de tortuga [tort**oo**ga]
turtle soup
sopa mallorquina [ma-york**ee**na]
soup with tomatoes, meat
and eggs
sopa sevillana [sebee-y**a**na] fish
and mayonnaise soup
sorbete [sorb**ay**tay] sorbet
soufflé de fresones [fres**o**ness]
strawberry soufflé

suplemento de verduras extra
vegetables
supremas de rodaballo
[soopr**ay**mass day rodab**a**-yo] fish
slices

tallarines [ta-yar**ee**ness] noodles
tallarines a la italiana [eetal-
y**a**na] tagliatelle
tapa de ternera rellena
[tairn**ai**ra ray-y**ay**na] stuffed veal
hock
tapas appetizers
tarta cake
tarta Alaska baked alaska
tarta de almendra almond tart
or gâteau
tarta de arroz [arr**oth**] cake or
tart containing rice
tarta de la casa tart or gâteau
baked on the premises
tarta helada [el**a**da] ice cream
gâteau
tarta moca mocha tart
tartar crudo raw minced steak,
steak tartare
tejos de queso [t**ay**-Hoss day
k**ay**so] cheese pastries
tencas tench
tencas con jamón [Ham**on**]
tench with ham
ternera [tairn**ai**ra] veal
ternera asada roast veal
tigres [t**ee**gress] mussels in
cayenne sauce
tocinillo de cielo [totheen**ee**-yo
day th-y**ay**lo] rich, thick crème
caramel
todo incluido all inclusive

tomate [tomatay] tomato

tomates rellenos [tomatess ray-yaynoss] stuffed tomatoes

tomatics a es forn baked tomatoes

tomillo [tomee-yo] thyme

tordo thrush

tordos braseados [brassay-adoss] grilled thrushes

tordos estofados braised thrushes

torrijas [torree-Hass] sweet pastries

torta de chicharrones [cheecharroness] pie filled with assorted cooked and cured meats

torta de sardinas sardine pie

tortilla [tortee-ya] omelette

tortilla a la paisana [pa-eesana] omelette containing a variety of vegetables

tortilla aliada [al-yada] omelette with mixed vegetables

tortilla al ron omlette with rum

tortilla a su gusto omlette made as the customer wishes

tortilla de bonito tuna fish omlette

tortilla de champiñones [champeen-yoness] mushroom omelette

tortilla de chorizo [choreetho] spicy sausage omelette

tortilla de escabeche [eskabechay] fish omelette

tortilla de espárragos asparagus omelette

tortilla de gambas prawn omelette

tortilla de jamón [Hamon] ham omelette

tortilla de morcilla [morthee-ya] black pudding omelette

tortilla de patata potato omelette

tortilla de sesos brains omelette

tortilla de setas mushroom omelette

tortilla española [espan-yola] (cold slice of) Spanish omelette with potato, onion and garlic

tortilla francesa [franthaysa] plain omelette

tortilla granadina omelette with artichokes, asparagus, brains and peppers

tortilla sacromonte [sakromontay] vegetable, brains and sausage omelette

tortillas variadas [bar-yadass] assorted omelettes

tostada toast

tostón sucking pig

tostón asado roast sucking pig

tournedó fillet steak

tournedó a la salsa foie [fwa] fillet steak in pâté sauce

trucha [troocha] trout

trucha ahumada [a-oomada] smoked trout

trucha con jamón [Hamon] trout with ham

trucha escabechada

marinated trout

truchas a la marinera
[mareenaira] trout in white
wine sauce

truchas molinera [moleenaira]
trout meunière – trout
coated in flour, fried and
served with butter, lemon
juice and parsley

trufas truffles (edible fungus)

trufas al jerez [Haireth] truffles
in sherry

turbante de arroz [toorbantay day
arroth] rice served with steak,
sausage, peppers and bacon

turrón [toorron] nougat

turrón de coco coconut
nougat

turrón de Alicante [aleekantay]
hard nougat

turrón de yema [yayma] nougat
with egg yolk

turrón de Jijona [HeeHona] soft
nougat

txangurro [changoorro] spider
crab cooked in its shell

uvas [oobass] grapes

vaca estofada [baka] stewed
beef

verduras [bairdoorass]
vegetables

vieiras [bee-ay-eerass] scallops

vinagre [beenagray] vinegar

xoric amb patates [soreek am
patatess] tern with potatoes
(type of swallow)

yogur [yo-goor] yoghurt

zanahoria [thana-or-ya] carrot

zanahorias a la crema [krayma]
carrots à la crème

zarzuela de mariscos
[tharthwayla day mareeskoss]
shellfish stew

**zarzuela de pescados y
mariscos** fish and shellfish
stew

Menu Reader: Drink

Essential Terms

beer la cerveza [thairb**ay**tha]
bottle la botella [bot**ay**-ya]
brandy el coñac [kon-yak]
coffee el café [kaf**ay**]
cup la taza [**ta**tha]
a cup of ... una taza de ...
gin la ginebra [Heen**ay**bra]
gin and tonic un gintónic [Heent**o**neek]
glass (wine glass) la copa
a glass of ... un vaso de [**ba**so day]
milk la leche [**le**chay]
mineral water el agua mineral [**a**gwa meen**ai**ral]
orange juice (fresh) el zumo de naranja [th**oo**mo day naran**Ha**]
port el Oporto
red wine el vino tinto [**bee**no t**ee**nto]
rosé el vino rosado [**bee**no]
soda (water) la soda [s**o**da]
soft drink el refresco
sugar el azúcar [ath**oo**kar]
tea el té [tay]
tonic (water) la tónica [t**o**nica]
vodka el vodka [b**o**dka]
water el agua [**a**gwa]
whisky el whisky
white wine el vino blanco [**bee**no]
wine el vino [**bee**no]
wine list la lista de vinos [**lee**sta day b**ee**noss]

another ..., please otro/otra ..., por favor [fab**o**r]

agua [**a**g-wa] water

agua mineral [meen**ai**ral] mineral water

agua mineral con gas fizzy mineral water

agua mineral sin gas [seen] still mineral water

agua potable [pot**a**blay] drinking water

Alella [al**ay**-ya] region near Barcelona producing red, white and rosé wines

Alicante [aleek**a**ntay] region in the south producing red and rosé wines matured in oak casks

Ampurdán region at the foot of the Pyrenees which produces rosé wine

anís [an**ee**ss] aniseed-flavoured alcoholic drink

año vintage

aperitivo aperitif

batido milkshake

batido de chocolate [day chok**o**latay] chocolate milkshake

batido de fresa [fr**ay**sa] strawberry milkshake

batido de frutas fruit milkshake

batido de plátano banana milkshake

batido de vainilla [ba-een**ee**-ya] vanilla milkshake

bebida drink

bebidas alcohólicas alcoholic drinks

bebidas refrescantes soft drinks

cacao [kak**ow**] cocoa

café con leche [l**e**chay] coffee with milk (large cup)

café cortado coffee with milk (small cup)

café descafeinado [deskafay-een**a**do] decaffeinated coffee

café escocés [eskoth**a**yss] black coffee, whisky and vanilla ice cream

café instantáneo [eenstant**a**nay-o] instant coffee

café irlandés [eerland**a**yss] black coffee, whisky, vanilla ice cream and whipped cream

café solo black coffee

café vienés [b-yen**a**yss] black coffee and whipped cream

caña (cerveza) [kan-ya thairb**ay**-tha] 250cc of draught beer

carajillo [karaH**ee**-yo] black coffee with brandy

carajillo de ron black coffee with rum

carajillo de vodka black coffee with vodka

Cariñena [kareen-y**ay**na] region in the north producing red and rosé wines

carta de vinos [day b**ee**noss] wine list

Cava [k**a**ba] Spanish champagne

cerveza [thairb**ay**-tha] beer, lager

227

cerveza de barril draught beer

Chacolí fruity white wine produced in the Basque Country

champán [champan] champagne

champaña [champan-ya] champagne

chato glass of red wine

Cheste [chestay] region to the west of Valencia producing dry and sweet white wines

chiquito [cheekeeto] glass of red wine

chocolate caliente [chokolatay kal-yentay] hot chocolate

Cigales [theegaless] region in Valladolid producing light rosé wines

clara shandy

cóctel cocktail

Conca de Barbera [barbaira] region in Catalonia producing red and white wines

Condado de Huelva [welba] region in the south producing dry, mellow and sweet white wines

con gas fizzy, sparkling

coñac [kon-yak] brandy

corto (de cerveza) [thairbay-tha] 125cc of draught beer (1/2 caña)

cosecha vintage

cosechero [kosechairo] red wine of the last vintage

cubalibre [koobaleebray] rum and cola

cubata a spirit with a soft drink of lemon or cola

cubito de hielo [yaylo] ice cube

cucaracha [kookaracha] tequila and coffee-flavoured strong alcoholic drink

destornillador [destornee-yador] vodka and orange juice

espumoso sparkling

gaseosa [gasay-osa] lemonade

ginebra [Heenay-bra] gin

granizada/granizado [graneethada] crushed ice drink

hielo [yaylo] ice

horchata (de chufas) [orchata day] milk drink flavoured with tiger nuts

infusión [eenfooss-yon] herb tea

jarra de vino [Harra day beeno] jug of wine

jerez [Haireth] sherry

jerez amontillado [amontee-yado] pale dry sherry

jerez fino pale light sherry

jerez oloroso sweet sherry

jugo [Hoogo] juice

jugo de albaricoque [day albareekokay] apricot juice

jugo de lima [leema] lime juice

jugo de limón lemon juice

jugo de melocotón peach juice

jugo de naranja [naran-Ha] orange juice

jugo de piña [peen-ya]
pineapple juice
jugo de tomate [tomatay]
tomato juice
Jumilla [Hoomee-ya] region in
the south producing dry,
light red wines and sweet
white wines

kirsch strong alcoholic drink
made from cherries

leche [lechay] milk
licor liqueur
licor de avellana [day abay-yana]
hazelnut-flavoured liqueur
licor de manzana [manthana]
apple-flavoured liqueur
licor de melocotón peach-
flavoured liqueur
licor de melón melon-
flavoured liqueur
licor de naranja [naran-Ha]
orange-flavoured liqueur
limonada lemonade
lista de precios [prayth-yoss]
price list

Málaga region on the south
coast producing sweet and
dry white wines
Mancha region of the interior
producing mainly white, but
also red wines
manzanilla [manthanee-ya] dry
sherry-type wine; camomile
tea
media de agua [mayd-ya day
ag-wa] half-bottle of mineral

water
menta poleo [polay-o] mint tea
Mentrida central region
producing dark-coloured red
wines
Montilla-Moriles [montee-ya-
moreeless] region in Andalusia
producing sherry-like white
wines
mosto grape juice

Oporto port
orujo [orooHo] colourless,
strong alcoholic drink made
from wine
orujo de miel [m-yayl] orujo
with honey

pacharán strong alcoholic
drink made from sloes
Penedés [penedayss] region
in Catalonia producing in
particular sparkling white
wines
Priorato [pree-orato] wine-
growing region near
Tarragona

refresco soft drink
reserva especial quality wine
matured in casks
Ribeiro [reebay-eero] region in
Galicia producing slightly
sparkling red and white
wines; type of white wine
Rioja [r-yoHa] region in the
north producing some of the
finest red and white wines
romeral wine

229

ron rum

sangría [sangree-a] mixture of red wine, lemonade, spirits and fruit

seco dry

semidulce [say-mee-doolthay] medium-sweet

sidra cider

sin gas [seen] still

sol y sombra [ee] brandy and anís

Tarragona region on the Mediterranean coast producing red and white wines

té [tay] tea

Tierra Alta [t-yairra] region in the province of Tarragona producing red and white wines

tila [teela] lime tea

tinto de Toro [teento] dry, red wine from Zamora

tónica tonic

tónica con ginebra [Heenebra] gin and tonic

Utiel-Requena [oot-yeel-rekayna] region in Valencia producing mild red and rosé wines

Valdeorras [balday-orrass] region in Galicia producing red and white wines

Valdepeñas [balday-payn-yass] central region producing pale and dark, fruity red wines;

type of fruity red wine

Valencia [balenth-ya] region on the Mediterranean producing red and white wines

Valle de Monterrey [ba-yay day montairray] region in Galicia producing full-bodied red and white wines

vino [beeno] wine

vino blanco white wine

vino de aguja [day agooHa] slightly sparkling rosé and white wines

vino de jerez [Haireth] sherry

vino del país [pa-eess] local wine

vino de mesa [maysa] table wine

vino rosado rosé wine

vino tinto red wine

viñedo vineyard

Yecla region in the south producing smooth red and light rosé wines

zumo [thoomo] fruit juice

zumo de albaricoque [day albareekokay] apricot juice

zumo de lima [leema] lime juice

zumo de limón lemon juice

zumo de melocotón peach juice

zumo de naranja [naranHa] orange juice

zumo de piña [peen-ya] pineapple juice

zumo de tomate [tomatay]

tomato juice

zurito [thoo**ree**to] 125 cc of draught beer (1/2 caña)

zurracapote [thoorrakap**o**tay] wine with sugar and cinammon

How the
Language
Works

Pronunciation

In this phrasebook, the Spanish has been written in a system of imitated pronunciation so that it can be read as though it were English, bearing in mind the notes on pronunciation given below:

air   as in h**air**
ay   as in m**ay**
e   as in g**e**t
g   always hard as in **g**oat
H   a harsh 'ch' as in the Scottish way of pronouncing lo**ch**
ī   as the 'i' sound in m**i**ght
ow   as in n**ow**
y   as in **y**es

Letters given in bold type indicate the part of the word to be stressed.

As i and u are always pronounced 'ee' and 'oo' in Spanish, pronunciation has not been given for all words containing these letters unless they present other problems for the learner. Thus María is pronounced 'mar**ee**-a' and fútbol is 'f**oo**tbol'.

Abbreviations

adj	adjective	pl	plural
f	feminine	pol	polite
fam	familiar	sing	singular
m	masculine		

Note

In the Spanish-English section and Menu Reader, the letter ñ is treated as a separate letter, as is customary in Spanish. Alphabetically, it comes after n.

An asterisk (★) next to a word in the English-Spanish section means that you should refer to the **How the Language Works** section or conversion tables for further information.

Nouns

All nouns in Spanish have one of two genders: masculine or feminine. Generally speaking, those ending in **-o** are masculine:

> **el zapato**
> el thap**a**to
> the shoe

Those ending in **-a**, **-d**, **-z** or **-ión** are usually feminine:

> **la cama**   **la pensión**
> la k**a**ma   la pens-**yo**n
> the bed   the boarding house

A small number of nouns ending in **-o** and **-a** (usually professions) can be either masculine or feminine:

> **el/la guía**   **el/la médico**
> el/la g**ee**-a   el/la **may**deeko
> the tourist guide   the doctor

Plural Nouns

If the noun ends in a vowel, the plural is formed by adding **-s**:

> **el camino**   **los caminos**
> el kam**ee**no   loss kam**ee**noss
> the path   the paths

> **la camarera**   **las camareras**
> la kamar**ai**ra   lass kamar**ai**rass
> the waitress   the waitresses

If the noun ends in a consonant, the plural is formed by adding **-es**:

el conductor	**los conductores**
el kondook**t**or	loss kondookt**or**ess
the driver	the drivers

la recepción	**las recepciones**
la rethepth-y**o**n	lass retheph-y**o**ness
the reception desk	the reception desks

If the noun ends in a **-z**, change the **-z** to **-ces** to form the plural:

el andaluz	**los andaluces**
el andal**oo**th	loss andal**oo**thess
the Andalusian	the Andalusians

Articles

There are different words for articles ('the' and 'a') in Spanish depending on the number (singular or plural) and gender of the noun. The definite article 'the' is as follows:

	singular	plural
masculine	**el**	**los**
feminine	**la**	**las**

el cuchillo/los cuchillos	**la piscina/las piscinas**
el koochee-yo/loss koochee-yoss	la peestheena/lass peestheenass
the knife/the knives	the swimming pool/
	the swimming pools

When the article **el** is used in combination with **a** (to) or **de** (of) it changes as follows:

a + el = al
de + el = del

vamos al museo	**cerca del hotel**
bamoss al moos**ay**-o	th**ai**rka del ot**e**l
let's go to the museum	near the hotel

Plural Articles

The indefinite article (a, an, some) also changes according to the gender and number of the accompanying noun:

	singular	plural
masculine	**un**	**unos**
	oon	**oo**noss
feminine	**una**	**unas**
	oona	**oo**nass

un sello	**unos sellos**
oon **say**-yo	**oo**noss **say**-yoss
a stamp	some stamps

una chica	**unas chicas**
oona **chee**ka	**oo**nass **chee**kass
a girl	some girls

Adjectives and Adverbs

Adjectives must agree in gender and number with the noun they refer to. In the English-Spanish section of this book, all adjectives are given in the masculine singular. Adjectives ending in -o change as follows for the plural:

el precio alto	**los precios altos**
el **preth**-yo **a**lto	loss **preth**-yoss **a**ltoss
the high price	the high prices

The feminine singular of the adjective is formed by changing the masculine endings as follows:

masculine	feminine
-o	-a
-or	-ora
-és	-esa

un cocinero estupendo
oon kotheen**ai**ro estoop**e**ndo
a wonderful cook

una cocinera estupenda
oona kotheen**ai**ra estoop**e**nda
a wonderful cook

un señor encantador
oon sen-y**o**r enkantad**o**r
a nice man

una señora encantadora
oona sen-y**o**ra enkantad**o**ra
a nice woman

un chico inglés
oon ch**ee**ko eengl**ay**ss
an English boy

una chica inglesa
oona ch**ee**ka eengl**ay**sa
an English girl

For other types of adjective, the feminine forms are the same as the masculine:

un hombre agradable
oon h**o**mbray agrad**a**blay
a nice man

una mujer agradable
oona mooH**ai**r agrad**a**blay
a nice woman

Unlike English, Spanish adjectives usually follow the noun.

The plurals of adjectives are formed in the same way as the plurals of nouns, by adding an **-s**:

una tumbona roja
oona toomb**o**na r**o**Ha
a red deckchair

dos tumbonas rojas
doss toomb**o**nass r**o**Hass
two red deckchairs

Comparatives

The comparative is formed by placing **más** (more) or **menos** (less) before the adjective or adverb and **que** (than) after it:

bonito
bon**ee**to
beautiful

más bonito
mass bon**ee**to
more beautiful

tranquilo
trank**ee**lo
quiet

menos tranquilo
m**ay**noss trank**ee**lo
less quiet

este hotel es más/menos caro que el otro
estay otel es mass/maynoss karo kay el otro
this hotel is more/less expensive than the other one

¿tiene una habitación más soleada?
t-yaynay oona abeetath-yon mass solay-ada
do you have a sunnier room?

¿podría conducir más deprisa, por favor?
podree-a kondootheer mass depreesa por fabor
could you drive faster please?

Superlatives

Superlatives are formed by placing one of the following before the adjective: **el más, la más, los más** or **las más** (depending on the noun's gender and number):

¿cuál es el más divertido?
kwal ess el mass deebairteedo
which is the most entertaining?

el día más caluroso   **el coche más rápido**
el dee-a mass kalooroso   el kochay mass rapido
the hottest day   the fastest car

The following adjectives have irregular comparatives and superlatives:

bueno	mejor	el mejor
bwayno	meHor	el meHor
good	better	the best

grande	mayor	el mayor
granday	mī-or	el mī-or
big	bigger	the biggest
	older	the oldest

malo	peor	el peor
malo	pay-or	el pay-or
bad	worse	the worst

pequeño	menor	el menor
pek**en**-yo	men**or**	el men**or**
small	younger	the youngest

Note that **más pequeño** means 'smaller'.

As ... as ... is translated as follows:

Madrid está tan bonita como siempre!
madr**ee**ta esta tan bon**ee**ta k**o**mo s-y**e**mpray
Madrid is as beautiful as ever!

The superlative form ending in **-ísimo** indicates that something is 'very/extremely ... ' without actually comparing it to something else:

guapo	guapísimo
gw**a**po	gwap**i**simo
attractive	very attractive

Adverbs

There are two ways to form an adverb. If the adjective ends in **-o**, take the feminine and add **-mente** to form the corresponding adverb:

exacto	exactamente
es**a**kto	esaktam**e**nte
accurate	accurately

If the adjective ends in any other letter, add **-mente** to the basic form:

feliz	felizmente
fel**ee**th	feleethm**e**ntay
happy	happily

Possessive Adjectives

Possessive adjectives, like other Spanish adjectives, agree with the noun in gender and number:

| | singular | | plural | |
	masc	fem	masc	fem
my	**mi**	**mi**	**mis**	**mis**
	mee	mee	meess	meess
your (sing, fam)	**tu**	**tu**	**tus**	**tus**
	too	too	tooss	tooss
his/her/its/your (sing, pol)	**su**	**su**	**sus**	**sus**
	soo	soo	sooss	sooss
our	**nuestro**	**nuestra**	**nuestros**	**nuestras**
	nwestro	nwestra	nwestross	nwestrass
your (pl, fam)	**vuestro**	**vuestra**	**vuestros**	**vuestras**
	bwestro	bwestra	bwestross	bwestrass
their/your (pl, pol)	**su**	**su**	**sus**	**sus**
	soo	soo	sooss	sooss

tu bolsa	**sus pastillas**
too bolsa	sooss pastee-yass
your bag	his/her/your tablets

vuestra maleta	**nuestros trajes de baño**
bwestra malayta	nwestross traHess day ban-yo
your suitcase	our swimming costumes

If when using **su/sus**, it is unclear whether you mean 'his', 'her', 'your' or 'their', you can use the following after the noun instead:

de él	day el	his
de ella	day ay-ya	her
de Usted	day oostay	your (sing, pol)
de ellos	day ay-yoss	their (masculine)
de ellas	day ay-yass	their (feminine)
de Ustedes	day oostaydess	your (pl, pol)

el dinero de usted	**el dinero de ella**	**el dinero de él**
el deenairo day oostay	el deenairo day ay-ya	el deenairo day el
your money	her money	his money

Possessive Pronouns

To translate 'mine', 'yours' 'theirs' etc, use one of the following forms. Like possessive adjectives, possessive pronouns must agree in gender and number with the object or objects referred to:

	singular		plural	
	masculine	feminine	masculine	feminine
mine	**el mío**	**la mía**	**los míos**	**las mías**
	el **mee**-o	la **mee**-a	los **mee**-oss	las **mee**-ass
yours (sing, fam)	**el tuyo**	**la tuya**	**los tuyos**	**las tuyas**
	el **too**-yo	la **too**-ya	loss **too**-yoss	lass **too**-yass
his/hers	**el suyo**	**la suya**	**los suyos**	**las suyas**
	el **soo**-yo	la **soo**-ya	loss **soo**-yoss	lass **soo**-yass
yours (sing, pol)	**el suyo**	**la suya**	**los suyos**	**las suyas**
	el **soo**-yo	la **soo**-ya	loss **soo**-yoss	lass **soo**-yass
ours	**el nuestro**	**la nuestra**	**los nuestros**	**las nuestras**
	el **nwestro**	la **nwestra**	loss **nwestross**	lass **nwestrass**
yours (pl, fam)	**el vuestro**	**la vuestra**	**los vuestros**	**las vuestras**
	el **bwestro**	la **bwestra**	loss **bwestross**	lass **bwestrass**
theirs	**el suyo**	**la suya**	**los suyos**	**las suyas**
	el **soo**-yo	la **soo**-ya	loss **soo**-yoss	lass **soo**-yass
yours (pl, pol)	**el suyo**	**la suya**	**los suyos**	**las suyas**
	el **soo**-yo	la **soo**-ya	loss **soo**-yoss	lass **soo**-yass

ésta es su llave y ésta la mía
esta ess soo ya**bay** ee **e**sta la **mee**-a
this is your key and this is mine

no es la suya, es de sus amigos
no ess la **soo**-ya ess day sooss ame**ee**goss
it's not his, it's his friends'

Personal Pronouns

Subject Pronouns

yo	yo	I
tú	too	you (sing, fam)
él	el	he/it
ella	**ay**-ya	she/it
ello	**ay**-yo	it
usted	oos**tay**	you (sing, pol)
nosotros	nos**o**tross	we (masculine)
nosotras	nos**o**trass	we (feminine)
vosotros	bos**o**tross	you (pl, fam, masculine)
vosotras	bos**o**trass	you (pl, fam, feminine)
ellos	**ay**-yoss	they (masculine)
ellas	**ay**-yass	they (feminine)
ustedes	oos**tay**dess	you (pl, pol)

Tú is used when speaking to one person and is the familiar form generally used when speaking to family, friends and children. **Vosotros/vosotras** is the plural form of **tú**.

Usted and **Ustedes** are the polite forms of address to be used when talking to someone you don't know. They take the third person forms of verbs: **Usted** takes the same form as 'he/she/it'; **Ustedes** takes the same form as 'they'.

In Spanish the subject pronoun is usually omitted:

no saben	está cansado
no s**a**ben	est**a** kans**a**do
they don't know	he is tired

although it may be retained for emphasis or to avoid confusion:

¡soy yo!	¡somos nosotros!
soy yo	s**o**moss nos**o**tross
it's me!	it's us!

yo pagaré los bocadillos, tú pagas las cervezas
yo pagar**ay** loss bokad**ee**-yoss too pa**g**ass lass thairb**ay**thass
I'll pay for the sandwiches, you pay for the beers

él es inglés y ella es americana
el ess eengl**ay**ss ee **ay**-ya ess amaireek**a**na
he's English and she's American

The pronouns as listed above are also used after prepositions:

para usted	**con él**
p**a**ra oost**ay**	kon el
for you	with him
sin ella	**después de usted**
seen **ay**-ya	despw**ay**ss day oost**ay**
without her	after you

The exceptions are **yo**, which is replaced by **mí**, and **tú** which is replaced by **ti**:

eso es para mí/ti
eso es p**a**ra mee/tee
that's for me/you

After **con** (with) **mí** and **ti** change as follows:

conmigo/contigo
konm**ee**go/kont**ee**go
with me/you

Object Pronouns

me	[may]	me
te	[tay]	you (sing, fam)
le	[lay]	him, you (pl, pol)
lo	[lo]	it
la	[la]	her/it, you (sing, pol)
nos	[noss]	us
os	[oss]	you (pl, fam)
les/los	[less/loss]	them, you (pl, pol, masculine)
las	[lass]	them, you (pl, pol, feminine)

Object pronouns generally precede the verb:

me la dio ayer	**las compré para ella**
may la d**ee**-o a-y**air**	lass k**o**mpray p**a**ra **ay**-ya
she gave it to me yesterday	I bought them for her

When used with infinitives, pronouns are added to the end of the infinitive:

¿puede llevarme al aeropuerto?
pw**ay**day yeb**a**rmay al airopw**air**to
can you take me to the airport?

intentaré recordarlo
eententar**ay** rekord**a**rlo
I'll try and remember it

When used with commands, pronouns are added to the end of the imperative form. See **Imperative** page 259.

If you are using an indirect pronoun to mean 'to me', 'to you' etc (although 'to' might not always be necessarily said in English), you generally use the following:

me	[may]	to me
te	[tay]	to you (sing, fam)
le	[lay]	to him/to her, to you (sing, pol)
nos	[noss]	to us
os	[oss]	to you (pl, fam)
les	[less]	to them, to you (pl, pol)

le compré flores	**le pedí su dirección**
lay k**o**mpray fl**o**ress	lay ped**ee** soo deerekth-y**o**n
I bought flowers for her	I asked him for his address

Reflexive Pronouns

These are used with reflexive verbs like **lavarse** 'to wash (one-self)', that is where the subject and the object are one and the same person:

me	[may]	myself (used with I)
te	[tay]	yourself (used with singular, familiar 'you')
se	[say]	him/her/itself (used with singular, polite 'you')
nos	[noss]	ourselves (used with 'we')
os	[oss]	yourselves (used with plural, familiar 'you')
se	[say]	themselves (used with 'they' and plural, polite 'you')

presentarse to introduce oneself
me presento: me llamo Richard
may pres**en**to: may y**a**mo Richard
may I introduce myself? my name's Richard

divertirse to enjoy oneself
nos divertimos mucho en la fiesta
noss deebair**tee**moss **moo**cho en la f-y**e**sta
we enjoyed ourselves a lot at the party

Demonstratives

The English demonstrative adjective 'this' is translated by the Spanish **este**. 'That' is translated by **ese** and 'that (over there/further away)' is translated by **aquel**.

Ese refers to something near to the person being spoken to. **Aquel** refers to something further away.

Like other adjectives, they agree with the noun they qualify in gender and number but they come in front of the noun. Their forms are:

masculine singular			feminine singular		
este	ese	aquel	esta	esa	aquella
estay	**ay**say	ak**el**	**e**sta	**ay**sa	ak**ay**-ya

masculine plural			feminine plural		
estos	esos	aquellos	estas	esas	aquellas
estoss	**ay**soss	ak**ay**-yoss	**e**stass	**ay**sass	ak**ay**-yass

este restaurante	ese camarero	aquella playa
estay restow**ra**ntay	**ay**say kamar**ai**ro	a**kay**-ya pl**a**-ya
this restaurant	that waiter	that beach (in the distance)

'This one', 'that one', 'those', 'these' etc (as pronouns) are translated by the same words as above only they are spelt with an **é**:

éste	ése	aquél
estay	**ay**say	ak**el**
this one	that one	that one (over there)

quisiera éstos/ésos/aquéllos
kees-y**ai**ra **e**stoss/**ay**soss/ak**ay**-yoss
I'd like these/those/those (over there)

The neuter forms **esto/eso/aquello** are used when no particular noun is being referred to:

esto	eso	aquello
esto	**ay**so	ak**ay**-yo

eso no es justo	¿qué es esto?
ayso no ess H**oo**sto	kay ess **e**sto
that's not fair	what is this?

Verbs

The basic form of the verb given in the English-Spanish and Spanish-English sections is the infinitive (e.g. to drive, to go etc). There are three verb types in Spanish which can be recognized by their infinitive endings: **-ar**, **-er**, **-ir**. For example:

hablar	[ablar]	to talk
comer	[komair]	to eat
abrir	[abrir]	to open

Present Tense

The present tense corresponds to 'I leave' and 'I am leaving' in English. To form the present tense for the three main types of verb in Spanish, remove the **-ar**, **-er** or **-ir** and add the following endings:

hablar to speak

habl-o	[**abl**o]	I speak
habl-as	[**abl**ass]	you speak (sing, fam)
habl-a	[**abl**a]	he/she speaks, you speak (sing, pol)
habl-amos	[abl**a**moss]	we speak
habl-áis	[abla-**ee**ss]	you speak (pl, fam)
habl-an	[**abl**an]	they speak, you speak (pl, pol)

comer to eat

com-o	[**ko**mo]	I eat
com-es	[**ko**mess]	you eat (sing, fam)
com-e	[**ko**may]	he/she eats, you eat (sing, pol)
com-emos	[kom**ay**moss]	we eat
com-éis	[kom**ay**-eess]	you eat (pl, fam)
com-en	[**ko**men]	they eat, you eat (pl, pol)

abrir to open

abr-o	[**abr**o]	I open
abr-es	[**abr**ess]	you open (sing, fam)
abr-e	[**abr**ay]	he/she opens, you open (sing, pol)
abr-imos	[abr**ee**moss]	we open
abr-ís	[abr**ee**ss]	you open (pl, fam)
abr-en	[**abr**en]	they open, you open (pl, pol)

Some common verbs are irregular:

haber to have

he	[ay]	I have
has	[ass]	you have (sing, fam)
ha	[a]	he/she/it has, you have (sing, pol)

hemos	[**ay**moss]	we have
habéis	[ab**ay**-eess]	you have (pl, fam)
han	[an]	they have, you have (pl, pol)

tener to have		**venir** to come	
tengo	[tengo]	vengo	[bengo]
tienes	[t-**yay**ness]	vienes	[b-**yay**ness]
tiene	[t-**yay**nay]	viene	[b-**yay**nay]
tenemos	[ten**ay**moss]	venimos	[ben**ee**moss]
tenéis	[ten**ay**-eess]	venís	[ben**ee**ss]
tienen	[t-**yay**nen]	vienen	[b-**yay**nen]

ir to go		**dar** to give	
voy	[boy]	doy	[doy]
vas	[bass]	das	[dass]
va	[ba]	da	[da]
vamos	[**ba**moss]	damos	[**da**moss]
vais	[ba-eess]	dais	[da-eess]
van	[ban]	dan	[dan]

poder to be able		**querer** to want	
puedo	[**pway**do]	quiero	[k-**yai**ro]
puedes	[**pway**dess]	quieres	[k-**yai**ress]
puede	[**pway**day]	quiere	[k-**yai**ray]
podemos	[pod**ay**mos]	queremos	[kair**ay**moss]
podéis	[pod**ay**-eess]	queréis	[kair**ay**-eess]
pueden	[**pway**den]	quieren	[k-**yai**ren]

The first person singular (the 'I' form) of the following verbs is irregular:

decir to say	digo	[**dee**go]
hacer to do, to make	hago	[**a**-go]
poner to put	pongo	[**pon**go]
saber to know	sé	[say]
salir to go out	salgo	[**sal**go]

See pages 256-257 for the present tense of the verbs **ser** and **estar** 'to be'.

Past Tense:

Perfect Tense

The perfect tense is used to express an action that has taken place in the past. It is formed with the present tense of **haber** (see page 249) and the past participle of the verb.

To form the past participles, make the following changes to the infinitive forms:

infinitive	past participle	
hablar	hablado	[ablado]
comer	comido	[komeedo]
encendir	encendido	[enthendeedo]

hemos dado una propina
aymoss d**a**do **oo**na prop**ee**na
we have given a tip

hemos comido bien
aymoss kom**ee**do b-yen
we've eaten well,
we've had a good meal

he encendido la luz
ay enthend**ee**do la looth
I (have) put the light on

Some common verbs are irregular in this past tense (including the verb 'abrir' used as a model for other tenses).

hacer to do/make	hecho	[**ay**cho]
abrir to open	abierto	[ab-**yai**rto]
decir to say	dicho	[**dee**cho]
volver to return	vuelto	[**bwel**to]
poner to put	puesto	[**pwes**to]
ver to see	visto	[**bees**to]
satisfacer to satisfy	satisfecho	[sateesf**ech**o]

Past Historic

The Past Historic is used to express what happened or what somebody did at a particular time in the past.

habl-é	[ablay]	I spoke
habl-aste	[ablastay]	you spoke (sing, fam)
habl-ó	[ablo]	he/she spoke, you spoke (sing, pol)
habl-amos	[ablamoss]	we spoke
habl-asteis	[ablastay-eess]	you spoke (pl, fam)
habl-aron	[ablaron]	they spoke, you spoke (pl, pol)

com-í	[komee]	I ate
com-iste	[komeestay]	you ate (sing, fam)
com-ió	[komi-o]	he/she ate, you ate (sing, pol)
com-imos	[komeemoss]	we ate
com-isteis	[komeestay-eess]	you ate (pl, fam)
com-ieron	[kom-yairon]	they ate, you ate (pl, pol)

abr-í	[abree]	I opened
abr-iste	[abreestay]	you opened (sing, fam)
abr-ió	[abri-o]	he/she opened, you opened (sing, pol)
abr-imos	[abreemoss]	we opened
abr-isteis	[abreestay-eess]	you opened (pl, fam)
abr-ieron	[abr-yairon]	they opened, you opened (pl, pol)

¿quién te dijo eso?	nos conocimos en Málaga
k-yen tay deeHo ayso	noss konotheemoss en malaga
who told you that?	we met each other in Málaga

lo compramos el año pasado
lo kompramoss el an-yo pasado
we bought it last year

Imperfect Tense

This tense is used to express what was going on regularly over an indefinite period of time and is sometimes translated by 'used to + infinitive'. It is formed as follows:

hablar to speak

habl-aba	[ablaba]	I was speaking
habl-abas	[ablabass]	you were speaking (sing, fam)
habl-aba	[ablaba]	he/she/it was speaking, you were speaking (sing, pol)
habl-ábamos	[ablabamoss]	we were speaking
habl-abais	[ablaba-eess]	you were speaking (pl, fam)
habl-aban	[ablaban]	they were speaking, you were speaking (pl, polite)

comer to eat

com-ía	[komee-a]	I was eating
com-ías	[komee-ass]	you were eating (sing, fam)
com-ía	[komee-a]	he/she/it was eating, you were eating (sing, pol)
com-íamos	[komee-amoss]	we were eating
com-íais	[komee-a-eess]	you were eating (pl, fam)
com-ían	[komee-an]	they were eating, you were eating (pl, pol)

abrir to open

abr-ía	[abree-a]	I was opening
abr-ías	[abree-ass]	you were opening (sing, fam)
abr-ía	[abree-a]	he/she/it was opening, you were opening (sing, pol)
abr-íamos	[abree-amoss]	we were opening
abr-íais	[abree-a-eess]	you were opening (pl, fam)
abr-ían	[abree-an]	they were opening, you were opening (pl, pol)

Two other useful regular verbs in the imperfect tense are:

tener to have

tenía	[ten**ee**-a]	I had
tenías	[ten**ee**-ass]	you had (sing, fam)
tenía	[ten**ee**-a]	he/she/it had, you had (sing, pol)
teníamos	[ten**ee**-amoss]	we had
teníais	[ten**ee**-a-eess]	you had (pl, fam)
tenían	[ten**ee**-an]	they had, you had (pl, pol)

estar to be

estaba	[est**a**ba]	I was
estabas	[est**a**bass]	you were (sing, fam)
estaba	[est**a**ba]	he/she/it was, you were (sing, pol)
estábamos	[est**a**bamoss]	we were
estabais	[est**a**ba-eess]	you were (pl, fam)
estaban	[est**a**ban]	they were, you were (pl, pol)

The following are irregular in the imperfect tense:

ir to go

iba	[**ee**ba]	I was going
ibas	[**ee**bass]	you were going (sing, fam)
iba	[**ee**ba]	he/she/it was going, you were going (sing, pol)
íbamos	[**ee**bamoss]	we were going
ibais	[**ee**ba-eess]	you were going (pl, fam)
iban	[**ee**ban]	they were going, you were going (pl, pol)

ser to be (see page 256 for more on this)

era	[**ai**ra]	I was
eras	[**ai**rass]	you were (sing, fam)
era	[**ai**ra]	he/she/it was, you were (sing, pol)
éramos	[**ai**ramoss]	we were
erais	[**ai**ra-eess]	you were (pl, fam)
eran	[**ai**ran]	they were, you were (pl, pol)

todos los viernes salíamos a dar un paseo

todos loss b-**ya**irness sal**ee**-amoss a dar oon pass**ay**-o

every Friday we used to go for a walk, every Friday we
    went for a walk

Future Tense

To form the future tense in Spanish (I will do, you will do etc)
add the following endings to the infinitive. The same endings
are used whether verbs end in **-ar**, **-er** or **-ir**:

hablar-**é**	[ablar**ay**]	I will speak
hablar-**ás**	[ablar**ass**]	you will speak
hablar-**á**	[ablar**a**]	he/she/you will speak
hablar-**emos**	[ablar**ay**moss]	we will speak
hablar-**éis**	[ablar**ay**-eess]	you will speak
hablar-**án**	[ablar**an**]	they/you will speak

volveré más tarde

bolbair**ay** mass t**a**rday

I'll come back later

The immediate future can also be translated by **ir** + **a** + infinitive:

vamos a comprar una botella de vino tinto

b**a**moss a komprar **oo**na bot**ay**-ya day b**ee**no t**ee**nto

we're going to buy a bottle of red wine

iré a recogerle

eer**ay** a raykoн**ai**rlay

I'll fetch him, I'll go and fetch him

Sometimes the future tense in Spanish indicates probability:

será verdad

sair**a** bair**da**

it might be true

In Spanish, as in English, the future can sometimes be
expressed by the present tense:

tu avión sale a la una
too aby-**on** s**a**lay a la **oo**na
your plane takes off at one o'clock

However, Spanish often uses the present tense where the future would be used in English:

le doy ochocientas pesetas
lay doy ochoth-y**e**ntass pes**ay**tass
I'll give you 800 pesetas

The following verbs are irregular in the future tense:

decir	to say	diré
		I will say
hacer	to do	haré
poder	to be able	podré
poner	to put	pondré
querer	to want	querré
saber	to know	sabré
salir	to leave	saldré
tener	to have	tendré
venir	to come	vendré

The Verb 'To Be'

There are two verbs 'to be' in Spanish: **ser** and **estar**. The present tense is as follows:

ser

soy	[soy]	I am
eres	[**ai**ress]	you are (sing, fam)
es	[ess]	he/she/it is, you are (sing, pol)
somos	[s**o**moss]	we are
sois	[soyss]	you are (pl, fam)
son	[son]	they are, you are (pl, pol)

estar

estoy	[estoy]	I am
estás	[estass]	you are (sing, fam)
está	[esta]	he/she/it is, you are (sing, pol)
estamos	[estamoss]	we are
estáis	[esta-eess]	you are (pl, fam)
están	[estan]	they are, you are (pl, pol)

Ser

Ser indicates an inherent quality, a permanent state or characteristic, something which is unlikely to change:

la nieve es blanca
la n-yaybay ess blanka
snow is white

Ser is also used with occupations, nationalities, the time and to indicate possession:

somos escoceses
somoss eskothaysess
we are Scottish

mi madre es profesora
mi madray ess profesora
my mum is a teacher

éste es nuestro coche
estay ess nwestro kochay
this is our car

son las cinco de la tarde
son lass theenko day la tarday
it's five o'clock in the afternoon

Estar, on the other hand, is used for temporary qualities, for things which could change:

estoy enfadado contigo
estoy enfadado konteego
I'm angry with you

estoy cansado
estoy kansado
I'm tired

este filete está frío
estay feelaytay esta free-o
this steak is cold

Notice the difference between the following two phrases:

Isabel es muy guapa	Isabel está muy guapa (esta noche)
Isabel ess mwee gwapa	Isabel esta mwee gwapa esta nochay
Isabel is very pretty	Isabel looks very pretty (tonight)

Estar is also used to indicate position and situation:

Barcelona está en Cataluña
barthelona esta en kataloon-ya
Barcelona is in Catalonia

Negatives

To express a negative in Spanish, to say 'I don't want', 'it's not here' etc, place the word **no** in front of the verb:

comprendo	no comprendo
komprendo	no komprendo
I understand	I don't understand

me gusta este helado	no me gusta este helado
may goosta aystay elado	no may goosta aystay elado
I like this ice cream	I don't like this ice cream

lo alquilé aquí	no lo alquilé aquí
lo alkeelay akee	no lo alkeelay akee
I rented it here	I didn't rent it here
van a cantar	no van a cantar
ban a kantar	no ban a kantar
they're going to sing	they're not going to sing

Unlike English, Spanish makes use of double negatives with words like nothing/anything or nobody/anybody:

no hay nadie ahí	no compramos nada
no ī nad-yay a-ee	no kompramoss nada
there's nobody there	we didn't buy anything

no sabemos nada de ella
no sabaymoss nada day **ay**-ya
we don't know anything about her

To say 'there's no …', 'I've no …' etc, make the accompanying verb negative:

no hay vino
no ī **bee**no
there's no wine

no tengo cerillas
no **te**ngo thai**ree**-yass
I've no matches

To say 'not him', 'not her' etc just use the personal pronoun followed by **no**:

nosotros, no
nos**o**tross no
not us

ella, no
ay-ya no
not her

yo, no
yo no
not me

Imperative

When speaking to people using the **Usted** or **Ustedes** forms, you make commands by removing the **-ar**, **-er** or **-ir** from the infinitive and adding these endings:

	singular		plural	
hablar to speak	habl-e	**a**blay	habl-en	**a**blen
comer to eat	com-a	**ko**ma	com-an	**ko**man
abrir to open	abr-a	**a**bra	abr-an	**a**bran

coma despacio
koma desp**a**th-yo
eat slowly

When you are telling someone not to do something, use the forms above and place **no** in front of the verb:

no me moleste, por favor
no may mol**e**stay por fab**o**r
don't disturb me, please

¡no beba alcohol!
no **ba**yba alk**o**hol
don't drink alcohol!

¡no venga esta noche!
no **be**nga **e**sta n**o**chay
don't come tonight

To form the imperative used to give commands to people you would normally address as **tú** and **vosotros**, remove the endings -ar, -er, and -ir from the verb and add these endings:

	tú		vosotros	
hablar (to speak)	**habl-a**	[abla]	**habl-ad**	[ablad]
comer (to eat)	**com-e**	[komay]	**com-ed**	[komayd]
abrir (to open)	**abr-e**	[abray]	**abr-id**	[abreed]

To form a negative imperative to people addressed as **tú** and **vosotros**, no is placed in front of the verb and the endings change:

tú		vosotros	
habla no **habl-es** [no abless]		hablad no **habl-éis** [no ablay-eess]	
come no **com-as** [no komass]		comed no **com-áis** [no koma-eess]	
abre no **abras** [no abrass]		abrid no **abr-áis** [no abra-eess]	

por favor, no hables tan rápido (to one person)
por fabor no abless tan rapeedo
please don't speak so fast

por favor, no habléis tan rápido (to several people)
por fabor no ablay-eess tan rapeedo
please don't speak so fast

Pronouns are added to the end of the imperative form:

despiérteme a las ocho, por favor
desp-yairtemay a lass ocho por fabor
wake me up at eight o'clock, please

bébelo   **ciérralas**
baybelo   th-yairalass
drink it   close them

ayúdeme, por favor
a-yoodemay por fabor
help me please

but when the imperative is negative, they are placed in front of it:

no lo bebas   **no las cierres**
no lo **bay**bass   no lass th-**yai**ress
don't drink it   don't close them

Questions

Often the word order remains the same in a question, but the intonation changes, the voice rising at the end of the question:

quiero bailar   **¿no quieres bailar?**
k-**yai**ro ba-eelar   no k-**yai**ress ba-eelar
I want to dance   don't you want to dance?

Dates

Use the numbers on pages 263-264 to express the date. In formal Spanish, the ordinal number may be used for 'the first', but not for other dates:

el uno/el primero de septiembre [**oo**no/el preema**i**ro day sept-**yem**bray] the first of September

el dos de diciembre [doss day deeth-**yem**bray] the second of December

el treinta de mayo [tray-**ee**nta day ma-yo] the thirtieth of May

el treinta y uno de mayo [tray-**ee**nti **oo**no day ma-yo] the thirty-first of May

Days

Sunday domingo
Monday lunes [**loo**ness]
Tuesday martes [**mar**tess]
Wednesday miércoles [m-**yair**koless]
Thursday jueves [Hway**bess**]
Friday viernes [b-**yair**ness]
Saturday sábado

Months

January enero [e**nairo**]
February febrero [feb**rairo**]
March marzo [**martho**]
April abril
May mayo [**mī**-yo]
June junio [Hoon-yo]
July julio [Hool-yo]
August agosto
September septiembre [sept-**yembray**]
October octubre [ok**toobray**]
November noviembre [nob-**yembray**]
December diciembre [deeth-**yembray**]

Time

what time is it? ¿qué hora es? [kay **o**ra ess]
one o'clock la una [la **oo**na]
two o'clock las dos [lass doss]
it's one o'clock es la una [ess la **oo**na]
it's two o'clock son las dos [son lass doss]
it's ten o'clock son las diez [son lass d-yeth]
five past one la una y cinco [la **oo**na ee **theen**ko]
ten past two las dos y diez [lass doss ee d-yeth]

quarter past one la una y cuarto [la **oo**na ee k**war**to]

quarter past two las dos y cuarto [lass doss ee k**war**to]

half past ten las diez y media [lass d-yeth ee m**ay**d-ya]

twenty to ten las diez menos veinte [lass d-yeth m**ay**noss b**ay-ee**ntay]

quarter to ten las diez menos cuarto [lass d-yeth m**ay**noss k**war**to]

at eight o'clock a las ocho [a lass **o**cho]

at half past four a las cuatro y media [a lass k**wa**tro ee m**ay**d-ya]

2 a.m. las dos de la mañana [lass doss day la man-y**a**na]

2 p.m. las dos de la tarde [lass doss day la **tar**day]

6 a.m. las seis de la mañana [lass s**ay-ee**ss day la man-y**a**na]

6 p.m. las seis de la tarde [lass s**ay-ee**ss day la **tar**day]

noon mediodía [m**ay**d-yo d**ee**-a]

midnight medianoche [m**ay**d-ya n**o**chay]

an hour una hora [**oo**na **o**ra]

a minute un minuto [oon meen**oo**to]

two minutes dos minutos [doss meen**oo**toss]

a second un segundo [oon seg**oo**ndo]

a quarter of an hour un cuarto de hora [k**war**to day **o**ra]

half an hour media hora [m**ay**d-ya **o**ra]

three quarters of an hour tres cuartos de hora [tress k**war**toss day **o**ra]

Numbers

0	cero [**thai**ro]	10	diez [d-yeth]
1	uno, una [**oo**no, **oo**na]	11	once [**on**thay]
2	dos [doss]	12	doce [**do**thay]
3	tres [tress]	13	trece [**tray**thay]
4	cuatro [k**wa**tro]	14	catorce [kat**or**thay]
5	cinco [**theen**ko]	15	quince [**keen**thay]
6	seis [s**ay-ee**ss]	16	dieciséis [d-yethees**ay-ee**ss]
7	siete [s-y**ay**tay]	17	diecisiete [d-yethees-y**ay**tay]
8	ocho [**o**cho]	18	dieciocho [d-yethee-**o**cho]
9	nueve [n**way**bay]		

19	diecinueve [d-yetheenwaybay]
20	veinte [bay-eentay]
21	veintiuno [bay-eentee-oono]
22	veintidós [bay-eenteedoss]
23	veintitrés [bay-eenteetress]
30	treinta [tray-eenta]
31	treinta y uno [tray-eenti oono]
40	cuarenta [kwarenta]
50	cincuenta [theenkwenta]
60	sesenta [sesenta]
70	setenta [setenta]
80	ochenta [ochenta]
90	noventa [nobenta]
100	cien [th-yen]
120	ciento veinte [th-yento bay-eentay]
200	doscientos, doscientas [dosth-yentoss, dosth-yentass]
300	trescientos, trescientas [tresth-yentoss, tresth-yentass]
400	cuatrocientos, cuatrocientas [kwatroth-yentoss, kwatroth-yentass]
500	quinientos, quinientas [keen-yentoss, keen-yentass]
600	seiscientos, seiscientas [say-eesth-yentoss, say-eesth-yentass]
700	setecientos, setecientas [seteth-yentoss, seteth-yentass]
800	ochocientos, ochocientas [ochoth-yentoss, ochoth-yentass]
900	novecientos, novecientas [nobeth-yentoss, nobeth-yentass]
1,000	mil [meel]
2,000	dos mil [doss meel]
5,000	cinco mil [theenko meel]
10,000	diez mil [d-yeth meel]
1,000,000	un millón [meel-yon]

When **uno** is used with a masculine noun, the final **-o** is dropped:

un coche
oon **ko**chay
one car

una is used with feminine nouns:

una bicicleta
oona beetheek**lay**ta
one bike

With multiples of a hundred, the -as ending is used with feminine nouns:

trescientos hombres
tresth-**yen**toss **o**mbress
300 men

quinientas mujeres
keen-**yen**tass mooн**ai**ress
500 women

Ordinals

1st	primero	[pree**mai**ro]
2nd	segundo	[se**goo**ndo]
3rd	tercero	[tair**thai**ro]
4th	cuarto	[**kwar**to]
5th	quinto	[**keen**to]
6th	sexto	[**ses**to]
7th	séptimo	[**sep**teemo]
8th	octavo	[ok**ta**bo]
9th	noveno	[no**bay**no]
10th	décimo	[**deth**eemo]

Conversion Tables

1 centimetre = 0.39 inches	1 inch = 2.54 cm
1 metre = 39.37 inches = 1.09 yards	1 foot = 30.48 cm
1 kilometre = 0.62 miles = 5/8 mile	1 yard = 0.91 m
	1 mile = 1.61 km

km	1	2	3	4	5	10	20	30	40	50	100
miles	0.6	1.2	1.9	2.5	3.1	6.2	12.4	18.6	24.8	31.0	62.1

miles	1	2	3	4	5	10	20	30	40	50	100
km	1.6	3.2	4.8	6.4	8.0	16.1	32.2	48.3	64.4	80.5	161

1 gram = 0.035 ounces	1 kilo = 1000 g = 2.2 pounds

g	100	250	500
oz	3.5	8.75	17.5

1 oz = 28.35 g
1 lb = 0.45 kg

kg	0.5	1	2	3	4	5	6	7	8	9	10
lb	1.1	2.2	4.4	6.6	8.8	11.0	13.2	15.4	17.6	19.8	22.0

kg	20	30	40	50	60	70	80	90	100
lb	44	66	88	110	132	154	176	198	220

lb	0.5	1	2	3	4	5	6	7	8	9	10	20
kg	0.2	0.5	0.9	1.4	1.8	2.3	2.7	3.2	3.6	4.1	4.5	9.0

1 litre = 1.75 UK pints / 2.13 US pints

1 UK pint = 0.57 l	1 UK gallon = 4.55 l
1 US pint = 0.47 l	1 US gallon = 3.79 l

centigrade / Celsius $°C = (°F - 32) \times 5/9$

°C	-5	0	5	10	15	18	20	25	30	36.8	38
°F	23	32	41	50	59	64	68	77	86	98.4	100.4

Fahrenheit $°F = (°C \times 9/5) + 32$

°F	23	32	40	50	60	65	70	80	85	98.4	101
°C	-5	0	4	10	16	18	21	27	29	36.8	38.3